D1575684

DRUNKS

ALSO BY CHRISTOPHER M. FINAN

*From the Palmer Raids to the Patriot Act:
A History of the Fight for Free Speech in America*

Alfred E. Smith: The Happy Warrior

DRUNKS

AN AMERICAN HISTORY

CHRISTOPHER M. FINAN

Beacon Press
BOSTON

362.292
F491

Beacon Press
Boston, Massachusetts
www.beacon.org

Beacon Press books
are published under the auspices of
the Unitarian Universalist Association of Congregations.

© 2017 by Christopher M. Finan
All rights reserved
Printed in the United States of America

20 19 18 17   8 7 6 5 4 3 2 1

This book is printed on acid-free paper that meets the uncoated paper
ANSI/NISO specifications for permanence as revised in 1992.

Text design and composition by Kim Arney

Library of Congress Cataloging-in-Publication Data
Names: Finan, Christopher M., author.
Title: Drunks : an American history / Christopher Finan.
Description: Boston, Massachusetts : Beacon Press, 2017. | Includes
    bibliographical references and index.
Identifiers: LCCN 2016048807 (print) | LCCN 2017008003 (ebook) |
    ISBN 9780807001790 (hardback) | ISBN 9780807001806 (e-book)
Subjects: LCSH: Alcoholism—United States—History. | Alcoholism—Treatment—
    United States—History. | Alcoholics—United States—History. | Alcoholics—
    Rehabilitation—United States—History. | BISAC: HISTORY / Social History. |
    PSYCHOLOGY / Psychopathology / Addiction. | PSYCHOLOGY / Mental Health.
Classification: LCC HV5292 .F555 2017 (print) | LCC HV5292 (ebook) | DDC
    362.2920973—dc23
LC record available at https://lccn.loc.gov/2016048807

For Sam and Al,
and our family ghosts

CONTENTS

PRESIDENT JOHN ADAMS had just discovered his son was an alcoholic. He was furious. Charles had been a handsome and charming nine-year-old when he accompanied his father on a diplomatic mission to Europe in 1779. "Charles wins the heart as usual, and is the most gentlemen of them all. . . . I love him too much," John wrote to his wife, Abigail. But in his midteens, Charles began to display disturbing behavior. While a student at Harvard College, he was caught running across Harvard Yard with several other boys. They may have been naked. They were probably drunk. Charles was able to graduate and became a lawyer, but John and Abigail remained concerned about the character of his friends. His father wrote him many admonishing letters.[1]

John learned the worst in 1799 during a visit to his daughter's home. He found Charles's wife and two young children living there: the family was bankrupt, and Charles had disappeared. He "is a mere rake, buck, blood, and beast . . . a madman possessed of the Devil," John told Abigail. "I renounce him." Abigail did not break with Charles, but she was also angry. When he reappeared, she told him that he was hurting his family and appealed to his pride and sense of honor. "But all is lost on him," she said. "The whole man [is] so changed that ruin and destruction have swallowed him up. Poor, poor, unhappy, wretched man."[2]

In November 1800, Abigail saw her son for the last time. His body was bloated. He was in great pain and often incoherent. He died a few weeks later at the age of thirty. "He was no man's enemy but his own," Abigail said. "He was beloved in spite of his errors." But Charles was not buried in the family vault. "Let silence reign forever over his tomb," his brother Thomas said.[3]

The country's First Family was not alone in feeling anger, shame, and guilt over the loss of an alcoholic family member. Americans had always been big drinkers. Even the Puritans had considered alcohol the "good Creature of God." Now the creature had turned. Cheap whiskey was flooding the market, and annual consumption of alcohol was climbing toward seven gallons per person, nearly three times what we drink today.[4]

Americans have been frustrated by alcoholism ever since. In 1808, a doctor and a minister organized a temperance society in a small town in upstate New York. Temperance became a national movement, as over two million people signed a pledge not to drink alcohol. When voluntary measures failed, state governments began banning the sale of alcohol, and prohibition was implemented nationally in 1920. Nothing could stop the drinking.

Many people blamed the drunks. Throughout history, they have frustrated every effort to force them to stay sober. In the first century AD, the Roman philosopher Seneca called alcoholism "a voluntary madness." Increase Mather, a Puritan minister in Boston, preached two sermons against drunkenness in 1673. "It is a sin that is rarely truly repented of and turned from," he said. "Blows cannot beat him out of it; but he will to it yet again, and that too the very next day after he hath smarted for it," he wrote. In 1871, a Massachusetts judge declared that drunks deserve no mercy. "[T]he *great truth* . . . remains that *the drunkard is self-made*, progressively self-taught, and obstinately self-immolated," he said.[5]

Even after the founding of Alcoholics Anonymous (AA) in 1935 proved that many drunks want to stop drinking, the major institutions of American life refused to help them. Hospitals would not admit alcoholics, turning away even those in need of emergency care. Most doctors, psychiatrists, and psychologists would not accept them as patients. They wound up in insane asylums and jails. The federal government finally recognized alcoholism as an illness in the 1960s, but many people were not convinced. The drunk's responsibility for abusing alcohol was still being debated at the dawn of the twenty-first century.

Yet the story of recovery from alcoholism is also one of the oldest in American history. In the same year that John Adams renounced his son, an alcoholic Native American on the verge of death experienced a vision that caused him to stop drinking. Handsome Lake became the leader of a religious revival that significantly reduced alcoholism among the Iroquois people. In 1840, six hard drinkers in Baltimore made their own pledge to stop drinking and founded a group to help alcoholics. Members of the Washington Temperance Society searched the streets of the nation's cities for homeless drunks and took them to meetings where they heard men like themselves describe how they got sober.

The Washingtonians were unable to sustain their movement, but they inspired others to open institutions where many drunks got sober. Doctors ran some of these "inebriate" homes and asylums. In the 1890s, tens of thousands of drunks found help in clinics that dispensed a drug called the "gold cure" for alcoholism. Others were able to stop with the help of religion. Drunks who had found sobriety played an important role in all of these efforts. In the 1940s, AA members began organizing groups around the United States. There were more than sixty thousand groups in 2016.

The fight against addiction is one of America's great liberation movements. Like the battles for racial equality, women's rights, and sexual freedom, its history is marked by periods of progress and devastating reverses. Several times, Americans have embraced humanitarianism, rejecting the view that drunks are to blame for abusing alcohol, only to return to the idea that addiction must be punished. Today we are expressing regret for our decision to send millions of addicts to prison during the 1980s and 1990s. Once again, there is hope that a more tolerant age is dawning. But after two centuries of struggle for the humane treatment of alcoholics, the fight continues.

CHAPTER ONE

Mountain of Bones

IN SPRING OF 1799, Handsome Lake, a Native American, joined members of his hunting party in making the long journey from western Pennsylvania to their home in New York. Handsome Lake was a member of the Seneca Nation, one of the six nations in the Haudenosaunee (Iroquois Confederacy). He had once been renowned for his fighting skill. But the Iroquois had been stripped of almost all their lands after the American Revolution. Now fifty years old, Handsome Lake, too, was a shadow of what he had been. He would later say that heavy drinking had reduced him to "but yellow skin and dried bones." After stopping in Pittsburgh to trade furs for several barrels of whiskey, the hunters lashed their canoes together and began to paddle up the Allegheny River. Only those in the outer canoes had to work. The rest of the party drank whiskey, yelling and singing "like demented people," Handsome Lake said. The good times didn't stop after they picked up their wives and children, who had accompanied them on the hunting trip and were waiting at a rendezvous. Everyone looked forward to being home in Cornplanter's Town, named for its Seneca Leader.[1]

The joy of their homecoming did not last long. There was enough whiskey to keep the men drunk for several weeks. Handsome Lake described the horror of that time:

> Now that the party is home the men revel in strong drink and are very quarrelsome. Because of this the families become frightened

and move away for safety. So from many places in the bushlands camp fires send up their smoke.

Now the drunken men run yelling through the village and there is no one there except the drunken men. Now they are beastlike and run about without clothing and all have weapons to injure those whom they meet.

Now there are no doors in the houses for they have all been kicked off. So, also, there are no fires in the village and have not been for many days. Now the men full of strong drink have trodden in the fireplaces. They alone track there and there are no fires and their footprints are in all the fireplaces.

Now the Dogs yelp and cry in all the houses for they are hungry.

Henry Simmons, one of three Quakers who had recently come to the village and had been contracted by the US War Department to "civilize" the Indians, said that some natives died. "One old Woman perrished out of doors in the night season with a bottle at her side," he wrote. In a community meeting later, Simmons denounced "the great Evil of Strong Drink." But the Indians did not need much persuading. After several days of deliberation, a council of Seneca elders announced that they were banning whiskey from the village.[2]

Handsome Lake was not present at the meeting or the deliberations of the council. He was suffering from the effects of so much alcohol and may even have been experiencing delirium tremens, which is caused by the sudden withdrawal of alcohol from someone who is addicted to it. For several weeks, he lay in a bed in the home of his daughter and son-in-law, consumed by thoughts of death. Handsome Lake described the ordeal, referring to himself in the third person. "Now as he lies in sickness he meditates and longs that he might rise again and walk upon the earth," he said. "And then he thinks how evil and loathsome he is before the Great Ruler. He thinks how he has been evil ever since he had strength in this world and done evil ever since he had been able to work." There must have been some alcohol in the village because Handsome Lake was able to get enough to ease his suffering. Drunk, he sang sacred songs to the dead. In more sober moments, he pondered the possible cause of his affliction:

Now it comes to his mind that perchance evil has arisen because of strong drink and he resolves to use it nevermore. Now he continually thinks of this every day and every hour. Yea, he continually thinks of this. Then a time comes and he craves drink again for he thinks he cannot recover his strength without it.

Now two ways he thinks: what once he did and whether he will ever recover.

While severely depressed, Handsome Lake was not hopeless. He was cheered by the mornings. "Now when he thinks of the sunshine and of the Creator who made it he feels a new hope within him and he feels that he may again be on his feet in this world," he wrote. But such feelings did not last long. "Then again he despairs that he will ever see the new day because of his great weakness."[3]

It was in this highly agitated state, seemingly torn between heaven and hell, that Handsome Lake was stricken by an apparently fatal attack. His daughter and her husband were sitting outside their cabin cleaning beans in preparation for planting when they heard Handsome Lake cry, "So be it!" As they looked toward the door, the old man staggered outside and collapsed in his daughter's arms. He appeared to be dead, and word was sent to Cornplanter, his half-brother, and Blacksnake, his nephew, who was the first to arrive. "Is he dead?" Blacksnake asked. Handsome Lake was not breathing and had no detectable heartbeat; his body was cool. But as they carried his body indoors, Blacksnake discovered a warm spot on his chest. A half hour later, Handsome Lake began breathing normally. Warmth began to return to the old man's body, and an hour and a half later, he opened his eyes. By this time, Handsome Lake was surrounded by his family. "My uncle, are you feeling well?" Blacksnake asked. "Yes, I believe myself well," he answered. "Never have I seen such wondrous visions!"[4]

Handsome Lake said his vision began when he heard a voice say, "Come out awhile." At first, he thought he had spoken the words himself in his delirium, but after hearing the words repeated two more times, he dragged himself from his bed and stepped outdoors. There he discovered three middle-aged Indian men; their cheeks had been painted red and they wore headpieces decorated with feathers. In one hand, they carried bows and arrows that they used as staffs; in the other were huckleberry bushes with berries of every color. "Never before have I seen such handsome commanding men," he said. The men told Handsome Lake that the Creator wanted to help mankind and had charged them with carrying his message to men:

> Four words tell a great story of wrong and the Creator is sad because of the trouble they bring, so go and tell your people. The first word is One'ga? [whiskey or rum]. It seems that you never have known that this word stands for a great and monstrous evil and has reared a high mound of bones. . . . [Y]ou lose your minds and one'ga? causes it all. . . . So now all must now say, "I will use it nevermore. As long as I live, as long as the number of my days is I will never use it again. I now stop."

The messengers explained that the Creator had made alcohol for white men to use as medicine. The white men also abused alcohol and "drink instead of work." But Indians should not use alcohol at all, they said. "No, the Creator did not make it for you."[5]

Alcohol was not the only evil that faced the Seneca, but the danger of alcohol was a recurring theme in the visions that Handsome Lake experienced over the next nine months. Six weeks after his first vision, a fourth messenger took Handsome Lake on a "sky journey" that included a stop in the domain of the Punisher, a monster whose shape was continually changing and occasionally took the form of the Christian devil, complete with horns, tails, and cloven hoofs. He lived in a vast iron lodge where sinners suffered torments that fit their crimes amid scorching blasts of wind: witches were plunged into boiling cauldrons and then frozen; women who had used love potions were forced to display their naked, rotting flesh. Drinkers swallowed molten metal.

The messenger also conducted Handsome Lake along the narrow path of the righteous, which was surrounded by flowers and delicious fruit. On their arrival in the land of the Creator, he was reunited with his dead son, grandchild, and niece. Even the beloved dog that he had sacrificed during the white dog ceremony greeted him rapturously.

Before sending Handsome Lake back to his people, the messenger repeated the warning against alcohol and witchcraft and said a "great sickness" would enter his village if the people did not mend their ways.

Handsome Lake's people appeared eager to obey. Cornplanter had described his brother's vision to the villagers soon after it was revealed in mid-June. Simmons, the Quaker adviser, said the Indians were deeply moved. They appeared "Solid and weighty in Spirit." Simmons also "felt the love of God flowing powerfully amongst us." Although he was regarded with suspicion by many of the natives, he felt he had to speak out in praise of Handsome Lake. Following the second vision in August, the Indians met in council again to hear the details of the sky journey. Handsome Lake was still too ill to attend.[6]

By the time of his third vision in February 1800, Handsome Lake was able to describe it to the council himself. The three angels had asked whether the people had given up whiskey, and Handsome Lake had admitted that he did not know. They told him to have his revelations written in a book and ordered him to carry the lessons of the *Gaiwiio* (Good Word) to all the towns of the Haudenosaunee. In June 2001, during a three-day meeting of representatives of five of the six nations in Buffalo Creek, Handsome Lake seized his chance, announcing that the Creator had revealed to him that "[w]hiskey is the great engine which the bad Spirit uses to introduce Witchcraft and many other evils amongst Indians." Handsome Lake's prophecy was believed. Before the council ended, it banned the use of alcohol and appointed Handsome Lake "High Priest, and principal Sachem [leader] in all things Civil and Religious."

Soon after, a whiskey seller named Webster witnessed the effect of Handsome Lake's prophecy. Eighteen Onondaga chiefs who had gladly accepted whiskey from him on their way to Buffalo Creek refused to touch the bottle he put before them on their way home. Webster feared that he might be attacked, but the Onondagas reassured him:

> The chiefs explained, that they had met at Buffalo, a Prophet of the Seneca nation, who had assured them, and in this assurance they had the most implicit confidence, that without total abstinence, from the use of ardent spirits, they and their race would shortly

become extinct; that they had entered upon a resolution, never again to taste the baneful article, and that they hoped to prevail on their nation to adopt the same salutary resolution.

The Iroquois had taken their first step on the path to becoming a sober people.[7]

Before they began to encounter European explorers and fishermen in the sixteenth century, very few indigenous people of the eastern coast of North America had ever tasted alcohol, and none had experienced anything more than the mild inebriation of fermented drinks used ceremonially. Nothing prepared them for the effects of distilled spirits. In 1609, explorer Henry Hudson offered alcohol to a group of Munsee Indians he encountered on Manhattan Island. His purpose in giving them drink was to determine "whether they had any treaherie in them," but he was surprised when one of the Munsee became intoxicated. "[T]hat was strange to them, for they could not tell how to take it." It must have been memorable for the Indians as well. (One theory of the origin of the word "Manhattan" is that the Indians named the island *manahactanienk*—the "place of general inebriation.")[8]

The experience of getting drunk for the first time could be terrifying for anyone. Not long after Hudson's encounter with the Munsee, Captain John Smith, the military leader of the colony at Jamestown, gave liquor to a native man who he was trying to revive. "[I]t pleased God to restore him againe to life, but so drunke and affrighted, that he seemed Lunaticke," Smith said. The man's brother was "tormented and grieved" by his wild behavior.[9]

Once the Indians lost their fear of alcohol, they fell in love with it. The euphoria of intoxication brought temporary relief from the pain of dispossession and death. A Jesuit attempting to convert the Cayuga Indians in the seventeenth century reported that they would announce their intention to get drunk before a drinking episode. "I am going to lose my head," a man would shout. "I am going to drink the water that takes away one's wits." Another missionary noted that the native people appeared to relish the disorientation that occurred as the alcohol took effect. "They rejoice, shouting, 'Good, good. My head is reeling!'" Once a man was drunk on alcohol, he found new powers in himself. When an Ottawa Indian was asked what brandy was made of, he said, "Of hearts and tongues. . . . [A]fter I have drank of it, I fear nothing and I talk like an angel." The drinker experienced a surge of self-confidence. "[I]n their drunkenness, . . . they become persons of importance, taking pleasure in seeing themselves dreaded by those who do not taste the poison," a third missionary said. Of course, inebriation also made Indians more vulnerable to manipulation by white men.[10]

The Europeans expressed shock over the self-destructive way the Indians drank. Alcohol abuse was certainly not unknown among whites, particularly those living on the frontier where many fur traders were killed in drunken brawls. But coming from cultures that had encountered alcohol centuries earlier, some of them had clear rules against abusing alcohol. Prohibitions against drunkenness were spelled out in Christian scripture, Western social etiquette, and even law, but the natives had no prohibitions against getting drunk. Wasn't that the point? One Indian observed: "The Great Spirit who made all things made everything for some use, and whatever use he design'd anything for, that use it should always be put to; Now, when he made rum, he said, Let this be for Indians to get drunk with. And it must be so."[11]

From the beginning, Indians drank to get drunk, to escape. "[G]ive two Savages two or three bottles of brandy. They will sit down and, without eating, will drink one after another until they have emptied them," a missionary said. At first, there were limited supplies of alcohol in America. But if the Indians didn't have enough brandy or rum to get everyone drunk, they gave it all to a chosen few. "And if any one chance to be drunk before he hath finisht his proportion (which is ordinarily a quart of Brandy, Rum or Strong-waters), the rest will pour the rest of his part down his throat," a colonist wrote. The Europeans agreed that the Indians had a drinking problem. "They will pawne their wits to purchase the acquaintance of it," Thomas Morton said in 1637. "Their paradise is drinking," Louis Antoine de Bougainville observed a century later.[12]

The Europeans would have continued simply to take advantage of Indians getting drunk if alcohol hadn't also sometimes made them aggressive. For the most part, early contact between the Puritans and the Indians had been peaceful. While the natives did not welcome the white man, they generally avoided attacking him and even offered critical assistance when the early settlers were on the verge of starvation. "The Natives are of two sorts, (as the English are)," Roger Williams, the founder of Rhode Island, reported. "Some are Rude and Clownish . . . , the Generall, are *sober* and *grave*, and yet chearfull in a meane. . . . There is a favour of *civility* and courtesie even amongst these wild Americans, both amongst *themselves* and towards strangers." But the behavior of drunken Indians was often terrifying, both to the colonists and other natives. In 1680, Jasper Danckaerts, who was visiting America in search of land for his religious community in Holland, experienced Indian drunkenness while staying with friends in what would later become Brooklyn, New York:

> When we arrived at Gouanes, we heard a great noise, shouting and singing in the huts of the Indians. . . . They were all lustily drunk, raving, striking, shouting, jumping, fighting each other, and foaming at the mouth like raging wild beasts. Some who did not participate with them, had fled with their wives and children to Simon's house, where the drunken brutes followed, bawling in the house and before the door, which we finally closed.

Danckaerts, a religious and fair-minded man, did not blame the Indians for getting drunk. The fault lay with the so-called Christians who sold them the liquor. He even lectured his hosts, who admitted that they had participated in the trade. "The subject is so painful and so abominable, that I will forbear saying anything more for the present," he wrote in his journal.[13]

Colonial authorities agreed with Danckaerts that the solution to the problem of native drunkenness was a prohibition against selling or trading spirits. The Massachusetts Bay Colony enacted the first ban in 1633, declaring that "no man shall sell or give any strong water to an Indian." New Netherlands approved a similar law a decade later. The most vigorous interdiction campaign was conducted in Canada, where Jesuit missionaries battled against the use of brandy in the fur trade. The Bishop of Quebec ordered the excommunication of any French trader who sold liquor to the Indians. A French governor had two traders shot for the offense. But the king of France ordered an end to restrictions on the liquor trade, and the laws elsewhere had little chance of success. As Danckaerts discovered, an Indian who wanted to buy alcohol didn't need to look farther than the next white homestead. Everyone was eager for his trade.[14]

The British and the French wooed the Indians with alcohol in an effort to gain an advantage in their continental rivalry. The records of colonial traders who operated in Indian country show that 80 percent of the charges to government accounts were for gifts of alcohol to the natives. The quantity of alcohol in Indian country increased dramatically after 1720 as the fur trade prospered. Thousands of gallons of rum were carried across the Allegheny Mountains to exchange for pelts at trading posts deep in the interior. At Detroit, three hundred thousand skins bought twenty-four thousand gallons in 1767. A government official estimated that Indians in the southern territories were consuming ten thousand gallons of rum every month in 1776. An Iroquois observed the rum flowed "so plentifully as if it ware water out of a fountain."[15]

It was obvious to all that drinking threatened the survival of the natives. Danckaerts had observed that the Indians were willing to trade anything for alcohol, including their blankets, leggings—"yes, their guns and hatchets, the very instruments by which they obtain their subsistence." The impact on the Indian economy was devastating. Little Turtle, a leader of the Miami, told a group of Quakers in 1801 that Indians returning from the hunt with furs were targeted by white men who invited them to drink. Even those who repeatedly refused found themselves weakening:

> [O]ne finally accepts it and takes a drink, and getting one he wants another, and then a third and fourth till his senses have left him. After reason comes back to him, he gets up and finds where he is. He asks for his peltry. The answer is, you have drunk them. Where is my gun? It is gone. Where is my blanket? It is gone. Where is my shirt? You have sold it for whiskey. Now, brothers, figure to yourself what a condition this man was in—he has a family at home, a wife and children that stand in need of the profits of his hunting. What must their wants be, when he is even without a shirt?

Furs were all the Indians had to trade. Guns were one of their few capital goods. When these were gone, the hunters and their families found themselves sinking into poverty. If the harvest had not been good, they faced starvation as well. In 1737, Conrad Weiser visited a village of Onondagas and Shawnees that had been hit hard by alcohol. "Their children looked like dead persons and suffered much from hunger," he reported.[16]

Many Indians didn't live long enough to starve to death. "When we drink it makes us mad," a Delaware Indian lamented. "We do not know what we do, we then abuse one another. We throw each other into the fire." Drinking-related injuries were common. "[S]ome falling into Fires, burn their legs and arms, contracting the sinews, and become Cripples all their Life-times. Precipices break their Bones and Joints, with abundance of Instances," explorer John Lawson wrote, describing natives in the Carolinas. Many drunks died of exposure after wandering away from their villages and passing out in the snow. John Josselyn, a naturalist, noted that the victims included women, "especially old women who dyed dead drunk." The number of alcohol-related deaths among Indians appears to have been shockingly high. A Choctaw leader estimated that his tribe had lost a thousand people in just eighteen months.[17]

The Indians began expressing fear of alcohol in the seventeenth century. Tequassino and Hatsawap, two Nanticoke sachems, persuaded the governor of Maryland to ban the sale of liquor to their tribe in 1679. William Penn, the founder of Pennsylvania, approved a similar law. When a new governor promised vigorous enforcement of the law twenty years later, the Indians reacted cautiously. One leader, Orettyagh, "Exprest a great Satisfaction and Desired that the Law might Effectually be put in Execucon and not only discoursed of as formerly it has been." The Indians would be disappointed again. Two decades later, Mingoes, Shawnees, and Conoys urged another governor to take action against the liquor dealers. Officials admitted they were powerless to enforce the law because "the Woods are so thick & dark we cannot see what is done in them."[18]

Recognizing that they could not count on the colonists to solve the problem, natives took matters in their own hands. In 1738, a hundred Shawnee warriors living along the Allegheny River signed a statement that was delivered to the Pennsylvania governor. "This day we have held a council, and it is agreed by the Shawnee in general that whatever rum is in our towns shall be broke and split and not drunk," they said. The Shawnee were as good as their word, spilling at least forty gallons of liquor in the streets. Indians in other places also took action: villagers at Otsinigo, New York, warned liquor dealers to stay away; some Iroquois chiefs banned the sale of rum in their communities as well. But even the most vigorously enforced Indian ban could not stop natives from purchasing liquor from the colonists. Indians who lived close to white communities were the most susceptible to alcohol abuse. According to one of their chiefs, the Tuscarora "lived but wretchedly being Surrounded by white People, and up to their Lips in Rum, so that they cou'd not turn their heads anyway but it ran into their mouths." To escape alcohol, they finally moved from the Carolinas to southern New York.[19]

The Indian efforts at self-policing generally failed. The natives were divided: for every sachem who saw the devastating impact of the trade on his people, there were a dozen young men who wanted to drink when they returned from months of hunting, and they had the pelts to trade. Some tribes fled into the wilderness to escape alcohol, but that didn't work for long as the white population moved westward. The great Indian leader Pontiac, who moved his followers from Detroit, admitted that their new home was close enough to whites "that when we want to drink, we can easily come for it." Aucus al Kanigut, the Tuscarora chief who had moved his people from the Carolinas to New York, feared that the victory over alcohol was only temporary. "We also request you would give us some medicine to cure us of our fondness for that destructive liquor," he said. The whites had no medicine and offered very little advice. In 1767, a group of Indians sought the counsel of William Johnson, the British superintendent of Indian affairs in the northern territories. "[T]he best Medicine I can think of to prevent your falling into your former Vice of drinking is to embrace Christianity," Sir William replied.[20]

Although Benjamin Franklin shared with his fellow colonists many stereotypes about Native Americans, he was also deeply concerned about the impact of alcohol on them. His newspaper periodically reported on the consequences of alcohol abuse among the natives, and in 1753 he issued a public warning of the danger. In his famous *Autobiography*, Franklin expressed fear for their future. "[I]f it be the Design of Providence to extirpate these Savages in order to make room for Cultivators of the Earth, it seems not improbable that Rum may be the appointed Means," he said.[21]

By the time of Handsome Lake's first vision in May 1799, America's indigenous people had lost most of their land in the East and Midwest. William Henry Harrison, a future US president who was governor of Indiana and the Louisiana territories, told his superior in Washington that the Indians were suffering a crisis of leadership:

> This poisonous liquor not only incapacitates them from obtaining a living by Hunting but it leads to the most atrocious crimes—killing each other has become so customary amongst them that it is no longer a crime to murder those whom they have been accustomed to esteem and regard. Their Chiefs and their nearest relatives fall under the strokes of their Tomahawks and Knives. This has been so much the case with the three Tribes nearest us—the Peankashaws, Weas, & Eel River Miamis that there is scarcely a Chief to be found amongst them.

Harrison blamed white settlers for corrupting the Indians with alcohol. "This is so certain that I can at once tell by looking at an Indian who I chance to meet whether he belong to a Neighboring or more distant Tribe," he wrote. "The latter is generally well Clothed healthy and vigorous, the former half naked, filthy and enfeebled with Intoxication, and many of them without arms except a Knife which they carry for the most villainous purposes." Harrison believed the Indians were close to "exterpation" and begged his superior to bring the problem to President Thomas Jefferson's attention. The following year Jefferson signed legislation banning the sale of alcohol to the Indians. Once again, the authorities lacked either the will or the resources to enforce the law.[22]

New, more militant Indians began to take the place of their discredited leaders. They opposed all efforts by white men to "help" them, believing that the Indians must arrive at their own solutions. Banning the consumption of alcohol was at the top of their list. In the 1750s, a Delaware woman who had been relocated to western Pennsylvania announced that she had been told by the "Great Power that they should destroy the poison from among them." Soon, other Delaware prophets emerged to urge the people to recapture the happiness of the days before the arrival of the white man by resisting incursions on their lands, rejecting Christian religion, and reviving the religious ceremonies of their forebearers. All the prophets agreed that it was essential for their people to stop drinking alcohol. "Hear what the Great Spirit has ordered me to tell you," the prophet Neolin announced:

> You are to make sacrifices, in the manner that I shall direct; to put off entirely from yourselves the customs which you have adopted since the white people came among us; you are to return to the former happy state, in which we lived in peace and plenty, before these strangers came to disturb us, and above all, you must abstain from drinking their deadly *beson* [poisonous, bewitched medicine, i.e., liquor], which they force upon us for the sake of increasing their gains.

The warrior Pontiac would later cite Neolin's teachings as an inspiration for the attacks that wiped out nine of the thirteen British forts from the frontier.[23]

Forty years later, the most militant of all Indian prophets began to speak. Ellskwata was the son of a Shawnee chief and the brother of Tecumseh, who would come as close as any man ever did to uniting the natives in opposition to the newly minted Americans during the War of 1812. Ellskwata was a known drunkard and braggart until one day in 1805 when he had his first vision. His visit to heaven bore several similarities to Handsome Lake's Sky Journey, which had occurred only a few years earlier. The drunkard was punished by "a cup of liquor resembling melted lead; if he refused to drink it he [the tormentor] would urge him, saying: Come, drink—you used to love whiskey. And upon drinking it, his bowels were seized with an exquisite burning."[24]

Like the prophets before him, Ellskwata, now calling himself Tenskwata (Open Door), urged the Indians to reject white ways, including alcohol. Indians and whites had separate origins, and "the Great Spirit did not mean that the white and red people should live near each other" because whites "poison'd the land." Tenskwata's preaching was not confined to the Shawnee; many Indians accepted his prophecy.[25]

By September 1807, Indian thirst for liquor was disappearing in Michigan. "All the Ottawas from L'abre au Croche adhere strictly to the Shawney Prophets advice they do not wear Hats Drink or Conjure," one trader reported. (Hats were a symbol of white settlers.) "Rum is a drug [on the market]. . . . Indians do not purchase One Galln per month," another complained. But Tenskwata's hopes for an Indian revival died with his brother during the Battle of Tippecanoe. He was exiled to Canada for ten years.[26]

Handsome Lake shared with other nativists a desire to save his people by restoring their pride in being Indians. Soon after awakening from his first vision, he said the messengers had told him that the Strawberry Festival, then under way, must always be held and that all must drink the berry juice. Later, he was instructed to revive the white dog ceremony, which involved eating the flesh of the sacrificed animal. The revival of Indian religion was crucial because Handsome Lake's vision had revealed that Christianity was not intended for Indians. He had seen a church with a spire but no door, which he saw as a symbol of the difficulty that Indians had in accepting the white man's religion. Jesus Christ also appeared in his dream and told him this in as many words. According to Handsome Lake, Christ said, "Now tell your people that they will become lost when they follow the ways of the white man." Handsome Lake was obsessed by the danger posed by magic and would soon lead a campaign against witches that would result in the murder of at least one woman.[27]

Handsome Lake also opposed the sale of any more land to the whites and was ambivalent about the arrival of the Quakers. The Quakers did not attempt to convert the Seneca. They wanted to help the Indians make the transition from hunting to farming. But this fundamentally changed Indian life, as the Quakers pushed the men toward the fields that women traditionally tended and attempted to move the women into strictly domestic duties. No less threatening was the opening of a school where the Quakers taught the children how to read and write English. Many worried that the students would cease to be Indians. Handsome Lake was not opposed to all English education, but he believed that it should be limited to enabling Indians to protect their interests by reading treaties and other contracts.

Handsome Lake sought to live peacefully with whites. This may have had something to do with the fact that the Iroquois resided on reservations encircled by whites, and thus they had no military options. But it also appears that he had never become embittered by whites. He disagreed with those who believed that the newcomers were trying to exterminate the Indians. He viewed whites as neither good nor bad. Indians and whites were different. Their religions were not opposed: the Christians followed the teachings of Jesus Christ, and the Indians had the Gaiwiio, and the two gospels did not appear to conflict. Handsome Lake even seemed willing to allow Christian Indians to keep their new religion as long as they were faithful to its moral code. This tolerance may have reflected his experience with the Quakers, who did not seek to judge the character of any man's faith. Handsome Lake was grateful for the Quakers' efforts to help his people and supported most of their economic reforms. In general, Handsome Lake believed that the Great Spirit wanted mutual respect between races and individuals. In time, he came to regret his attack on witches.

Handsome Lake saw that many of the Indians' problems were the result of a breakdown in their sense of obligation to each other and to the community. Some members of the younger generation had lost respect for their elders, provoking arguments between fathers and sons. Some mothers were interfering too much in the lives of their daughters and disrupting the relationship between husbands and wives. Too many men were refusing to marry in order to avoid responsibility for raising children or were "putting aside their wives" through divorce. Women were sometimes guilty of being jealous of other women and brutal to their children. Much of Handsome Lake's visions bore on the importance of strengthening the bonds between family members. Husbands must be the heads of their families. It was no longer enough to participate in the hunt and spend the rest of the year in idleness. They must "harvest food for [the] family" and take care of the livestock. Women must be good housewives, caring for their husband and children, welcoming guests, and looking out for orphans. Mothers-in-law should mind their own business.

It was obvious to Handsome Lake that alcohol worsened all of the Indians' problems. Alcohol had played a key role in defrauding Indians of their lands. Heavy drinking was a major source of violence in the community and contributed to a decline in economic productivity, while undermining some families by increasing philandering, fueling arguments between husbands and wives, and occasionally leading to child abuse. But where other prophets blamed the white men for using drink to destroy the Indians, Handsome Lake explained how they were destroying themselves:

> Good food is turned into evil drink. Now some have said that there is no harm in partaking of fermented liquids.
>
> Then let this plan be followed: let men gather in two parties, one having a feast of food, apples and corn, and the other have cider and whiskey. Let the parties be equally matched and let them commence their feasting at the same time. When the feast is finished you will see those who drank the fermented juices murder one of their own part but not so with those who ate food only.

Handsome Lake was offering his people an alternative: they didn't have to drink. A white man later asked an Onondaga man why his people had suddenly stopped drinking when they had been urged to do it for years. "[T]hey had no power," he replied. "[B]ut when the Great Spirit forbid such conduct by their prophet, he gave them the power to comply with their request."

The Quakers were the first to notice the change in the Seneca. Henry Simmons had been living in Cornplanter's Town when Handsome Lake and his drunken compatriots had torn it up. Soon after Handsome Lake's first vision, Cornplanter told Simmons that the Allegheny Seneca "now drank much less than formerly." Over the next year, "the Indians now became very sober, generally refraining from the use of strong liquor, both at home and abroad among the white people," Simmons said. One of them told another Quaker, "no more get drunk here, now this two year."

In 1803, Handsome Lake suffered the first of several setbacks, losing his title as the supreme leader of the Six Nations to Red Jacket, the leader of the Seneca in the Buffalo Creek reservation. But the loss of political power did not undermine Handsome Lake's moral authority. He made annual visits to many of the Seneca reservations where his following continued to grow. A Quaker delegation that toured Handsome Lake's stronghold in the Allegheny Valley discovered that white settlers in the area were amazed that the Seneca "entirely refused liquor when offered to them. The Indians said . . . that when white people urged them to drink whiskey, they would ask for bread or provisions in its stead."

The Indians' main tool for enforcing the ban on alcohol was community pressure. Occasionally, they resorted to threats, like the one they issued to a white trader who sold cider to some Seneca without telling them that it contained alcohol. When the fraud was discovered, sober Indians told him that they would break his barrels if he did not get out of town, which he promptly did. With their own people, the Indian enforcers confined their efforts to verbal harassment. If the chiefs discovered that someone had gotten drunk "when they were out in the white settlements, they were sharply reproved by the chiefs on their return, which had nearly the same effect among Indians, as committing a man to the workhouse among white people."

Handsome Lake recognized that it would not be easy for his people to keep away from sin, and he showed tolerance for their weakness. He endorsed public confession as a way of relieving guilt and was willing to meet with individuals privately if their behavior had been particularly heinous. He preached that even people who confessed on their deathbeds could save themselves from damnation. So the community never concluded that a drunk was beyond saving. In 1809, the Quakers were told by residents of the Cattaraugus reservation that all the men there had stopped drinking. "[B]ut there were yet three women who would sometimes become intoxicated, yet they did not intend to cease labouring with them till they become reformed."

Sobriety spread beyond the Seneca to other Iroquois tribes. The Onondaga chiefs who had scared the whiskey trader Webster on their way home from the grand council in 1801 succeeded in their goal of carrying the Prophet's words to their people. Two years later, a missionary wrote that the Onondaga had "for two years greatly reformed in their intemperate drinking." The Oneida, who were divided between native and Christian factions, were somewhat less successful. But Handsome Lake's message was preached even to the Christian Indians. Their white minister acknowledged that the native religion "absolutely forbid the use of rum, and assert[ed] that no Indian can be a good man who takes even a spoonful."

Seven years after Handsome Lake's visions, the Indians had begun to recognize the full extent of the damage that alcohol had done to their people. At a Seneca reservation, the leaders told William Allinson that "since they had got their eyes open to see they were sensible that strong drink had done them a great deal of mischief and kept them poor but now they had got hold of it and was determined never to let it raise again." Allinson was one of the Quakers who were encouraging the Iroquois to accept white values, and he praised the Seneca for embracing the profit motive. "They are naturally avaricious and saving & not being so liable to Imposition as when they drank Spirits, some of them are growing rich."

Handsome Lake never succeeded in reforming all of the Iroquois or even all of the Seneca. Red Jacket, the leader of the large Seneca reservation at Buffalo Creek, remained a political foe. While he denounced demon rum, he was known to drink. There were also small Seneca reservations along the Genesee River that lay close to white settlements. In these places, "we are almost discouraged about our Brothers," Handsome Lake admitted. But these were the exceptions. Every year, Handsome Lake walked hundreds of miles to visit his followers and make new converts. It was obvious to all but the most cynical observers that a great change had occurred among the Iroquois. In 1809, Quaker Jacob Taylor attended a meeting of the Council of the Six Nations at Buffalo Creek. "I think I never saw so many Indians together before that conducted with so much propriety—the number could not be well ascertained, but it was thought there were about One Thousand, and I don't remember seeing one Drunken Indian among them," he said.

Handsome Lake died on August 10, 1815, at the age of sixty-six. It had been sixteen years since he launched his campaign to save the Iroquois people by preaching the Gaiwiio. He had been making his annual tour, when he received an invitation to speak at the Onondaga reservation in central New York. Although it was 150 miles away, he made the journey by foot, speaking at villages as he traveled. He was sick and depressed by thoughts of death by the time he arrived at Onondaga. The meeting that he had hoped to address had to be canceled, but he emerged from the small cabin to make a final address:

I will soon go to my new home. Soon I will step into the new world for there is a plain pathway before me leading there. Whoever follows my teachings will follow in my footsteps and I will look back upon him with outstretched arms inviting him into the new world of our Creator. Alas, I fear that a pall of smoke will obscure the eyes of many from the truth of the *Gaiwiio* but I pray that when I am gone that all may do what I have taught.

Handsome Lake was buried in the center of the council house in Onondaga.

When the news reached the outside world, the *Buffalo Gazette* published an obituary that began by carefully distinguishing between Handsome Lake and Tenskwata. It called him "the Peace Prophet" and recounted how a fifty-year-old man who was "remarkable only for stupidity and beastly drunkenness" had experienced his great dream. "The chief immediately abandoned his habits, visited the tribes—related his story—which was believed, and the consequence has been, that from a filthy, lazy drunken set of beings, they have become cleanly, industrious, sober, and happy," the obituary said.

A few months before his death, Handsome Lake had experienced his final vision. He was walking in a field of corn. "Suddenly a damsel appeared and threw her arms about my neck and as she clasped me she spoke saying, 'When you leave this earth for the new world above, it is our wish to follow you,'" he recalled. "I looked for the damsel but saw only the long leaves of corn twining around my shoulders. And then I understood that it was the spirit of the corn who had spoken, she the sustainer of life."

So I replied, "O spirit of the corn, follow not me but abide still upon the earth and be strong and be faithful to your purpose. Ever endure and do not fail the children of women. It is not time for you to follow for the *Gaiwiio* is only in its beginning."

Handsome Lake knew he had fulfilled his mission.

CHAPTER TWO

Out of the Gutter

THE METHODIST CHURCH on Greene Street in New York City was packed on the wintry evening of March 23, 1841. New Yorkers had been hearing reports from Baltimore that a group of drunks had gotten themselves sober and had launched a movement to save the lives of alcoholics. The reformed drunks were members of the Washington Temperance Society and called themselves Washingtonians to identify their struggle against the slavery of alcohol with the nation's war of liberation from British despotism. There was some trepidation among New York temperance advocates about inviting even sober drunks to address one of their meetings. They feared that tales of debauchery would offend the middle-class audience. But the full pews of the church revealed the enormous curiosity to hear their stories. John H. W. Hawkins, an unemployed hatter who had been sober less than a year, was the first to speak.

Hawkins would become the Washingtonians' greatest orator, but he had made his first speech only a few weeks earlier. At the age of forty-three, he was not a young man, and his nose was too large for a handsome one. He had large expressive eyes and dark bushy eyebrows. As he spoke in the Greene Street church, his audience was struck by the simplicity and sincerity with which he told about his terrible degradation and nearly miraculous recovery. They were also moved by his passionate commitment to saving the lives of alcoholics by getting them to sign a pledge not to drink alcoholic beverages. "If there is a man on earth who deserves the sympathy of the world it is the poor drunkard," Hawkins said. "He is poisoned, degraded, cast out, knows not what to do, and must be helped or he is lost. . . . I feel for drunkards. I want them to come and sign the pledge and be saved."[1]

Suddenly, Hawkins was interrupted by a voice from the gallery. "Can I be saved?" a man asked. "I am a poor drunkard. I would give the world if I was as you." "Yes, there is, my friend," Hawkins replied. "Come down and sign the pledge, and you will be a man. Come down and I will meet you, and we will take you by the hand." A minister who was present later described the scene for William George Hawkins, John's son and biographer. There was silence as the man made his way to the stairs and began to descend. "Your father sprang from the stand, and, followed by others, met the poor man literally half way, escorted him to the desk, and guided his hand as he signed his name . . . ," the minister wrote. "[T]hen such a shout broke forth from the friends of temperance as must have reached the angels above."[2]

More drunks now rose and came forward—"five or six others of this miserable class . . . and some 30 or 40 others, well known as hard drinkers and drunkards," the Reverend John Marsh, secretary of the American Temperance Union, reported. News of the Greene Street meeting soon spread through the city. The Washingtonians addressed "immense meetings" in the largest churches every night for the next two weeks. Three thousand people heard them at a meeting in City Hall Park. More than twenty-five hundred signed the Washingtonian pledge. "The victory was now gained," Marsh said. "The work of redemption among the poor drunkards had commenced."[3]

The Washingtonians were an exuberant expression of America's most optimistic age. The ideas of the European Enlightenment were expressed in the Declaration of Independence: that all men are created equal; that they are endowed by God with inalienable rights, including the right to life, liberty, and the pursuit of happiness. The American Revolution did not produce a democracy immediately, but in the following decades, the advocates of rule by the high born and well educated lost ground to those who believed that the common man should govern. In 1828, universal manhood suffrage helped elect President

Andrew Jackson. The United States was growing rapidly, both economically and geographically, and experiencing its first great wave of immigrants. In such a dynamic society, most Americans agreed that change was a good thing.

Changes in American religion contributed strongly to this dynamism. For more than a century, Protestant ministers had endeavored to convince believers that they were naturally sinful and that most people were destined for hell. But this bleak philosophy was challenged by a series of revivals that were sweeping the country. The sermons preached by the revivalists were no less frightening in evoking the horrors of damnation. Before large meetings, often held outdoors to accommodate the crowds, they did their best to create an emotional response that caused people to scream, fall to the floor, jerk uncontrollably, even bark like dogs. But the revivalists offered their listeners the promise of salvation. If they let God enter their hearts, the revivalists said, they would shed their evil nature and become new, guaranteeing eternal life.

As Americans became increasingly hopeful about improving their condition, they embraced reform. By the 1830s, they acknowledged that they had many problems to confront. Rapid growth had made many men rich, but it had also created a growing class of impoverished workers who had nowhere to turn during the frequent recessions. Crime was a growing threat to social order. Yet Americans believed in progress. If man was essentially good, then social problems were not inevitable. "It is to the defects of our social organization . . . that we chiefly owe the increase of evil doers," declared Dorothea Dix, a pioneer in seeking more humane treatment for the mentally ill. She was joined by a generation of reformers who sought to improve conditions through education, universal peace, prison reform, equal rights for women, and the end of slavery.[4]

During this period of hopefulness, the movement to curb the consumption of liquor emerged. In 1808, as Handsome Lake worked to spread sobriety among the Iroquois in western New York, a doctor and a minister started the first temperance society in the small town of Moreau in eastern New York. The first state temperance organization, the Massachusetts Society for the Suppression of Intemperance, was organized a few years later. The meaning of "temperance" would evolve in the following decades. At first, it meant abstinence from rum, whiskey, and other distilled liquors. Many who signed a temperance pledge continued to enjoy their glass of beer or wine in good conscience. The predominant role that the clergy would play in the temperance movement throughout its history is apparent in the fact that the Massachusetts society addressed itself to the problems of Sabbath breaking and profanity as well as drinking whiskey.

The movement grew rapidly after the launch of a national organization, the American Society for the Promotion of Temperance, which soon included a thousand local temperance groups with a membership of a hundred thousand. In 1835, the American Temperance Society claimed that more than two million people had signed pledges promising that they would not drink distilled liquor, forcing four thousand distilleries to close. Alcohol consumption fell from seven gallons per person in 1830 to slightly more than three gallons in 1840, the biggest decline during a ten-year period in American history. This amazing success convinced the leaders of the temperance movement that the goal of national sobriety was within reach. But the movement stalled when a split developed between those who opposed only hard liquor and those demanding total abstinence ("teetotalers").

Worried temperance leaders saw the emergence of the Washingtonians as almost miraculous. For centuries, it had been assumed that little could be done to help alcoholics, and the temperance movement had directed its energy to preventing the creation of new drunkards, rather than the reclamation of those who were afflicted. The Reverend Justin Edwards, a founder of the American Temperance Society, explained:

> We are at present fast hold of a project for making all people in this country, and in all other countries, temperate; or rather, a plan to induce those who are now temperate to continue so. Then, as all who are intemperate will soon be dead, the earth will be eased of an amazing evil.

Not all temperance leaders were so pessimistic about the possibility of recovery. One leader, Gerritt Smith, presented case studies of how temperance had improved the lives of thirty-eight of his neighbors in a small town in upstate New York, including men and women who were certainly alcoholic.[5]

But no one expected to see the day when an alcoholic like John Hawkins would step on a public stage and proclaim his intention to save other drunks. Hawkins certainly never expected it. He had been struggling with alcoholism for half of his life. Hawkins's father, a tailor in the Fell's Point section of Baltimore, died when John was thirteen. Hawkins had already displayed a "daring, brave and restless spirit" in frequent clashes with the minister who had been given the responsibility of educating him. During the War of 1812, at the age of sixteen, he picked up a gun and rushed to meet invading British troops during the Battle of North Point. Later, to help curb his adventurous spirit, Hawkins was apprenticed to a hatmaker. Although his master was strict, Hawkins took to the work eagerly. During his apprenticeship, he began to drink regularly. Employers served their workers alcohol during the workday, and apprentices received the same liquor as adults. Hawkins later described his first place of employment as "perfect a grog-shop as ever existed." He said that eight of his twelve fellow apprentices "died drunkards."[6]

After Hawkins completed his apprenticeship, he was unable to find work. Like so many other young men, he decided to look for opportunity in the West. He arrived in Pittsburgh after ten days of travel by foot, stagecoach, and boat. He found a job, but two months later, he was on the move again, traveling south along the Ohio River to Cincinnati. Hawkins wrote to his mother that it was "a beautiful place" of fourteen thousand people. He found a job there, too, but left after just a couple of weeks to join relatives in Madison, Indiana. "I have had sore conflicts since I left home," he wrote his mother, without providing any details. His relatives were more forthcoming. They told his mother that Hawkins was drinking. "As soon as I was away from parental care, I gave way; all went by the board, and my sufferings commenced," Hawkins explained later.[7]

With hard times spreading west, he found little work over the next two years. For six months, he had only the clothes he wore and no shoes. But if jobs were dear, liquor was cheap. By the time he made it back to Baltimore, his health was beginning to break. "John, I am afraid you are bloated," his mother said. His stomach may have been distended by malnutrition. It is also possible that he was suffering from a swollen liver that had been damaged by heavy drinking.[8]

Hawkins was able to stop drinking for extended periods. He returned to the Methodist Church and married. He tried to tackle the West again, loading his wife and three children into a Conestoga wagon. Thirteen months later, the covered wagon returned to Baltimore. Business had been slow, and his wife was in poor health. Hawkins was also drinking again. When his wife died, leaving him with three young children, he got sober again. For four years, he enjoyed the luxury of steady work and remarried. Even a new wife and his religious faith could not prevent another relapse.

Hawkins had never known such hard times. In 1837, the country entered a depression that would last for six years. Unable to work in his own trade, he was forced to take any job he could find. A job in a bakery paid just a dollar for a day of work that started just after midnight and continued almost nonstop until seven or eight at night. He had to quit after three weeks because he could not stand the pace. "You cannot imagine the trouble of mind I have and am still passing through for the want of employment at my own business," he wrote his parents.[9]

Poverty did not stop Hawkins's drinking. His consumption of alcohol was actually increasing. By June 1840, he was buying whiskey by the gallon and drinking a quart and a half a day. On the morning of June 12, Hawkins was in agony as he lay in bed listening to the sounds of his family preparing breakfast below. "I was a wonder to myself; astonished I had any mind left; and yet it seemed in the goodness of God uncommonly clear," he said.

> I laid in bed long after my wife and daughter were up, and my *conscience* drove me to madness. I hated the darkness of the night, and when light came I hated the light. I hated myself, my existence. I asked myself, "Can I restrain? Is it possible? Not a being to take me by the hand and lead or help me along, and say, '*you can*.'" I was friendless, without help or light; an outcast.

His wife, Ann, came upstairs and asked Hawkins to come down to breakfast. He told her he would, but he remained in bed, trying to decide whether to drink his last pint of whiskey. "I knew it was life or death with me, as I decided," he said. His thirteen-year-old daughter Hannah appeared at the door next. Hannah was her father's favorite.

When he stumbled home at night, collapsing in the hallway, she fetched a blanket and pillow and watched over him until he was sober enough to drag himself to bed. She also bought him liquor. "[S]he was a drunkard's friend—my only friend," Hawkins said.[10]

Hannah also tried to get her father to come down to breakfast, but she added a new plea. "Father, don't send me after whiskey today," she said. Hawkins was stung. "I was tormented before, but this was unexpected torture," he said. He ordered her from the room, and she left in tears. Hawkins pulled the bedcovers over his head, but a short time later, he heard someone enter the room. Peeping out, he saw that Hannah had returned. Filled with remorse and shame, he called to her. "Hannah, I am not angry with you, and I shall not drink any more," he said. "She cried, and so did I." There was still a pint of whiskey in the bedroom cupboard. As he rose and dressed, Hawkins looked at the bottle several times. "Is it possible I can be restored," he asked himself. He was sure that if he drank it, he was doomed. "I suffered all the horrors of the pit that day," Hawkins said. But his family supported him. "Hold on—hold on," Ann said.[11]

Hawkins had quit drinking on a Friday. By Saturday, he was feeling better, but there was no guarantee that he could remain sober. Ann must have been alarmed when he left the house on Monday night without telling her where he was going. Soon after, he arrived at his first meeting of "the society of drunkards." The men in the room included the founders of the Washington Temperance Society. He also found some old friends. "We had fished together—got drunk together," he said. "One said, 'There is Hawkins, the "regulator," the old *bruiser*,' and they clapped and laughed." Hawkins was not in a laughing mood. "I was too sober and solemn for that," he said.

One of the goals of the Washingtonian meeting was to persuade newcomers to sign a pledge not to drink alcoholic beverages of any kind, whether distilled or fermented. "The pledge was read for my accommodation; they did not say so, and yet I knew it," Hawkins said. "They all looked over my shoulder to see me sign my name. I never had such feeling before. It was a great battle." At home, Ann listened for her husband's return, fearing the worst. She was astonished to see him sober when he opened the door. "I told her quick—I could not keep it back—'I have put my name to the temperance pledge never to drink as long as I live!'" Their celebration woke Hannah, who joined in the tears.[12]

After a life of misfortune, Hawkins had finally gotten lucky. The Washingtonian movement was only two months old when he decided to get sober. The whole thing had started in a bar. On the evening of April 2, 1840, six friends sat in the Chase Tavern in Baltimore discussing a lecture by a well-known temperance advocate that was scheduled for later that night. They met at the tavern almost every night and often drank to excess. One of them, William K. Mitchell, would later say that he had been trying to control his drinking for fifteen years without success. Four of the party decided to go hear what the temperance advocate had to say. They were impressed. "After all temperance is a good thing," one said when the group had returned to the bar. They decided to form their own temperance society and to make Mitchell the president.[13]

Two days later, on a Sunday, the six men met again and discussed the project over drinks. Mitchell, who had not attended the lecture, agreed to serve as president and to draft a pledge. On Monday, he carried the pledge to his friends, finding the first still in bed nursing a hangover. On the evening of April 5, they held the first meeting of the Washington Temperance Society in the home of one of the members.

The number of Washingtonians grew rapidly. With the exception of Mitchell, who owned his own tailoring business, all of the founders were workingmen—two blacksmiths, a carpenter, a coach-maker, and silver-plater. Members were required to participate in recruitment, and they found many prospects among their heavy-drinking friends. Anyone could join by signing the pledge; a significant number were not drunks. They joined out of sympathy for the cause and because the meetings were so interesting. Mitchell suggested that the way to keep the meetings lively was for members to stand and describe their problem with alcohol. Mitchell was the first to tell his story, and soon several men were sharing at every meeting. John Zug, an early historian of the movement, described the meetings: "[A]fter their regular business is transacted, the several members rise promiscuously and state their temperance experience for each other's warning, instruction and encouragement. . . . To hear the tales of degradation, woe, and crime, which some describe as the condition to which they had reduced themselves by strong drink, is enough to melt the heart of stone."[14]

When the meetings grew too large to be held in private homes, the Washingtonians held their first public meeting in the Masonic Hall on November 19. Zug estimated that in just eight months, the Washingtonians had recruited three hundred members, including as many as two hundred "reformed drunkards." A subscription campaign was launched to raise funds for the construction of a permanent home for the movement.

After their overwhelming reception in New York, Hawkins and his comrades returned to Baltimore to join a celebration of the first anniversary of the group's founding. More than six thousand men paraded on crowded streets, marching to the music of brass bands under temperance banners that, in some cases, had been sewn by the wives of reformed men. Hawkins, who estimated that half of the marchers had quit drinking in the past year, described what the day had meant to them and their families. After years of suffering poverty and shame, they had emerged from their garrets to conquer the city:

> [W]here were our wives on that occasion? at home, shut up with hungry children in rags, as a year ago? No, no! but in carriages, riding round the streets to see their sober husbands! My family were in a hack, and I carried apples, cakes, &c. to them, and my wife said "How happy all look; why, husband, there is———all dressed up; and only think, I saw old———in the procession, as happy and smart as any of them." . . . We cut down the rum tree that day in Baltimore, under ground . . . roots and all!

Hawkins was not home for long. Washingtonian delegates were carrying the news about their movement to major cities around the country, and he headed to Boston.[15]

Hawkins and another Washingtonian, William E. Wright, encountered packed houses everywhere. They spoke at the Odeon, on Thursday, April 15, where 82 signed the pledge; 279 signed on Friday, 141 on Saturday, and 429 on Sunday. The biggest meeting yet was held at Faneuil Hall, known as the "cradle of liberty" for the role it had played in rallying Bostonians during the American Revolution. The circumstances of the meeting were not ideal. President William Henry Harrison had died in office two weeks earlier, and the hall was hung with black bunting. The city had also been hit by a storm that brought heavy rain. But the large hall was full, men occupying the seats on the main floor and women in the galleries along the side walls and rear of the room.

Hawkins's speech shared nothing of the gloom and melancholy of his surroundings. He began by confessing his amazement to find himself on such a famous stage. "When I compare the past with the present, my days of intemperance with my present peace and sobriety, my past degradation with my present position in this hall, the Cradle of Liberty—I am overwhelmed," he said. "It seems to me holy ground." At the same time, it was the perfect place to make a second declaration of independence:

> Drunkard! Come up here; you can reform;—take the pledge in the Cradle of Liberty and be free! Delay not. I met a gentleman this morning who reformed four weeks ago, rejoicing in his reforma- tion. He brought a man with him who took the pledge, and this man has already brought two others. This is the way we do the business up in Baltimore; we reformed drunkards are a *Committee of the Whole on the State of the Union!* are all missionaries—don't slight the drunkard, but love him. No; we *nurse* him as the mother does her infant learning to walk. We go right up to him and say, How do you do? and he remembers our kindness.

Hawkins told the story of one Baltimore drunk—"a real wharf rat" whose family was starving, their clothes "not fit for paper rags." The Washingtonians persuaded his brother to lend him the money to buy a horse and cart. "He has paid for his horse and cart, his family and him- self are well clothed, cellar full of wood, a barrel of flour, and he has be- come a Christian gentleman. All this in one short year," Hawkins said.[16]

Hawkins explained that the Washingtonians were not a new class of philanthropists. They saw the problem through the eyes of drunks. They knew all the tricks of the "grog-sellers," who put out free plates of salted fish, cheese, herring, and crackers. "Well the stuff is very apt to stick in the throat, so it is washed down, and then the breath must be changed, and a little more fish or cheese is taken, and that must be washed out of the throat; and so it goes," he said. Hawkins added that the tavern keeper was not the only one guilty of mistreating the drunk. When a man finally developed an unquenchable thirst for alcohol, he found himself an outcast:

> This making the drunkard by a thousand temptations and induce-ments, and then shutting him up in prison, is a cruel and horrible business. You make the drunkard, and then let him come into your house, and you turn him out; let him come to the church, and you turn him out; friends cast him off; the grog-seller turns him out when his money is gone, or midnight comes. When he serves his time out in the prison, he is turned out with the threat of a flogging if he is ever caught again; and yet you keep open the place where he is entangled and destroyed.

The Washingtonians were able to help drunks because they knew their problems and because they continued to need help themselves. "I tell you that we keep close watch of each other," Hawkins said. At times, this meant being in smelling distance. "We are very loving, and we take care to get along-side the mouth and know what has been going on there."[17]

The Washingtonians were missionaries to the wider world as well. They were fully committed to the philosophy of teetotalism. They be-lieved that alcohol had made them drunks and that abstinence was the only way to avoid the danger of alcoholism. "Is there a moderate drinker who says he can use 'a little,' or 'much' and 'quit when he pleases?'" Haw-kins asked.

> I tell him from experience he can't do it. Well, he can *if he will*, but HE WON'T WILL! that is the difficulty, and there is the fatal mistake. Does he want to know whether he can? I ask him to go without his accustomed morning bitters or his eleven-o'clock, to-morrow, and he will find how he loves it! We have come up out of the gutter, to tell him how much he loves it, and how he can escape.

Hawkins warned against "the pretty drink, the genteel and the fash-ionable." Hawkins spoke for over an hour, his powerful voice reaching every corner of the great hall. He then introduced a local man named Johnson, a shoemaker who had only recently quit drinking. Johnson was speaking publicly for the first time and was apparently too nervous to talk for more than a few minutes. Applause filled the hall. "Everybody manifested joy at his perfect emancipation from the slavery of intemperance, and wished him 'God speed,'" a reporter for the *Mercantile Journal* wrote. With three cheers, the meeting was adjourned, and "pledges were then taken in great numbers."[18]

Hawkins and his partner delivered dozens of speeches in all kinds of venues during their two-week visit. One Sunday, Hawkins addressed three hundred men in the state prison in Charlestown. "He was listened to with closest attention when he described what he *knew* of the evils of intemperance, of the terrible effects it had produced upon himself and his family . . . ," a reporter wrote. "[H]e showed that the drunkard, although by many regarded as incorrigible, and treated as an outcast from society, *can be reformed*, and become a respectable and useful member of society."

> Those convicts seemed to feel the force of this language; this appeal to their feelings, to their better nature, was not in vain. All of them seemed to regard him as a friend, as a monitor, who came among them to fortify their souls against crimes; and many of them wept, yes, those rough-looking despised men, wept like children, and those were precious tears.

A week later, Hawkins started for home, speaking and collecting pledges as he went: 318 in Worcester, Massachusetts; 520 in Norwich, Connecticut; 315 in Paterson, New Jersey. On the dock in Philadelphia, preparing to board a boat to Baltimore, Hawkins was arrested for an old bar bill. But he paid his tab and was soon on his way. The money probably came from donations collected at the meetings he addressed. Hawkins never returned to his trade as a hatter. He supported himself and his family with speaking fees.[19]

It seemed that nothing could stop the headlong progress of the Washingtonians. In Baltimore, membership nearly doubled to more than twenty-two hundred in 1841, leading to the formation of new weekly meetings around the city and plans to construct a central meeting place that would hold twenty-five hundred people. The growth of the Washingtonians was even more explosive in New York, the largest city in the nation. "The reformed drunkards are becoming missionaries—scouring the streets and lanes, penetrating the haunts of vice, and by encouraging words and kindness are pressing persuasion, leading the poor, wretched inebriate up to the pledge," the *New York Herald* reported in August 1841. Six months after the Greene Street meeting, there were fifty Washingtonian societies meeting around the city. Washingtonians claimed as many as twenty thousand members. A number of prominent merchants, professionals, and master craftsmen who owned their own shops helped lead the New York societies, but the majority of members were workers. Bakers, butchers, hatters, printers, and shipwrights established their own societies, helping make New York the "banner city" of Washingtonianism.[20]

Baltimore, New York, and Boston became hubs, sending delegates to surrounding communities. The first society in Philadelphia was established by some of the men who were on their way home to Baltimore after their speaking engagements in New York. The Washington Total Abstinence Society of Boston sent delegates to 160 towns in Massachusetts, New Hampshire, Maine, Vermont, and Rhode Island. William Wright, who had accompanied Hawkins to New York and Boston, toured upstate New York as far west as Buffalo in the summer of 1841 and later made several trips to Virginia. By early 1842, there were Washingtonian societies in Chicago, New Orleans, and Mobile, Alabama. New hubs emerged in Washington, DC, Philadelphia, Pittsburgh, Cleveland, Cincinnati, and St. Louis.

The remarkable growth of Washingtonianism is partly explained by the enthusiasm of men whose lives had been saved by sobriety. A single delegate could work miracles. During a four-month tour of Georgia, one man visited 13 counties, delivered 142 addresses, and organized 31 societies. Among the 6,300 who signed the pledge, there were 600 reformed drunkards, 2,000 moderate drinkers, and 1,600 "temperate" men and 2,000 women. These figures are only suggestive. How were "drunkards" distinguished from moderate drinkers or "temperate" men? All we can say with certainty is that the country was in a temperance fever, and many of those who were running a temperature were alcoholics who believed for a time that they had a real chance for sobriety.

The participation of women was a surprise. Women embraced the Washingtonian movement so strongly that they were often a majority of the audience at the meetings where reformed men spoke about their experience as drunks. They began to organize their own groups, often within days of the arrival of the Washingtonians. They were known collectively as Martha Washington societies, and the members called themselves Marthas. There was a precedent for female participation in the temperance movement, but like temperance men of the period, they were mostly middle- and upper-class women. The Marthas were from the working and lower-middle classes. Most were the mothers, wives, and daughters of alcoholics who had intimate knowledge of the devastation that drinking could cause. They could be seen at Washingtonian meetings urging their men to sign the pledge. Hawkins helped start a Martha Washington society during his trip to Boston and another in Paterson, New Jersey, on his way home to Baltimore. By 1843, there were thousands of Marthas around the country.

Like the Washingtonians, the Marthas attempted to relieve the suffering of alcoholics and their families. Their groups met as often as every week, sewing and repairing clothing that they distributed to people who were almost naked. They also helped with furniture, bedding, and even cash. The Marthas were particularly interested in helping women alcoholics. While men were far more likely to be drunks, more than two hundred women were arrested for drunkenness in New York City every week. The Lady Mount Vernon Temperance Benevolent Society explained how it tried to help them:

> Instead of reproaching the fallen of our sex with harsh rebukes, we offer the friendship and confidence of our ladies. After signing the pledge, they are visited and their immediate wants supplied, as far as possible, and employment secured for them. Thus, real and efficient sympathy give them a motive for good action and rarely do they disappoint us.

Marthas sometimes risked their lives trying to help. In Utica, New York, they knocked on a door that the neighbors were too frightened to try and discovered a drunken woman whose eyes were swollen shut from a beating administered by her inebriated husband. The woman promised to renew her broken pledge, and her husband signed, too. She may soon have been making calls herself. Martha Washington societies welcomed reformed drunks as members, including "inveterate cases." Membership was no guarantee that a woman would stay sober, but the support of her fellow Marthas undoubtedly improved her chances.[21]

Catholics also joined the Washingtonians. This was not a small matter. The many Protestant sects in the United States didn't agree on much, but they all feared the Catholic Church. Rhode Island and Pennsylvania had been the only colonies that allowed Catholics to vote, and restrictions on the civil liberties of Catholics and Jews remained on the books as late as 1820. Fear of Catholics grew as they began to arrive in large numbers from Ireland and Germany in the 1820s and 1830s. In 1834, a mob burned a Catholic convent to the ground in Charlestown, Massachusetts. Anti-Catholic literature proliferated, including the notorious *Awful Disclosures of the Hotel Dieu Nunnery of Montreal*, which accused priests and nuns of sexual perversion. Lecturers carried the warning of the Catholic threat to every village, and attacks on Catholic churches became so frequent that insurers refused to issue policies for any buildings that were not constructed of brick. Hatred for Catholics also grew among white, native-born workingmen who competed for jobs with the foreigners. The competition only became more intense during the depression of 1837.

The leaders of the temperance movement before 1840 were predominantly Protestant ministers who naturally shared the anti-Catholicism of their countrymen. But they were ready to embrace Catholics who signed the abstinence pledge. They were thrilled by news of the great temperance movement that was then sweeping Ireland under the direction of a Capuchin priest from Cork, the Reverend Theobald Matthew. Rev. Matthew began his crusade by founding the Cork Total Abstinence Society in 1838. He was soon conducting mass meetings and collecting pledges by the thousands—25,000 in Cork alone in just three months; the number reached 130,000 just a few months later. Rev. Matthew's influence soon became apparent on the other side of the Atlantic. The Reverend John Marsh, the secretary of the American Temperance Union, reported in November 1839 that five thousand to ten thousand Irish immigrants had taken the total abstinence pledge.

The Washingtonians welcomed Catholics as they did any man who wanted to quit drinking. It was a part of their creed that membership was open to adherents of any religion and no religion. While the overwhelming majority of Washingtonians were practicing Christians, they feared that evangelicals proselytizing for a variety of denominations would attempt to take over their movement, creating dissension and diverting their efforts to save drunks. For this reason, the Baltimore Washingtonians initially barred prayers from their meetings. This made them a target for criticism by the older temperance leaders as well as a growing nativist movement. In 1841, when the Washingtonians were drawing large crowds in Baltimore, a correspondent for the *New York Herald* criticized them for allowing a Philadelphia priest to address a meeting of two thousand. The reporter also referred scornfully to the audience as "including darkeys, women and children." The reference to African Americans is significant because blacks outside the slave states were active in the temperance movement and apparently organized their own Washingtonian groups, although little is known about them.[22]

According to his son's biography, Hawkins was always ready to address a Catholic audience. During a tour of the South, he was approached by a priest in Savannah, Georgia, who told him that drunkenness was a big problem for his parishioners and urged him to speak at his church. Hawkins was surprised to find that every seat in the large church was filled. The sexton had placed a table below the altar. When the priest asked why, he replied, "And sure, sir, it is for the spaker [sic] to stand upon." The priest ordered the table removed and told Hawkins to speak in front of the altar where he himself normally stood. The priest sat in the first pew and joined many in the audience in weeping as Hawkins described the sad fate of the alcoholic and his family. He jumped to his feet as soon as Hawkins had finished. "Fasten every door of the church," he ordered. "Let not a man or a woman leave the house until you have all signed the pledge!"[23]

In the winter of 1842, it appeared that the Washingtonians had permanently changed the nation. Temperance leaders estimated that a half-million people had signed the pledge during the preceding twelve months and that whiskey consumption had been cut in half. Many bars had closed: in Lynn, Massachusetts, only 3 of the 18 that had existed six months earlier were still operating; in Portland, Maine, only 24 of 130. Bars were closing even in neighborhoods that had once been notorious for drunkenness. "In one block, on Wednesday last, we counted 'To Let' on eight rum-shops, hardly a stone's-throw from the Five Points," reported a Washingtonian newspaper in New York City. Many hard-pressed retailers attempted to catch the prevailing wind by banning liquor from their premises. In Elyria, Ohio, General Griffith, the largest distiller and vendor in the area, had signed the pledge with his family and held a teetotalers' dinner to celebrate the conversion of his inn into a temperance hotel.[24]

Elaborate celebrations of the success of Washingtonianism were held throughout the country on February 22, 1843, Washington's birthday. The largest celebration occurred in New York City, where the Washingtonians took over all four of the halls that had been built over one of the city's largest public markets. Three thousand people thronged the doors, eventually making their way into an area the size of a modern football field. The space was so vast that speaking platforms were erected at both ends of the building to ensure that most of the crowd could hear. Reformed drunks dominated the early part of the evening. Hawkins spoke, and so did the young man who had pleaded for his help at the Greene Street church a year earlier. During the first break in the program, the crowd descended on the hundreds of tables filled with food that lined the walls, washing everything down with two thousand tumblers of clear, cold water. The evening ended with a round of toasts that were responded to with music, instead of drink. A temperance glee club sang, and recently reformed firemen entertained with "appropriate and animated songs." The entire audience joined in three temperance anthems before the evening ended.[25]

The Washingtonians celebrated in frontier towns as well as big cities. In Springfield, Illinois, a rapidly growing community of fifteen hundred, the Washington Temperance Society of Springfield invited State Representative Abraham Lincoln to deliver an address. Lincoln had moved to Springfield in 1837 when it became the state capitol and had begun to practice law. At six feet four, the swarthy and beardless twenty-eight-year-old never failed to make an impression on those he met. He made friends easily, relying on a seemingly limitless supply of jokes and stories to smooth the way. He was already a leader of the Whig Party in the state legislature.

Lincoln seemed like a perfect choice to speak to the Washingtonians. He didn't drink, and he fully supported the goal of temperance. "Whether or not the world would be vastly benefitted by a total and final banishment from it of all intoxicating drinks, seems to me not *now* to be an open question," Lincoln told his Springfield neighbors. "Three-fourths of mankind confess the affirmative with their *tongues*, and I believe, all the rest acknowledge it in their *hearts*." But Lincoln was not a prohibitionist. He was highly critical of the leaders of the temperance movement before the emergence of the Washingtonians. They assumed that drunks couldn't be saved and consigned them to the devil, alienating potential supporters. "There is something so repugnant to humanity, so uncharitable, so cold-blooded and feelingless [*sic*], that it never did, nor ever can enlist the enthusiasm of a popular cause," Lincoln said. He believed that helping drunks should be the main goal.[26]

One of the great advantages the Washingtonians had over the old temperance leaders was that they recognized the humanity in every drunk. "Those whom they desire to convince and persuade, are their old friends and companions," Lincoln said. "They know that generally, they are kind, generous and charitable, even beyond the example of their more staid and sober neighbors."

> I believe, if we take habitual drunks as a class, their heads and hearts will bear an advantageous comparison with those of any other class. There seems ever to have been a proneness in the brilliant, and the warm-blooded, to fall into this vice.—The demon of intemperance ever seems to have delighted in sucking the blood of genius and of generosity. What one of us but can call to mind some dear relative, more promising in his youth than all of his fellows, who has fallen a sacrifice to his rapacity?

In Lincoln's opinion, the main purpose for normal drinkers to take the pledge was to provide moral support for the newly sober man. "[T]o break off from the use of drams, who has indulged in them for a long course of years, and until his appetite for them has become ten or a hundred-fold stronger . . . requires a more powerful moral effort," Lincoln said. His neighbors and relatives could help by showing him there was no necessity for drink. "When he casts his eyes around him, he should be able to see all that he respects, all that his admires, and all that he loves, kindly and anxiously pointing him onward; and none beckoning him back, to his former miserable 'wallowing in the mire.'"[27]

Lincoln believed that the Washingtonians were succeeding not only because they were more sympathetic to the drunk but because they had found a way to appeal to the reason of men who appeared to have lost it forever. Convincing a drunk that you were his friend was the critical first step. "Therein is a drop of honey that catches his heart, which, say what he will, is the great high road to his reason, and which, when once gained, you will find but little trouble in convincing his judgment of the justice of your cause," Lincoln said. No one was better suited for this job than another drunk. Reformed drunks had many lessons to teach about how to rebuild one's life. But their greatest gift was hope:

> They teach hope to all—despair to none . . . And what is a matter of the most profound gratulation [sic], they, by experiment upon experiment, and example upon example, prove the maxim to be no less true in one case than in the other. On every hand we behold those who but yesterday were the chief sinners, now the chief apostles of the cause. Drunken devils are cast out by ones, by sevens, and by legions. And their unfortunate victims, like the poor possessed, who was redeemed from his long and lonely wanderings in the tombs, are publishing to the ends of the earth, how great things have been done for them.

Lincoln believed that the Washingtonians had proved that anyone could get sober, although he would certainly have acknowledged that not all of them would stay sober.[28]

Lincoln hoped the Washingtonians would do more than save drunken lives. The conflict over slavery was beginning to erupt in acts of violence. In Illinois, an abolitionist editor had been murdered by a proslavery mob. Lincoln believed the solution was for his countrymen to adhere to what he described in another speech as "cold, calculating, unimpassioned" reason. Temperance could help the nation subdue the growing passions over slavery:

> With such an aid, its march cannot fail to be on and on, till every son of earth shall drink in rich fruition the sorrow-quenching draughts of perfect liberty. Happy day, when, all appetites controlled, all passions subdued, all matter subjected, mind, all-conquering mind, shall live and move, the monarch of the world! Glorious consummation! Hail, fall of fury! Reign of reason, all hail!

But the Washingtonians were already encountering strong headwinds.[29]

There wasn't a cloud in the sky on May 30, 1844, when Boston celebrated the third anniversary of the city's first Washingtonian meetings. "It was a brilliant day, in the most beautiful of months," John B. Gough, a reformed drunk, recalled. "The sun shone from a sky of cloudless azure, and the young May flowers rejoiced in his beams; the river sparkled as it flowed along, bearing on its broad bosom majestic barques decorated from trucks to main-chains with gay flags and streamers." Boston was a thriving mercantile port and the state capital, but all private and government business had been adjourned, allowing thousands to converge on the route of a grand parade. Under colorful banners and strings of uncorked bottles hung upside down, the Boston Brigade Band led the parade playing "triumphant music." It was followed by the Washington Light Infantry and then a four-horse carriage bearing Governor George Briggs and William K. Mitchell, who had helped launch the Washingtonians. Then came many members of local temperance societies, who formed a "long and imposing procession." If any excitement was lost, it rekindled at the appearance of a corps of marching children. "Some were there who had once known the misery of having a drunken parent; who had long been strangers to the kind word and approving smile . . . ," Gough said. "[H]appily the little things trooped on, waving . . . banners, and shouting for very joy." The marchers finally reached Boston Common, where a huge crowd was waiting to hear the governor and other dignitaries extol the rapid growth of the temperance movement.[30]

Appearances were deceiving. Riding at the front of the parade with Governor Briggs and Mitchell was the Reverend John Marsh. Marsh had been a strong supporter of the Washingtonians in the beginning. They had given a lift to the temperance movement at a critical moment. But he saw troubling signs of decline. Fewer people were attending Washingtonian meetings, and the number of bars was rising again. The *Journal of the American Temperance Union* said that the public was growing bored listening to drunks tell their life stories. The Washingtonian "experience" meetings had produced "a new and most important era in the temperance reformation." The *Journal* continued:

> There has been nothing like it. But like everything else, it has its day; and, when repeated and long continued, becomes stale and wearisome. In spite of various characters introduced, there is a sameness in the tale, for every drunkard's life is in its leading features the same.

Six months later, a Cincinnati minister confirmed this view. "[T]hough the Washingtonians have endured, and worked well, their thunder is worn out," he said.[31]

Marsh and other ministers were also unhappy about signs of religious indifference among the Washingtonians. In 1843, during a Washingtonian meeting in Newark, a Rev. Scott complained about the Washingtonians holding meetings on Sundays. A Washingtonian newspaper, the *Crystal Fount and Rechabite Recorder*, reported that this irritated some members of Scott's audience, and the minister was chastised by the next speaker. "Mr. Segue, of Morris County . . . gave us a thorough-going Washingtonian address, in which he gave [Scott] two or three severe, but at the same time very polite 'raps on the knuckles,'" it said. The newspaper's editor explained that while the Washingtonians wanted to work with ministers, they feared that religion could be an obstacle to getting men sober:

> For the propagation of the temperance cause we wish to meet on common ground, but if we agree to unite with temperance anything which should be kept separate, we must fail in accomplishing

the object we have in view. Our object is to reform the inebriate, and if the infidel or the skeptic will unite with us effecting his redemption from rum drinking, we give them the right hand of fellowship.

The Washingtonians concerned themselves with saving lives, not saving souls. Therefore, the Sunday meetings would continue. "We believe it is 'lawful to do good on Sabbath Day,' and as our Sabbath evening meetings are eminently calculated 'to do good,' they will most assuredly be continued," the editor wrote.[32]

The opinions of the Washingtonians were becoming irrelevant. Temperance leaders were preparing to move forward without them. As attendance at Washingtonian meetings continued to decline, groups began to close. "Where are all the Washingtonian societies, which sprang up in a night? Dead or breathing their last!" the American Temperance Union journal wrote just five months after the huge Boston demonstration. But the temperance movement would live on, it insisted.

Is not this evidence of a retrograde feeling in the temperance community? We say, No. Amid all these declines and changes and deaths, the temperance cause has moved onward. Each new organization has given it a new impulse for the time, and when it has accomplished its work, it has given way to something more acceptable to the community and perhaps more efficient.

The *Journal* was right. The temperance movement's first major victories were just around the corner. In 1851, Maine approved the first statewide ban on the sale of alcohol; twelve more states and two Canadian provinces soon followed. Despite the boasts of the Washingtonians, "moral suasion" was not the wave of the future.[33]

The Washingtonians were probably doomed from the beginning. The explosion of popularity that greeted their arrival was both a blessing and a curse. It filled their meetings with eager recruits, but the overwhelming majority of men who signed the pledge did not have a deep personal interest in sobriety. They signed because they were moved by the spectacle of alcoholics reclaiming their lives, because they thought it would be good for the country and might improve the quality of their lives. Some signed because everyone else was signing, and they wanted to share the excitement. But only a small minority of the signers were people who had a serious problem with alcohol.

There are no precise numbers. Rev. Marsh estimated that 4 million people signed the pledge during the 1840s, including 500,000 hard drinkers and 100,000 "sots." A modern student of the Washingtonians estimates that fewer than 150,000 heavy drinkers joined the movement. In any case, the reformed drunks constituted a small minority of the people who took the pledge. They made up a larger percentage of the membership of the Washingtonian groups, but they probably weren't a majority. As a result, many Washingtonians were never more than fair-weather friends who quickly lost interest in the organization.[34]

When the nonalcoholics deserted, the Washingtonian movement was left in the hands of the reformed men. They did not lose interest in the "drunkalogues" that were spoken at meetings. The many similarities in the life histories of alcoholics were actually a source of strength for the recovering drunks, encouraging them to see themselves as part of a larger group with a responsibility to support men who were struggling and to reach out to alcoholics who were still drinking. But they faced temptation every day. There were three thousand bars in New York City. Temperance leaders were so alarmed by the number of new bars opening in Boston that they held a series of meetings in late 1842 and early 1843 to study the problem. The only explanation appeared to be that men were beginning to break their pledges. "Backsliding" was a growing threat.

Politics made matters worse. Politicians in the early American republic were novices in the democratic arts, but it didn't take them long to recognize that the shortest route to a man's vote was through a shot glass. The Founding Fathers had been the first to "treat" their constituents to hard cider or whiskey. The advent of universal male suffrage propelled election-related drinking to new heights. "In many counties the candidates would hire all the groceries in the county seats and other considerable villages, where the people could get liquor without cost for several weeks before election . . . ," a former governor of Illinois recalled. "[L]ong before night a large portion of the voters would be drunk and staggering about town, cursing, swearing, halloing, yelling, huzzaing for their favorite candidates." The importance of alcohol was clear on the day that Andrew Jackson was inaugurated in 1829. The rowdiness of his supporters at a reception threatened serious damage to the White House until the punch bowl was carried out to the lawn, drawing the crowd with it.[35]

The excesses of election year drinking were no laughing matter for the Washingtonians, especially the members who were newly sober alcoholics. It was hard enough to remain abstinent in normal times. The elections of the time were tremendously exciting events. "The minds of all men seem filled with but one idea—'How our party goes,' and who will be elected," the *Crystal Fount* reported during the final days of the 1844 presidential campaign. "Such excitement we have seldom witnessed—so much singing, speaking, aye, and drinking and carousing, fighting and quarreling. Night and day have both been made hideous by the men *and boys* of both parties." The problem was exacerbated by the fact that political meetings were "almost invariably" held in taverns, which also served as polling places. The editor of the *Crystal Fount* believed that the election had undone several years of hard work:

> The evil done to the cause of temperance, during the past few months, is almost incalculable. . . . Men have broken their pledge in this city, who have held prominent stations in the temperance cause, and who have defied the tempter for two or three years, and boasted that they knew the blessing of temperance too well to break the pledge; yet carried away by excitement, and mingling in the company of rum-drinkers, and frequenting taverns, they have fallen lamentably low.

He insisted he was not discouraged. "Our army is great and vast compared with the few noble souls who began the work about four years since," he said. Even then, the army was melting away.[36]

A strong organization might have enabled the Washingtonians to survive the loss of most of its members, but it was a grassroots movement consisting of hundreds of independent groups. The Washingtonians never seemed to think they needed a national organization. The local groups were marked by an extreme democracy. Officers were elected every quarter. As a result, there were no generally accepted rules or guidelines to direct groups whose members included both former drunks and lifelong teetotalers, workers and paragons of the middle class. They were vulnerable to factionalism and internal disputes.

Americans had lost their zeal to save the alcoholic. Even the Marthas withdrew from their charity work. Virginia Allen, a newspaper editor, lamented the loss. In 1846, she reported that two hundred New York City women were arrested for drunkenness in a single week:

> Where are our Martha Washingtonians? Where those who once waited not for such objects to meet their sight, but rather sought them out and encouraged them in the pure joys of the paths of Temperance? Alas, alas, we are becoming selfish and care no more for the wretched beings whom we once delighted to rescue from misery and starvation.

The revolution was over.[37]

Yet the efforts of the Washingtonians were not wasted. It is unreasonable to expect them to have permanently erased the stigma of alcoholism. They did change the lives of thousands of drunks, at least briefly. The closing of their meetings was a serious blow because it deprived them of a regular opportunity to meet with other alcoholics, offering support to the wavering and receiving it themselves in times of need. A majority, perhaps the overwhelming majority, began drinking again. But there were men and women who remained abstinent, drawing strength wherever they could find it—from active participation in the temperance movement, religion, family, friends, and sheer willpower.

The Washingtonians had proved that many drunks wanted to get sober, but they had also learned the lesson that it is easier to get sober than to stay sober. The testimonials of reformed men speaking at meetings had inspired many drunks to try. They had signed the pledge with every intention of quitting forever. But addiction is powerful. The drunks needed a source of strength to resist temptation. The Seneca and other Iroquois tribes had found that power in a new religion. As the *Gaiwiio* or Good Word won the support of a growing number of Iroquois, it created an environment in which it was easier to resist the temptation to drink and to raise children who never acquired the habit.

The former Washingtonians were not entirely without alternatives. Many of them joined a new organization, the Sons of Temperance. All the founders were workingmen. Brothers John and Isaac Oliver were printers who were prospering on business generated by the Washingtonian phenomenon, producing sheet music, handbills, and their own newspaper, the *New York Organ*. The Olivers started the Sons of Temperance in an effort to stem backsliding by providing material incentives for membership. In return for a payment of five cents in weekly dues, the group provided medical and burial insurance for the members and their wives.

Like the Freemasons and other fraternal organizations, the Sons of Temperance developed secret rituals. They initiated members in special ceremonies, used codes and symbols, and honored members with special titles and other marks of distinction. Such affectations were necessary to compete with other fraternal organizations, but they also made it easier for drunks to seek help. The Washingtonians admitted their alcoholism in public meetings, but membership in the Sons of Temperance was secret. So a drunk could join without revealing to the world that he had a problem. Secrecy also protected the Sons from the bad publicity that visited the Washingtonians whenever one of their members got drunk. The rituals strengthened the social bond between the Sons, who were expected to help brothers who had started drinking again.

The Sons of Temperance grew rapidly, enrolling 221,578 members in chapters around the United States in just six years. As in the case of the Washingtonians, most of these men were not alcoholics. But probably thousands of drunks found refuge there or in the other fraternal temperance groups that were active at the time—the Rechabites, the Independent Order of Good Samaritans, and the Independent Order of Good Templars.

Members of the Samaritans were almost all reformed drunks. The Samaritans and their female auxiliary, the Daughters of Samaria, banned any discussion of political issues, including prohibition, and became the first group of reformed drinkers to welcome all alcoholics, including African Americans. Notwithstanding their open-door policy, the membership of the Samaritans peaked at fourteen thousand.

The Independent Order of Good Templars, which was founded in 1851, was by far the largest of the fraternal temperance societies.

Its first great leader was an ex-drunk, Nathaniel Curtis, a middle-aged baker from upstate New York. Curtis had stopped drinking during the Washingtonian movement and then joined the Sons of Temperance. But he disliked the requirement that members of the Sons pay for sickness and burial insurance because it excluded people who couldn't afford the dues. He also persuaded the Templars to welcome women as members. As a result, the Templars grew rapidly by recruiting groups that lacked social standing, including women, manual laborers, and young people.

The Templars actively recruited reformed drunks, but their ambition was larger. They wanted to help all their members remain abstinent from alcohol and strongly supported legal prohibition. The focus of their meetings was on temperance education, and members were required to follow a course of study on the subject and to pass an exam testing their knowledge. Reformed drunks do not appear to have shared their stories during the meetings. Nevertheless, the Templars helped many of them. In 1885, a former leader of the Templars estimated that four hundred thousand of the five million members who had joined since the group's founding had been "hard drinkers." As many as half of the hard drinkers were reported to have stayed sober.[38]

One Washingtonian never surrendered. Even as his comrades followed new paths, John Hawkins stuck to the old road, carrying the promise of recovery to alcoholics. The life of a Washingtonian lecturer was never easy. Travel often involved great hardship. There were no railroads in the 1840s. People traveled on sailing ships, steamboats, canal boats, and in carriages and on horseback; passage was frequently delayed by bad weather and impassable roads. Hawkins was willing to speak anywhere there was at least a promise that his expenses would be covered. These contracts were not always honored. In one town, news of a poor collection following one of Hawkins's speeches prompted the local saloon keepers to send him some money. Hawkins smiled at the joke and kept the change. At the time, he was speaking almost every day and traveling an average of ten thousand miles a year.[39]

Hawkins did more than give speeches. He met with alcoholics wherever he could find them, often in jails. Since colonial times, local communities had responded to the problem of drunkenness with punishment. During the eighteenth century, Massachusetts fined drunks five shillings, and those who were unable to pay were confined in the stocks for three hours. Whipping was also used for minor crimes. These punishments were not intended to reform the offenders but to maintain public order. With the rise of humanitarianism in the early nineteenth century, the focus of criminal justice became reformation. But the change did not benefit drunks, who were arrested repeatedly and sent to jail.

During a tour of the South in the winter of 1844, the mayor of Charleston, South Carolina, asked Hawkins to visit the court where the drunks who had been arrested the night before were processed. First offenders and others who were "not so bad" were released after signing the pledge. "The others, the worst, are sent to the poorhouse, a kind of workhouse and prison," Hawkins wrote his son. "I visit them every day, talk to them, encourage them." Visiting the prison one day, Hawkins met a young man who had been confined for more than fifty days, living on bread and water in a cold, dirty cell.

Hawkins received a constant stream of requests for help from the relatives of alcoholics. It was no different in Charleston. "I have also visited with a great many families who have sent for me, to talk to the father, husband, brother, or son, as the case may be and with few exceptions, I have been successful," he told his son.[40]

To modern ears, Hawkins can sound foolish, even messianic. How could he claim success after talking with a drunk for only a few minutes? He probably did not believe he had permanently changed the men whose lives he touched. Because he was a drunk himself, he was all too aware of the danger of relapse, and he became a strong supporter of prohibition when it was clear that moral suasion could not keep men sober.

On the other hand, it is true that Hawkins and his fellow Washingtonians underestimated the difficulty of keeping men sober. They believed that alcohol was the drunk's biggest problem, and that he would become like other men when he stopped drinking. This ignored the damage that had been done by years of abusing alcohol. Drunks were seriously flawed individuals who required help to conquer what Alcoholics Anonymous would later characterize as a threefold disease— physical, mental, and spiritual. Their only hope was the growth of institutions that could provide a solution to these long-term problems.

Given enough time, the Washingtonians might have begun to provide the answers that alcoholics needed, but they were unable to sustain their movement.

Hawkins was naturally distressed by the signs of decline. Despite the success of his tours in the Midwest and the South, there was continued evidence of deterioration in the East. Even Massachusetts, a Washingtonian stronghold, was in danger. In January 1847, Hawkins wrote a letter to the editor of the *Mercantile Journal*, proposing the creation of a fund to hire a "suitable person who would be willing to devote his whole time in finding out and visiting the unfortunate drunkard and endeavor so to reform him that he may be kept out of the Police Court and House of Correction ... and make him a useful citizen, by watching over him for good." The suggestion that someone should be paid to help alcoholics was farsighted, but it was also an acknowledgment that the popular support that had once lifted the alcoholic had disappeared.[41]

Hawkins never stopped insisting on everyone's duty to help the drunkard. He delivered another call to arms in March at what was probably the last Washingtonian convention in Massachusetts:

> When I look at the nature of man, and consider the passions, like the flint and steel, ready to burst into flame at the slightest collision, I wonder that so many have been saved. I have now lived seven years a sober life, and enjoyed for seven years a sober sleep. There is nothing now to make me tremble. There is one sweet thought at morning and night, in summer and in winter, in sickness and in health, that my heart involuntarily and continually utters, and it is this, "*Thank God I am a sober man.*" Let us go on, brethren, nor cease our labors, until the last drunkard is saved. Never give up a man while there is life; but struggle on, and lift him up again and yet again, nor relinquish your hold on him, until he is dead, dead, dead![42]

In the winter of 1858, at the age of sixty, Hawkins toured Vermont, refusing to allow bad weather to prevent him from speaking on 107 days in succession. When he died later that year, his son estimated that he had traveled over 200,000 miles, spoken at more than 5,400 meetings, and addressed 1.5 million people.[43]

The Washingtonians deserve great credit for what they accomplished. They showed the country that drunks had not ceased to be human, that many desired sobriety, and that at least some could achieve it. This would inspire new efforts to help alcoholics in the years ahead. The long journey of John Hawkins was not in vain.

CHAPTER THREE

Discovery of the Disease

J. EDWARD TURNER was an irresistible force. In 1843, with the Washingtonian excitement near its peak, Turner sailed to Europe to interrogate the world's leading medical authorities about the problem of drunkenness. He was only twenty-one, but the young doctor already held strong opinions. During his medical studies and first two years of practice, he had cared for an alcoholic uncle who was given to periodic binges. His uncle's case convinced him that alcoholism was a disease, and he hoped that he would find support in Europe, which had pioneered the creation of institutions for the treatment of insanity. He spent two years in Edinburgh, London, and Paris, but he found little sympathy at a time when Europe was largely untouched by the temperance movement.

On his return to the United States, Turner resolved to gather facts to prove his theory. Abandoning his medical practice, he spent four years conducting surveys of doctors, clergymen, judges, and coroners. At first, he met indifference. During the first three years, 3,000 letters to doctors received just 134 replies. But the Washingtonians were making Americans reconsider their views. More than a third of his correspondents responded in 1848. "[E]very year thereafter there was an increased interest manifested by those addressed," Turner wrote.[1]

Turner was making progress, but he was still many years away from achieving his dream of curing alcoholism. He returned to Europe to study the design of insane asylums and hospitals in Germany, Italy, and

France. Back in America, he conducted an intense lobbying campaign in the New York State legislature that finally secured a charter for an institution to be called the "United States Inebriate Asylum." Even then, he had trouble getting anyone to serve on the board of trustees, and the men he found failed completely in their efforts to sell stock in the institution. The construction of the asylum only became possible after another lobbying campaign forced the legislature to part with some of the money that the state collected in taxes on the sale of liquor. It took him sixteen years to get that far. He estimated that there had been seventy thousand meetings.

Turner spent years perfecting the design of his asylum. He envisioned an immense institution, measuring 1,453 feet across the front of five attached buildings. There would be ten wards with twenty beds in each. He adopted a grand style to match its great size. Simple brick structures would never do for Turner. He had developed a taste for Gothic architecture during his tours of Europe, and the facade of his building would feature towers surmounted by turrets, cathedral windows, and buttresses studding the entire length of the roof. Everything was to be faced in limestone drawn from local quarries. The amenities inside would be equally lavish:

> A spacious dining hall; a reading room and library with shelving capacity for 20,000 volumes; a chapel with stained-glass windows and seating for 500 worshipers; a stage for lectures and dramatic entertainments; three expansive reception parlors; lavatories "furnished with all the appliances of the Russian bath"; numerous industrial workshops as well as diverse recreation facilities, including bowling alleys, a billiard room, and a gymnasium (patients could also go rowing on the river or riding on the grounds), a kitchen and a bakery; and a conservatory or winter garden to accommodate 100,000 plants.

Turner didn't omit a single detail.[2]

Construction of the renamed New York State Inebriate Asylum began in 1858 on a hill overlooking Binghamton, a picturesque city of eight thousand located at the confluence of two rivers in upstate New York. Five of its leading citizens arranged for the city to donate

250 acres of land. They may have seen it as a solution to the frequent drunkenness of canal boatmen who had settled in town following the completion of a local canal. They may also have believed that being the home of a pioneering medical institution would be a source of prestige. At the very least, it would encourage commerce and provide jobs. But in the beginning, it was just a source of speculation. The asylum wouldn't open for another six years.

Doctors had recognized the danger of alcohol almost a century before Turner had begun to dream. One of the first was Dr. George Cheyne, who knew the problem of addiction from the inside. Cheyne was born in Scotland in 1671 and attended the University of Edinburgh. He enrolled at the Royal College of Surgeons, which had recently been established in Edinburgh, and was such a successful student that he became a protégé of Archibald Pitcairne, one of the most celebrated doctors of his day. Pitcairne was also a somewhat scandalous figure in Edinburgh, which was under the stern eye of the Presbyterian Church. He was known as a hard drinker who wrote sometimes ribald verse satirizing the Scottish ministers. Cheyne, too, loved to drink, and his hands began to shake in the mornings while he was still a medical student.

Things got worse after Cheyne moved to London to establish a practice. He sought his clients in taverns where he spent most of his time, eating and drinking so much that his health soon failed. His weight ballooned to over four hundred pounds, and he fled to the country to avoid further temptation. His old friends appeared to forget him. "Being thus forsaken, dejected, melancholy, and confined in my country retirement, my body melting away like a snow-ball in summer, I had a long season for reflection," Cheyne recalled. In his search for guidance, he began to purchase and study religious books recommended by a clergyman he admired. He also committed himself to temperance in both food and drink. After his return to London, Cheyne wrote extensively about health and had a lot to say about the role of food and drink.[3]

In 1724, Cheyne warned that drinking was dangerous. The process usually began innocently with someone prescribing a little liquor to deal with depression caused by misfortune. But the drinking soon became compulsive:

> A little Lowness requires Drops, which pass readily down under the Notion of Physick; Drops beget Drams, and Drams beget more Drams,' till they come to be without Weight and without Measure; so that at last the miserable Creature suffers a true Martyrdom, between its natural modesty, the great Necessity of concealing its Cravings, and the still greater one of getting them satisfied some how.

"It has very often raised in me the most melancholy Reflections, to see even the Virtuous, and the Sensible, bound in such Chains and Fetters, as nothing less than omnipotent Grace or the unrelenting Grave could release them," Cheyne said. The doctor had advised patients again and again that they were killing themselves with drink. But it was no use. "They were deaf to Reason and Medicine, to their own Experience, and even to the express Words of Scripture, that says, the Drunkard shall not inherit the Kingdom of Heaven," he said.[4]

The first American doctor to notice the problem of alcoholism was Benjamin Rush, who had also studied at the University of Edinburgh, receiving his medical degree in 1768. Rush was an unusually ambitious young man with a high, domed forehead and piercing blue eyes. His evenings were devoted to reading and writing, which sometimes lasted until the early hours of the morning. He was one of the most active correspondents in the American colonies, writing friends on both sides of the Atlantic. By the time he was twenty-seven, Rush had already written more articles and pamphlets on medical subjects than almost any physician in America. "Many, many times have I heard the watchman cry 3 o'clock before I had put out my candle," he said.[5]

Rush was also a rebel. He rejected the medical theory embraced by most Philadelphia doctors and did not hesitate to insult them. Unfortunately for Rush's patients, the new theory he embraced continued to employ the traditional remedy of bloodletting. When he was establishing a practice in Philadelphia, he wrote a pamphlet attacking slavery, even though many of the people he hoped would become clients owned slaves. For years, Rush's friends had warned him to be more discreet in revealing his opinions. But he was undeterred, even as the number of visits to his office fell in the months after the publication of his pamphlet. Prudence "is a rascally virtue," Rush said.[6]

The young rebel was also an ardent believer in American independence and played a key role in bringing Pennsylvania into the revolution. He suggested to Thomas Paine that he consider writing a pamphlet and even came up with the title: *Common Sense*. Rush's efforts were rewarded by election to the Second Continental Congress shortly after the adoption of the Declaration of Independence. He took his seat in time to participate in the signing. As the Congress members waited for their turn, one joked that they might be signing their own death warrants.

However, Rush was no politician. His gift for cultivating friendships was undermined by his quick temper and lack of discretion. He supported George Washington for commander in chief and joined him in a small celebration when he won the job. Rush visited Washington in the field on Christmas Eve, 1776, when the war was going badly, and the commander was "much depressed." The next day, Washington led his troops across the Delaware and won an important victory at Princeton. However, more reverses followed, and Rush began to lose confidence in Washington. With the troops suffering at Valley Forge, Rush criticized Washington behind his back. His friendship with the father of his country ended when Washington found out what he had said. Rush, who was a surgeon general in the army, also challenged his direct superior and was forced to resign his commission.[7]

After several years of attending to his practice, Rush began to return to public life by writing anonymous articles about a variety of issues, including a piece, "Against Spirituous Liquors," that was published by the *Pennsylvania Journal* in June 1782. The article was a brief argument against the custom of serving hard liquor to farmworkers during the harvest. He did not know it at the time, but he was about to declare another war.

Rush was well aware that drinking could be harmful. At Edinburgh, he had learned about the relationship between drinking and the abdominal swelling caused by cirrhosis of the liver. He had patients who died from alcohol abuse. But it was a ten-day trip to western Pennsylvania in 1784 that convinced Rush that he must attack whiskey, rum, and other distilled liquor. During the journey, he was struck by the contrast between neat and well-ordered German farms and the usually rundown condition of those owned by Scotch Irish families. Rush thought that the explanation was that so many of the Scotch Irish farms included a still. "The quantity of rye destroyed and of whisky drunk in these places is immense, and its effects upon their industry, health and morals are terrible," Rush said.[8]

Back in Philadelphia, Rush began writing about the problem of alcohol abuse. Just two weeks later, he completed *An Enquiry into the Effects of Spirituous Liquors on the Human Body, And Their Influence upon the Happiness of Society*. Only eleven pages, the pamphlet was not a scientific treatise. Rush merely noted that since the invention of distilled spirits with high alcoholic content, "physicians have remarked that a number of new diseases have appeared among us." He described them briefly: a stomach sickness "known by tremors in the hands, insomuch that persons who labour under it, are hardly able to lift a tea cup to their heads"; "an universal dropsy" or swelling of the limbs; obstruction of the liver; "madness," "palsy," and "apoplexy." There was no need to elaborate because "the danger to life from the disease which have been mentioned is well known," Rush wrote.[9]

The solution to the problem was obvious: people must stop drinking hard liquor. Rush proceeded with his customary optimism to challenge the nearly universal view that liquor was essential and to offer a variety of alternatives. The common arguments for the use of liquor were that it staved off the effects of both extreme cold and heat and that it made hard labor easier. A drink might warm you, but it did not have nearly the lasting effect of a full meal, Rush said. The idea that fiery liquor could have a cooling effect was "absurd." "Half the diseases which are said to be produced by warm weather, I am persuaded are produced by the spirits which are swallowed to lessen its effects," he said. Rush did not expect people to stop drinking all alcoholic beverages. He considered beer healthful and supported removing the tax on it to encourage people to switch from rum and whiskey. He was also enthusiastic about wine. With such good substitutes available, why wouldn't almost everyone prefer them once they understood the dangers of liquor?[10]

Rush recognized that people who were addicted to alcohol would not find it easy to switch. None of the authors who had written about alcohol abuse had much hope for the "habitual drunkard." Rush was not so gloomy. He had known alcoholics who had quit drinking and were "restored to health, to character, and to usefulness to their families and to society." His suggestion to those who wished to quit drinking was that they quit "suddenly and entirely." "No man was ever gradually reformed from drinking spirits," he said. He even suggested "a few glasses of sound old wine every day" to help alcoholics with the side effects of withdrawal. Nevertheless, Rush recognized that some compulsion would be helpful to his cause. He wanted to see higher taxes on distilled liquor. It might also be necessary that "some mark of publick infamy" should be "inflicted by law upon every man convicted . . . of drunkenness."[11]

Over the next two decades, Rush's knowledge about alcoholism deepened. In 1804, he published an expanded version of his pamphlet that provided a detailed description of the symptoms of acute and chronic drunkenness. Rush also provided a more detailed list of diseases caused by drinking, noting that postmortem examination had revealed that the bodies of drunkards exhibited differences from those of nondrinkers. "[E]ven the hair of the head possesses a crispness which renders it less valuable to wigmakers than the hair of sober people," Rush wrote. While retaining the strong, propagandizing tone of its predecessor, Rush's new *Inquiry* made an important contribution to the medical knowledge about excessive drinking.[12]

The boldest scientific claim was that drunkenness was a disease with its own symptoms and stages of progression. The key symptom was the loss of control: both men and women felt compelled to drink until intoxicated, even knowing the damage they were doing to their loved ones and that death was near. A few years later, Rush would characterize the loss of control as "a disease of the will" and quote a drunk to drive home his point. "Were a keg of rum in one corner of a room, and were a cannon constantly discharging balls between me and it, I could not refrain from passing before that cannon, in order to get at the rum," the drunk said. Most people believed that drunks were morally weak. But Rush insisted that the loss of control was involuntary—the final stage of a process in which a person experiences drunken "paroxysms" with increasing frequency. It was not moral weakness that made people drink: it was the disease of drunkenness that made them morally weak. Anyone could be a victim—husbands, wives, judges.[13]

Rush observed that alcoholism also appeared to be hereditary. "I have once known it to descend from a father to four out of five of his children," he wrote. "I have seen three, and once four, brothers who were born of sober ancestors, affected by it." Rush could not explain this phenomena, but he thought it was significant enough to issue a warning. "These facts . . . should not be overlooked by parents, in deciding upon the matrimonial connexions to their children," he concluded.[14]

As Rush learned more about the disease of intemperance, he began to pay closer attention to its victims. What he discovered made him increasingly hopeful. The title of his 1804 pamphlet is *An Inquiry into the Effects of Ardent Spirits: An Account of the Means of Preventing, and of the Remedies for Curing Them.* It contains a new section that describes a dozen "religious, metaphysical and medical" ways in which drunks had regained their sobriety. "Examples of the divine efficacy of Christianity for this purpose have lately occurred in many parts of the United States," he wrote, apparently referring to the fact that Quakers and Methodists were urging their members not to drink. People stopped drinking because they felt guilt; Rush knew one man who recovered after he attacked his beloved wife in a drunken fit. Others were shamed into stopping by their children or their servants. A farmer was brought to his senses when his favorite goat, which had accompanied him to the tavern and got as drunk as his master, refused to follow him across the same threshold on the following day.

While Rush was willing to recommend things that had worked in the past, he was also suggesting something new. Religious cures and moral appeals were obviously inadequate to stop an epidemic. What was needed was a medical approach. Rush told how he had cured "a negro man," probably his slave, by putting tartar emetic in his rum, causing him to vomit so much that he could no longer stand the smell or taste of liquor. He also urged doctors to make "frequent representations . . . to drunkards, not only of the certainty, but of the *suddenness* of death from habits of intemperance."[15]

By 1810, Rush had become convinced that the best way to cure drunkards was to establish a separate institution where they could receive medical treatment. Rush's "Plan for an Asylum for Drunkards to be called Sober House" does not appear to have ever amounted to more than a rough draft that was found in his papers. Nevertheless, it was a bold plan that authorized county courts to inquire into the behavior of heavy drinkers to determine whether they were a danger to themselves or others and to confine drunks until they were cured. A Sober House was not to be a jail. Each inmate was to have his own "apartment." "Such diet, drink, and employments and means of moral and religious instruction should be contrived for them as are calculated to promote their reformation," he wrote.[16]

Rush apparently intended the Sober House to be a public institution; the cost of treating paupers was to be paid from local taxes. Rush later described it as a "hospital" that he hoped to see established "in every city and town in the United States." He anticipated criticism from people who would see a Sober House as "an infringement upon personal liberty, incompatible with the freedoms of our governments."

> We do not use this argument when we confine a thief in jail, and yet, taking the aggregate evil of the greater number of drunkards than thieves into consideration, and the greater evils which the influence of their immoral example and conduct introduce into society than stealing, it must be obvious, that the safety and prosperity of a community will be more promoted by confining them than a common thief.

Rush said that no one should be confined without being examined by a doctor and two or three judges or commissioners appointed for that purpose. Presumably, the same officials would determine when the reformed drunk could be released.[17]

Rush did not see a lot of progress in his lifetime. The temperance movement was just getting under way when he died in 1813. But he was not discouraged. "The seeds of truth upon all subjects are imperishable," he wrote to John Adams. While some ideas are instantly popular, "the more profound they are and the more interesting they are to human happiness, the more slowly they come to maturity," he said. The idea that chronic drunkenness was a disease and that its victims deserved compassion was certainly one of these. "I am aware that the efforts of science and humanity, in applying their resources to the cure of a disease induced by an act of vice, will meet with a cold reception from many people," Rush had written in his expanded *Inquiry*. "But let such people remember, the subjects of our remedies, are their fellow creatures. . . . Let us not then, pass by the prostrate sufferer from strong drink, but administer to him the same relief we would afford to a fellow creature in a similar state, from an accidence and innocent cause." Benjamin Rush, a signer of the Declaration of Independence, was a founding father of the movement for alcoholism recovery as well.[18]

Slowly, doctors began to respond to Rush's leadership. A doctor was one of the organizers of the first temperance society in Moreau, New York, in 1808. Others became active in the temperance movement as it spread across the country over the next two decades. In the early 1830s, Dr. Samuel B. Woodward, the superintendent of the Worcester State Lunatic Hospital in Massachusetts and a renowned temperance lecturer, published a series of articles in a Boston newspaper that called for the creation of public institutions for "inebriates." Woodward claimed to have successfully treated "many hundreds" of drunks who had been confined either for insanity or for committing crimes while drunk. "The result of this experience has been the fullest conviction, that a large proportion of the intemperate in a well-conducted institution would be radically cured," he wrote. The treatment he had in mind was not much different than the talk therapy that all the patients in his hospital received, but he believed that the drunks had a better chance of permanent recovery than those who were suffering from other kinds of mental illness, particularly if they were treated in separate institutions.[19]

The Washingtonians were the first to provide beds for homeless drunks, building bunks in the basements of their New York and Boston headquarters. In the winter of 1857, there was a new effort to create a home for men who were trying to get sober. The wife of a clergyman, Mrs. Charles Spears, petitioned the Massachusetts legislature to establish such a place. As a part of their ministry, Mrs. Spears and her husband worked with prisoners and their families. They became convinced that drunkenness was responsible for much of the city's crime and misery. More than six thousand people signed their petition. Before the state could act, a group of Mrs. Spears's supporters rented a suite of rooms in Boston that they offered to drunks as the Home for the Fallen.

The Home for the Fallen was clearly inspired by the optimism of the Washingtonians and was renamed the Washingtonian Home a few years later. One of its founders was a young businessman from Maine named Albert Day. Day was not a reformed drunk: he had never had an alcoholic drink in his life. Born in 1821, he had been exposed to the temperance movement at an early age and, before the age of ten, had spurned an offer to take his first drink. Day was deeply sympathetic to the plight of alcoholics and was active in the Washingtonian movement before he moved to Boston. He was a member of the committee that opened the Washingtonian Home in 1857 and a year later gave up his business to become its superintendent.

The Washingtonian Home could not have found a better leader. At thirty-six, Day was still boyish looking, with long dark hair combed back from his forehead. His eyes were deep-set and inquiring, but the corners of his mouth often turned up in a small smile. He had been convinced that alcoholism could be cured ever since he met a drunk named Jack Watts. He went to Watts's cottage when he heard that the man, his wife, and three young children were starving. "Mr. Watts, I hear you are in straitened circumstances," Day said. Watts admitted that he had spent his last three cents in a bar and that his children were hungry. Day immediately left to buy food for the family, and after delivering the groceries, he promised to return.

The next day Watts told Day that he had been unemployed for a long time. Day spoke about the importance of temperance—"kindly, respectfully, hopefully, strongly"—and offered to pay him a dollar for a day of chopping wood. Day gave Watts the money that night, and when he visited the next morning, Watts was still sober. Day spoke again about the necessity of total abstinence, and Watts said he would never drink again. Day helped him get a job. When Watts died many years later, he was still sober.[20]

Watts was the first of thirty thousand alcoholics that Day would treat over the next forty years. From the start, he was convinced that drunks could not be forced to stay sober. People had been putting them in jails, workhouses, and insane asylums for years, only to see them return to drinking on their release. They couldn't stop drinking until they wanted to stop drinking. For this reason, the Washingtonian Home adopted a policy that "those only can be admitted who have a sincere desire to reform."

Because of their frequent incarcerations, drunks had a hard time understanding that the Washingtonian Home was not a jail. David Harrisson Jr., a lawyer and an alcoholic who spent four months in the home, described the commotion that ensued when a newly arrived alcoholic became convinced that he was being held against his will:

> I have heard the superintendent smilingly address him, "Why, my dear fellow, what is the matter?" The reply would be shrieked out, "I won't and shan't be kept in here." "Why, who wants to keep you?—there is the door. Come, I will show you the way out." To see the look of drunken and stupid astonishment which the poor fellow would put on was ludicrous in the extreme. For a few minutes he would stare around in imbecile astonishment, and then, with a long drawn sigh, and "Well, I'll be blowed if this don't beat cats," sink back, overcome into the nearest chair."

The superintendent offered more reassuring words. "We don't intend to restrain you, sir," Day said. "If you intend to stop here, and try to reform, you can do so, and we will do all in our power to help you." "That's just my gait," the drunk replied. "Say, old chap, ain't you going to treat?" Like Rush, Day used a nauseant as part of the detoxification process. He handed the man whiskey spiked with ipecac to induce vomiting. The patient soon became "as docile as a lamb and almost as helpless as a child," Harrisson wrote.[21]

With few exceptions, residents of the Washingtonian Home were never confined. Almost all of them paid for room and board during three to six months of treatment, so they usually left the building to work during the day. They might be temporarily restrained if they got drunk again and became violent or were in danger of hurting themselves when they were suffering delirium tremens, the illness that struck many drunks during the first days after they quit drinking. In these cases, Day would sometimes administer ipecac or potassium bromide, a sedative.

Treatment at the Washingtonian Home primarily involved psychological counseling. At the time he became superintendent, Day was hardly qualified to do anything else. Although he would later graduate from Harvard Medical School, he was just a businessman who wanted to help alcoholics. But he had a clearer understanding of what needed to be done than most doctors. They thought their job was over when they had nursed the drunk back to health. Day disagreed. "It may safely be laid down as a rule, that no man has thus needed his care that does not stand in need of further assistance and advice," he wrote in *Methomania*, a slim volume that was his only contribution to scientific literature. Day was never a theorist. His great gift was his ability to see each patient as an individual. "[M]y experience has convinced me, that each case must be approached with rare discernment of individual characteristics and circumstances, and that no rule of treatment throughout is capable of universal application," he said.[22]

While every drunk was different, the therapeutic goals were the same. The first objective was to convince the sick man that he could get better. This wasn't easy when most people believed that alcoholics were incurable. No one believed it more than the drunks themselves. "[I]t follows that the element of hope should be carefully nourished as a powerful stimulant to other methods employed," Day said. Next, the patient must be shown that he had to stop drinking alcohol. Rush had believed that the high concentration of alcohol in distilled liquor caused alcoholism and that drunks could continue to consume wine and beer. But this view had been abandoned by the temperance movement. Day wrote that it was a "physiological fact" that the "physical effects of the poison" made it impossible for the alcoholic to drink alcohol. Like Rush, he believed that drunkenness was a disease, but not a disease that could be cured by medicine:

> [I]t is well to impress upon the patient, by all the means at command, the vital interests to himself that hang upon his total and continued abstinence; to encourage and increase as far as possible his self-respect; and to stimulate into active exercise that family affection and domestic disposition which will of themselves act as a powerful restraint. The usually exciting and demoralizing character of the past life should be avoided; while a habit of mind should be sought, calm, even in temperament, cheerful in disposition, and free from unusually or unnecessary excitement.

Everything depended on the alcoholic's decision to stop drinking. "The patient should be encouraged, that his disease can be cured, and at the same time impressed with the belief that it rests mostly with himself, and that 'eternal vigilance is the price of liberty,'" Day said.[23]

Day used every opportunity to educate his patients about the nature of their disease. The size of the Washingtonian Home made this easy. In 1860, twenty men were in residence at any one time, giving the superintendent many opportunities to speak with them individually. He also delivered informal talks on Wednesday evenings, often using the experience of recent patients as a starting point. One evening, Day discussed the case of a man who had left the home after several months of treatment. He was full of confidence that he could stay sober, congratulating himself for not even thinking about a drink during a long delay at a train station. It seemed to prove that he had licked his problem, but he decided to test himself. "Here goes, then, for the last glass of whiskey I shall take as long as I live, and I take it purely as a scientific experiment," he said. The scientist was discovered dead drunk an hour later and escorted back to the Washingtonian Home. Day drew the following conclusions:

> 1. No hope for the inebriate until he thoroughly distrusts the strength of his own resolution. 2. No hope for the inebriate except in total abstinence as long as he lives, both in sickness and in health. 3. Little hope for the inebriate unless he avoids, on system and on principle, the occasions of temptation, the places where liquor is sold, and the persons who will urge it upon him.

Day was not discouraged by relapses, and he urged his patients to remain hopeful. "Some men, he said, *must* fall, at least once, before the last rag of confidence is torn from them." Day said he knew men who had relapsed three times before they finally got sober.[24]

The Wednesday evening lectures were delivered in the chapel of the Washingtonian Home. Religion played a prominent role in the life of the institution. There were both morning and evening prayers. These nonsectarian services were probably agreeable to most residents, who were largely drawn from the middle and upper classes and therefore accustomed to regular church attendance. "[T]hey had been ornaments to the society in which they moved . . . were of excellent education, superior abilities, and no small experience in the walks of life," Harrisson said. Many were ministers. The home also welcomed workingmen if they could afford to pay room and board, and some beds were reserved for the poor.[25]

Superintendent Day believed religion helped men stay sober. He presented every departing patient with a Bible and urged him to read it daily. He did this to encourage his "moral elevation" but also to strengthen resistance to the "unavoidable temptations" of society. One of Day's patients was a fireman from Philadelphia who had gloried in the drunken battles fought with rival engine companies when they arrived at a fire simultaneously. Once he sobered up, the man "proved to be a good, simple soul, very ignorant, not naturally intelligent, and therefore more capable of faith than of knowledge," according to a writer who visited the Washingtonian Home after the Civil War. He began to read the Bible while still a resident of the home. By the time he left six months later, "this daily reading being associated in his mind with his reform, the book became a kind of talisman to him, and he felt safe as long as he continued the practice." The fireman stayed sober throughout his service in the Civil War and earned a reputation for bravery. After his return from one especially harrowing mission that included swimming across the Potomac River under fire, he was offered whiskey. "Don't offer me *that*," he said. "I dread that more than bullets." He was killed at the Battle of Antietam.[26]

The residents of the Washingtonian Home also helped each other. Twenty percent of the men in treatment either arrived in the throes of delirium tremens or soon fell victims to it, providing an object lesson for those who were not so badly off. There were positive role models, too. From the beginning, the managers observed that a fellowship developed among the residents. A new man was surprised to meet alcoholics who had been sober for months. As he talked to his neighbors, he began to think about the implications for himself. "They gradually feel that what others have done they can do; that, after all, the whole difficulty is a disease, which simply needs correcting," Day wrote in his first report in 1858. "A spirit of emulation is engendered among the inmates, and each gives countenance and strength to the other." The drunks shared their life stories with each other and also spoke during public meetings on Tuesdays. Graduates of the home often attended the public meetings to steel themselves against relapse and served as role models for the men in treatment.[27]

The Washingtonian Home was a success from the beginning. In the spring of 1858, Day reported that not more than ten of the several hundred men who had been treated had relapsed. By 1860, it had treated five hundred men. He would probably have acknowledged that the number of relapses would grow over time as the reformed men faced repeated temptations. But he was confident that most would stay sober as long as they remembered what they had learned. Graduates who lived in the Boston area could take a refresher course by attending the Tuesday night meetings at the home. But even those whose homes were far away had options. Many of those whose stories are told in Harrisson's *A Voice from the Washingtonian Home* became active in the temperance movement. One graduate returned to his home in New Bedford, Massachusetts, to discover that a former resident of the home was scheduled to address a local temperance convention. Others joined local groups of the Sons of Temperance, and some became leaders.[28]

Many graduates also maintained a correspondence with Day. It often began with a letter reporting their safe arrival home. One man assured Day that he had arrived "without accident and clear of whiskey." His family gave him a rapturous reception. "My cheeks were almost blistered, and my arms quite lame from the kisses and shaking of the hands that I got," he said. Another graduate of the home waited a day before he showed himself on Main Street:

> On the corner of the square . . . was a constant crowd, renewed as fast as one left by another filling his place, and which was composed of persons anxious to shake hands with me. I can assure you that no politician, on returning to his constituents, could have been made to feel more the elevation of success, and the pride of station, than I have been compelled to feel since my advent on Saturday.

The joy at being restored to the affection of their family and friends naturally made the reformed men deeply grateful to Day and his institution. They also felt a strong sense of obligation. "I trust that my course in the future may be such as never to bring the Home into disrepute, and myself and friends again to disgrace and ruin," another said. Some men wrote to Day every year on the anniversary of the day they stopped drinking.[29]

There was never a shortage of patients. The home's alumni were walking advertisements for its success, and they recommended it enthusiastically to their drinking buddies. "There is a gentleman in the office now asking me what you have been doing to make me look so well," a recovered man wrote Day. "I tell him it takes you to do it, and he had better start." Being the only institution of its kind certainly helped. As news of its existence spread, men from all over the country began to apply for admission. "[I]ts former inmates may be found . . . in almost every State of the Union and territory of the United States, from the icy coast of Northern Maine to the Pacific shores of far-off California," Harrisson wrote. A majority of the patients were from places that were closer to Boston, including everyone associated with the publication of Harrisson's book—the publisher, the printer, the manufacturer of the paper, and the man who engraved the images.[30]

Soon people in other parts of the country began to create institutions where drunks could get sober. Just two years after the founding of the Washingtonian Home, a group of volunteer firemen calling themselves the Dashaways opened the San Francisco Home for the Care of Inebriates. Like the Bostonians, the Dashaways also drew their inspiration from the Washingtonian movement and grew to nearly five thousand members who were dedicated to rescuing drunks. They built a large headquarters that included a reading room and an auditorium where Washingtonian-style experience meetings were held. On an upper floor, they created a dormitory that housed up to fifty-six men, many of whom had been picked up on the streets. During four weeks of treatment, the rescued men rested, ate nourishing meals, and received the attention of doctors who had volunteered their services. They also attended meetings where they heard recovering alcoholics tell their stories and could tell their own if they were so inclined. On their release, they could join the Dashaways, who promised to help them start their new lives.

In 1863, a third refuge was established in Chicago. Robert A. Law, a member of the Independent Order of Good Templars of Cook County, persuaded his fellow Templars to sponsor a Washingtonian Home for the Cure of Inebriates. Templars in Quincy, Massachusetts, followed their example, opening the Good Templars' Asylum the next year. Two homes opened in 1867—in Brooklyn, New York, and Media, Pennsylvania, a suburb of Philadelphia.

None of these fledgling institutions captured the public's attention like Turner's New York State Inebriate Asylum, which had finally opened in 1864. The accommodations in the asylum lived up to Turner's high standards. Writing anonymously, John W. Palmer, a doctor who was a resident, described his room to readers of the *Atlantic Monthly* in 1869:

> Walls lofty and sky-colored; door and double window tall and dignified—the latter provided with liberal panes and inside latticed shutters; wood-work of oak and dark cherry, handsomely molded and paneled; a portly oaken wardrobe with double doors and drawers . . . a hospitable carpet in warm colors; "all the modern improvements" for ablution, represented by a marble tank and silver-plated turn-cock; a double register for hot air and ventilation; pendent gas-fixtures, in good style, with globes and side-light . . .

There were two tables for periodicals, papers, and writing material; a wide iron bed on rollers; a rocking chair, two black walnut desk chairs (one with arms and one without); a mirror, "not palatial," but large enough and "neatly framed"; and a shelf with three "blue and gold" volumes of verse and a picture of a lovely child. On the walls hung reproductions of well-known photographs and watercolors.[31]

Considering the great care and expense that Turner lavished on the asylum, it is natural to assume that he had a high regard for his patients. But Turner appears to have shared little of Day's love for his fellow man. Day was a businessman who became a doctor in order to be a better caregiver. Turner was a doctor who abandoned his practice after only a few years to pursue his dream of curing alcoholism with a passion that bordered on fanaticism. If the New York State Inebriate Asylum was located in a beautiful place and offered every comfort, it was because Turner believed that this was essential to the successful treatment of alcoholics. In Europe, he had learned that insane asylums were located in the countryside to isolate patients from the influences that contributed to their illness. Some things they were happy to leave behind, but others were more difficult. Turner did not allow residents to receive visitors, believing that family and friends may have contributed to their alcoholism. Their incoming mail was censored, and they were not allowed to send replies.

Turner and Day had very different approaches to alcoholism. They both called it a disease, but they did not agree on the cure. Although Day believed that recovery depended on a patient's willingness to stop drinking, Turner had no faith in willpower. He was unimpressed by what he saw when he visited the Washingtonian Home in 1859. Turner believed that alcoholism was strictly a medical problem and that it could be cured only by following a doctor's orders. Dr. T. D. Crothers, another pioneer in the medical treatment of alcoholism, described Turner's treatment philosophy many years later:

> His ideal asylum . . . was practically a workhouse hospital on a military basis, restraint and control being the corner-stone. Each case was regarded as a suicidal mania needing positive restraint and constant care and watching. . . . Elaborate rules were laid down regulating all the conduct and care of the patient, and a most thorough system of medical and military treatment enforced.

Asylum residents were held to a tight schedule: they rose at the same hour every day, ate breakfast, attended mandatory religious services, and then began their day, which included four hours of outdoor exercise. Dinner was followed by evening services and lights out at 10 p.m. Turner believed that what alcoholics needed above all was "discipline." He thought they could be forced to get sober.[32]

From the start, there was evidence that this wouldn't work. Unlike the Washingtonian Home, which required drunks to apply for admission, many of the residents of the asylum were there against their will. Some had reluctantly agreed under pressure from their families, and even voluntary patients often became dissatisfied under the restraint that Turner insisted was necessary. An antagonistic relationship developed between the patients and staff. The alcoholics used bribes to buy liquor and then hid their bottles around the grounds. Some escaped, while others pleaded with family until they were finally removed.

Turner's response to rebellion was to seek greater control. At his urging, the New York State legislature passed a law giving judges the power to involuntarily commit drunks to the asylum for three months. A year later, Turner was back in Albany, and the term of commitment was extended to one year.

Turner might have had his way with the legislature, but he soon found himself in conflict with the new president of the asylum's board of trustees, Dr. Willard Parker. Parker was one of the most eminent surgeons in the country. Although he had been an early supporter of the asylum, he had not served on the board before he was elected president and did not have any experience with drunks. What he discovered when he visited the asylum a few months after his election made him question whether Turner should continue as superintendent. In conversation with some of the patients, he found many were very unhappy.

At the time of Parker's visit, most of the residents of the asylum were middle-aged men who came from good families, including "professional men, well educated, of refined taste and decided ability." It is not surprising that they bridled at Turner's restrictions. Parker believed that Turner was also jeopardizing the institution. Although the asylum was chartered by the state, it was a private institution and depended on its patients to pay the bills. Despite Turner's ambition to treat hundreds of men at a time, the asylum had managed to attract only forty patients during the first year.[33]

Parker told Turner that he was being too strict with his patients. He suggested "their having a larger liberty and their being placed upon their honor, as they were all gentlemen belonging to Christian households," Turner wrote. The superintendent thought Parker was being naive and proceeded to instruct him in the nature of alcoholism. While the drunks seemed normal when they were sober, "he should remember that among the patients under treatment in the Asylum were homicidal and suicidal dipsomaniacs, thieves and liars, the destroyers of home and violators of the marriage vows." They were victims of "morbid conditions of the stomach and the brain" that produced an unquenchable thirst for alcohol that they would do anything to satisfy. Clearly, drunks could not be trusted.[34]

Turner could barely conceal his contempt for Parker. "It is not strange . . . that the inebriate, under such an ungovernable thirst, will pour into your ear, and also into the ear of his friends, his invented wrongs and misrepresentations for the purpose of regaining his liberty and satisfying his morbid appetite," he told Parker, who was also getting angry. "As the discussion was prolonged, it became more and more intensified," Turner remembered. But this was not a mere clash of egos. The bigger problem was that Parker was the president of the asylum, charged with the responsibility for ensuring its financial success, and Turner's treatment philosophy seemed guaranteed to drive patients away. Soon after visiting Binghamton, Parker began working to oust Turner. For two years, the founder of "the first inebriate asylum in the world" fought to keep his job but finally resigned in 1867.[35]

Parker turned to Day to save the asylum. Day arrived with five patients from the Washingtonian Home in the spring of 1867. Amid the beauty of the budding countryside, the asylum must have seemed like paradise to the drunks from Boston. The mood of the institution changed dramatically as the suspicion and strictness of the Turner regime was replaced by Day's benevolent despotism. John Palmer described an almost idyllic life:

> I awake to the music of the rising bell, on which an Ethiopian minstrel, naturally corked, is ringing cheerful changes in the halls; and my first conscious sensation is a pleasant one as, turning over for a fresh thrill, and applauding my pillow with a sensuous pat, I cast a complacent glance and thought about my room.

As they washed and dressed in their rooms, some inmates greeted the day with music, "No. 7 . . . whistles 'Champagne Charlie,' with expression, while 'Mary Had a Little Lamb,' with variations is pensively executed on a comb by Number 21," Palmer wrote. Others joined the chorus with animal noises, imitating cuckoos, parrots, and cows.[36]

While the asylum was perhaps not the paradise that Palmer describes, it was undoubtedly more pleasant. As the number of patients grew to a hundred, Day continued to counsel them individually and to lecture on some aspect of alcoholism on Wednesday evenings. But because he had less time for each man, the patients began to play a larger role in the treatment process. There had been a dramatic change since the days when smuggling liquor into the asylum was applauded. "An inmate who should now attempt such a crime would be shunned by the best two thirds of the whole institution," one writer observed. The new attitude was symbolized by the formation of a new patient organization, the Ollapod Club. Membership in the club was by invitation only, but Palmer insisted that it was never intended to be exclusive. "Whosoever is companionable, genial, sympathetic, co-operative, of us and with us and for us, he is the man for the votes of our understandings and our hearts," he said. The excluded appear to be men who were not making the effort to get sober. Two-thirds of the residents were members of the club.[37]

One of the important functions of the Ollapods was to provide recreation for men who were often bored. (The delivery of the mail, now untouched by censorship, was the highlight of their day.) Meetings were held on Tuesdays and Saturdays and usually consisted of the reading of papers on literary and other subjects. The essays were written by the residents, and one visitor noted that this gave the asylum a "college-like" atmosphere, "especially when you get about among the rooms of the inmates, and see them cramming for next Monday's debate, or writing a lecture." The topics were meaty—"Meteoric Phenomena, and Theories concerning them," "Curiosities of Music," and "Wit and Humor, English and American." But Palmer said that the bill of fare was never too heavy. "[T]here is a preference for the satirical handling of social absurdities," he said. Once a month, Binghamton residents were invited to hear them. The members spent the rest of their evenings gathered around small tables in the Club Room, "reading, chatting or engaged in games of chess, whist, euchre and cribbage."[38]

The Ollapods were participating in their own recovery by organizing meetings and obeying rules that they had established for themselves. Their brief bylaws forbid a member to bring the club into disrepute "by presenting himself at any time or place under the influence of liquor." An offender was required to offer the club "a becoming apology" in writing that would be read by the secretary at the next meeting. The bylaws did not provide for expulsion. If the errant drunk was truly sorry, there could be no question of cutting him off. "[O]n the contrary, we do hold ourselves bound, collectively and individually, to extend to him all necessary protection and aid, with prompt and cheerful goodwill," the bylaws read.[39]

The Ollapods did not expel members because they recognized them as brothers. "It is a favorite phrase of the house, that we are all 'tarred with the same stick,' and by that same token we stick together," Palmer said. It was a tremendous relief for a man to learn that he was not alone in his inability to stop drinking; that he drank not because he was weak or evil but because he suffered from an illness that was shared by other men. It lifted a terrible burden of guilt and shame. It also made it possible for him to examine his life with a new honesty, acknowledging the harm that his drinking had done to himself and others.[40]

Not everyone experienced a change of heart. Palmer reported that as many as ten of his fellow inmates "habitually practice deception or otherwise break faith with us." There was also a gap between newcomers and the men who had been sober for a while. But the old hands took it on themselves to school the recent arrivals. The new man was "introduced to himself by those who quickly get to know him better than himself," Palmer said.

> Humbly he comes down from the stilts of his presumption, modestly he modifies the strut of his obtrusiveness—a man good-humoredly snubbed. His unappreciated qualities are developed; the mystery of hidden good in him is solved; he learns to rate himself lower than his own price, higher than the appraisal of his friends. The test of shrewd insight we apply to his temper precipitates the true from the bogus.

These conversations were probably unpleasant at times. The sober drunk must have felt frustration in educating an obstinate new arrival, while the newcomer bridled at what he saw as the condescension of someone who had been sober for only a few weeks or months. But the relationships between the residents were central to the recovery process. "If I were asked wherein lies the peculiar healing of this place, I should answer in the profound impressions of its sympathetic intercourse," Palmer said.[41]

The stories of the drunks who had been rehabilitated in the Binghamton asylum and the inebriate homes in Boston, Chicago, and San

Francisco helped rekindle optimism about curing alcoholism. This time, doctors would play the leading role in convincing Americans that there was hope for drunks. In the decade after the opening of the New York State Inebriate Asylum in 1864, six institutions for alcoholics were launched, and the majority were headed by doctors who believed that drunkenness should be treated as a medical problem. In 1867, the Kings County Home opened in Brooklyn, New York, and the Pennsylvania Sanitarium for Inebriates began treating patients in suburban Philadelphia. For the first time, women were also getting help. Four hundred applied for admission to Turner's asylum before it decided it would only treat men. Neither of the Washingtonian Homes admitted women. Alcoholic women in Chicago were cared for in the home of Charles Hull. (It would later become Hull House, the settlement house headed by Jane Addams.) Finally, in 1869, the Martha Washington Home opened in Chicago, the first facility dedicated to helping women. Later, women were also admitted to the Kings County Home.

Dr. Joseph Parrish, the founder of the Pennsylvania Sanitarium, wanted to do more than treat patients. He was a reformer. As a young doctor, he had traveled to Europe to continue his education and had been appalled by the treatment of the insane in Rome. He also did something about it by getting the pope to support improvements. He returned to the United States with a new interest in psychology and developed a reputation as an "alienist," the precursor to the modern psychiatrist. Parrish also had a long-standing concern for drunks, who he got to know intimately during his work in Philadelphia's Jeffersonian Home. The Jeffersonian Home had opened during the Washingtonian era to provide a place for drunks to dry out. What Parrish learned there made him a temperance advocate and strong supporter of prohibition. But he did not believe that either pledges to stay sober or laws banning alcohol could help the alcoholic. He wanted to change how people thought about intemperance and how society treated drunks.

Just a few years after opening his own asylum, he wrote to Willard Parker, the president of the New York State Inebriate Asylum, to propose the formation of the American Association for the Cure of Inebriety (AACI), "an association with the single object of advocating the disease theory as applied to certain forms of alcoholic inebriety." Parker supported the idea, and Parrish issued an invitation to the superintendents, physicians, and board members of institutions that were treating drunks. A meeting was called for November 29, 1870, at the headquarters of the Young Men's Christian Association in New York City. Parrish and Parker were surprised by the strong turnout. Sixteen men attended.[42]

Parker encouraged Parrish to prepare a keynote address and "present the subject as it now appears to you." In his speech, Parrish laid out the evidence for believing that drunks were suffering from an illness. Some men inherited a "constitutional susceptibility" to alcohol in the same way others were afflicted with other physical defects, like deafness or blindness. "Such predisposition is often exhibited by a sense of unrest and nervous depression," Parrish said. "He is suffering from the effects of an organization that he did not create, and from infirmities which he did not knowingly promote." But, according to Parrish, not all alcoholism was inherited. Anything that depleted the nervous system could create a vulnerability—a "forcing system of education . . . the struggle for wealth, power or position, the unhealthy rivalry for display, and all the excitements which produce the 'wear and tear in our life.'" Whether inherited or acquired, the constitutional susceptibility produced "a desire for speedy relief, and a strong tendency to seek artificial support in the most convenient form, which is alcohol."[43]

What defined the disease was the inability to stop drinking. "[N]otwithstanding the knowledge of the danger of resorting to alcoholic stimulants, the popular condemnation of the practice, and the inward convictions on the subject, there is an overwhelming impulse which drives its victims to indulgence," Parrish wrote. People accused drunks of failing to exercise willpower, but it was a disease that robbed them of the power to quit. He continued, "If our philosophy be true, we have primarily, a defective condition of body or mind, and an impaired will, among its earliest evidences; then an appetite, and lastly drunkenness with all its resulting evils." Thus, the drunk suffered twin defects—a need for alcohol to soothe his restless and depressive nature and an inability to stop drinking once he started. Powerless over his own life, he was in dire need of medical attention. "When drunkenness is the result of an impaired moral nature, or of a defective physical organization . . . it is to be considered as a disease, and treated accordingly," Parrish said.[44]

Parrish argued that alcoholics had been treated unfairly. Their disease shared characteristics with other illnesses. Insanity was the result of "excess or irregularity of some kind." Rheumatism, gout, and consumption could be inherited or acquired. Dyspepsia, colic, and cholera were sometimes the result of abusing the "goodly fruits of the earth." But science ignored the drunk. "[U]pon what principle can this class of person be excluded from the common ranks of men who are diseased," Parrish asked. While acknowledging that "many inebriates" did not seek recovery and that some had to be confined in institutions for the rest of their lives, Parrish insisted that many more could get sober if they had help. He urged his colleagues to publicize the new things they were discovering about alcoholism every day. "These should be so many centers of light and information, from which may radiate truth, which our people, who are already scourged to sadness by this evil, are eagerly waiting for," he said.[45]

The next paper read at the conference was "a remarkable document" that made "a profound impression," Parrish said many years later. Framed as a letter to the attendees, it was the product of a meeting of the inmates at the Parrish's Pennsylvania Sanitarium. The recovering drunks wanted to express their support for the goal of expanding medical treatment for alcoholism. In the process, they provided an intimate view of their lives as alcoholics and as recovering men. They began by confessing ignorance about how they became drunks. "Doubtless, to ourselves, as well as to others, the cause of our condition is a mystery," the letter said. How was it that they became alcoholics, while other members of the family could drink without danger? What was it that made it possible for the hard-drinking friends of their youth to moderate their drinking as they became responsible adults? Their sense of grievance was strong. They had a list:

1. That a social ostracism is practiced towards us, which is not practiced towards other members of families or society, who have vices and diseases, that are equally offensive to morals, and equally damaging to the community.

2. That church ostracism in many instances, deprives us of the very sympathies and forces, that should combine, for our relief and restoration.

They complained that the law treated them unfairly, excusing acts committed by the insane while applying the full force of the law to crimes committed during alcoholic blackouts. "[O]ur sorrows and sins, are made texts for sermons; our symptoms and misfortunes are caricatured by lecturers and performers, and we are exposed to odium and ridicule," they said.[46]

They expressed their gratitude for the inebriate asylum. "[W]e need places of refuge . . . where we may escape the depressing influences to which we have referred," the letter continued. But they weren't seeking merely to escape. Drunks needed time to "regain that moral tone, and power of will, which can alone fit us for the duties and responsibilities of life." They thanked Parrish and quoted extensively from his annual report to the board of the sanitarium. The letter concluded with a blessing:

> We earnestly desire that the spirit of your counsels may be just and right, and sincerely hope that through them, society and government, may be so led, that while relieving them of one of the most terrible evils uncontrolled appetite inflicts, the victims themselves may be gently led back to the prodigal's home.

It is certain that Day and the other men at the conference were deeply moved.[47]

The founders of the AACI believed they had started something new. "It is not a temperance, but a scientific gathering," Willard Parker told his colleagues at the opening of their meeting. But the declaration of principles that it adopted after hearing from the drunks at Parrish's asylum made it clear that the AACI was just as committed to advocacy as the activists who had resumed their fight for prohibition:

1. Intemperance is a disease.
2. It is curable in the same sense that other diseases are.
3. Its primary cause is a constitutional susceptibility to the alcoholic impression.
4. The constitutional impression may be inherited or acquired.

5. Alcohol has its true place in the arts and sciences. It is valuable as a remedy, and like other remedies may be abused. In excessive quantity it is a poison, and always acts as such when it produces inebriety.

6. All methods hitherto employed having proved insufficient for the cure of inebriates, the establishment of asylums for such a purpose is the great demand of the age.

7. Every large city should have its local or temporary home for inebriates, and every state, one or more asylums for the treatment and care of such persons.

8. The law should recognize intemperance as a disease, and provide other means for its management than fines, station-houses and jails.[48]

The advocates of the disease theory of alcoholism knew that they would encounter opposition. "[T]here need be no controversy with the doctrine of sin or law," Parrish wrote, clearly expecting trouble. One of the first shots was fired by a police judge from Lowell, Massachusetts, just a few months after the AACI was organized. Nathan Crosby was a rock-ribbed conservative whose view of human nature had not improved during his twenty-five years on the bench. He strongly disapproved of the idea that criminals could be reformed by more humane treatment. He was particularly hard on drunks, who he believed were entirely responsible for their behavior. "The American Association for the cure of inebriates [*sic*] say *inebriety is a disease . . . ,*" Crosby told a committee of the Massachusetts legislature. "[B]ut the *great truth . . .* remains that *the drunkard is self-made,* progressively self-taught, and obstinately self-immolated."[49]

The committee was considering legislation to create government-operated inebriate asylums. Crosby objected:

Sir, instead of asylums, would it not be better to build places more odious than our jails and houses of correction, to bring back again the stocks and pillory and iron cage, that the people might be terror stricken at the view and flee as for their lives, from every approach of the appetite.

Crosby believed that only banning the sale of alcohol would solve the problem of drunkenness. He urged the legislators "to barricade all grog shops, cracker-and-salt-fish saloons, all gambling houses and club rooms." The police could take care of the drunks they found in these establishments. "Let them put the men within into the pest house, to drink worm-wood tea and eat soups or chain them to the nearest lamp-post, till sober," he said.[50]

Crosby was not the only critic of the AACI and its supporters. By its second annual meeting, there had been so much "influential opposition" from temperance advocates and religious leaders that Parrish felt he had to respond. During an opening address, he noted that the critics were not doctors and therefore had "a very superficial and false notion of what disease is." "If intemperance is not a disease, how comes it that so many tens of thousands of people die from it every year?" he asked. Parrish categorically rejected the charge made by Crosby and others that recognizing alcoholism as a disease relieved drunks of the responsibility to stop drinking. "When a person knows that he has a disease, he applies himself to its relief or cure," he said. "He takes counsel, changes his mode of life and does what his physician may prescribe." Parrish expressed amazement that the AACI's efforts had been made the target of "ungenerous assault." "It seems to me that every good citizen, and especially every Christian citizen, should rejoice over the recovery of intemperate persons, by any instrumentality that may be made available for that purpose," he said.[51]

The reference to Christians is significant because many of the AACI's critics were religious leaders. Like the prohibitionists, ministers felt threatened by the prospect of an organized recovery movement. They believed that drunkenness originated in the sinful nature of man and that the only hope for sobriety lay in religious conversion. The disease theory of alcoholism removed God from the central place in the recovery process. The Washingtonians had encountered opposition from the same source. Their reply had been that it was the churches that had abandoned the drunks. Thirty years later, Parrish echoed their complaint. "[H]as the church put itself directly to the work of reaching these offensive children of our common family, and attempted to do them good, and make them wiser and better? Has it not too often cast them off?" he asked.[52]

The closing of the New York State Inebriate Asylum in 1879 was a blow to the AACI. But the asylum had been plagued by poor management from the beginning, and the problems did not disappear after Day took over. Turner's dream had been grandiose. He was followed by men with a better understanding of alcoholism and a more modest model of treatment. AACI members found reason for hope in the fact that the number of inebriate asylums had grown since 1870. The Franklin Reformatory Home for Inebriates opened in Philadelphia in 1872, the Appleton Temporary Home in South Boston in 1873, and the Walnut Lodge Hospital for Inebriates in Hartford, Connecticut, in 1878. In 1876, the AACI founded the first scientific journal devoted to the subject, the *Quarterly Journal of Inebriety*. In 1888, Parrish expressed his satisfaction. "When I look back over the years that have passed since 1870, I am amazed at the progress the cause has made," he wrote.[53]

CHAPTER FOUR

Search for Higher Power

THE ENEMIES OF THE Water Street Mission attacked on July 4. Jerry McAuley, a reformed drunk, had been under no illusions when he opened the mission in a New York City slum in 1872. Water Street was one of the most notorious streets in the city. Located just a block from the crowded East River docks, it was known for its many seedy bars and the prostitutes who made themselves available to sailors and other passersby at all hours. He knew he had enemies. The saloon keepers hated him because he welcomed drunks, and many of them were getting sober. The police hated him because they took bribes from the saloon keepers, so they joined in the harassment directed at McAuley and his mission. But he never expected the mission to be attacked with fireworks.

On Independence Day, a barrel appeared in the street in front of the mission before the evening service. A ruffian posted at the mission door signaled to men in the street whenever someone stood to testify to the blessings he had received from God. Fireworks were lit and dropped in the drum, exploding so loudly they drowned the voices inside. But McAuley was resourceful:

> I said to the congregation, "Now I want you to watch me: I'll select a hymn ahead of time, and the moment I say 'Sing!' just sing with *all your might*, and when I say, '*Testify!*' be ready and spring right up." A convert arose and opened his mouth, when bang! bang! bang!

went the fireworks in the barrel. "Sing!" I shouted, and they fairly roared; my! What lungs they had, and you couldn't hear the fireworks at all! Just as soon as that pack was out I called "Testify!" and a brother jumped up, and before they could get the next pack ready and rightly on fire he was through, and then we drowned the racket again with a grand old hymn.

When the hooligans ran out of firecrackers, they were reduced to shooting some Roman candles against the back of the house. "[W]e never had a better meeting," McAuley insisted. "Several were helped spiritually, and among others one soul was *gloriously saved!*"[1]

The saloon keeper across the street who had orchestrated the disruption eventually moved elsewhere, and so did many others who tried to do business in the same space. "We carried the matter to God, and prayed him to break up whoever came in there to sell rum; and that prayer was heard, for 15 or 16 failed one after another," McAuley explained. The Water Street Mission had opened two years after the founding of the AACI. Its success was an early indication that religion would be a powerful force for recovery in the last half of the nineteenth century.

His neighbors in County Kerry, Ireland, would probably have said that McAuley was born bad. He was certainly angry. According to a brief autobiography McAuley wrote in 1875, his father was a counterfeiter who fled home to avoid arrest. He said nothing about his mother. He was raised by a grandmother whose prayers he mocked by throwing things at her head as she knelt. He did not attend school but spent his time getting into trouble. "I got blows for me meat and drink till I wished myself dead many a time," he said. At thirteen, he was shipped to a married sister in New York but lived with her only a short time before meeting two boys who became his partners in crime. They made their living as river pirates, launching a boat under the cover of darkness to steal what they could from the many ships moored in one of the world's busiest ports. At nineteen, he was arrested for a robbery and sentenced to fifteen years of hard labor in Sing Sing prison.[2]

As McAuley entered the strong stone walls of Sing Sing, he noted a sign above the door. "The way of the transgressor is hard," it read. Prisons were intended as reformatory institutions, but they used harsh measures to accomplish their goal. When McAuley arrived, Sing Sing still banned prisoners from all conversation and punished infractions with techniques that are regarded as torture today. The punishment didn't work on McAuley. "[I]t only made me harder and harder," he said.[3]

But prison did change him. One Sunday, about five years into his sentence, he was shocked to hear one of his criminal confederates address the inmates during religious services. Orville Gardner, a former prizefighter and thief, had such a terrible reputation that he was known as "Awful Gardner" in the New York newspapers. He was also an alcoholic, but the death of his young son had forced him to take a hard look at his life, including his drinking. He put a two-quart jug of whiskey in a boat and rowed to a clearing on the Brooklyn shore. "Now it is give you up forever or never leave this place alive," Gardner said, addressing the jug. He fought temptation for nine hours, praying for help. He rejected the idea of smashing the jug, fearing the smell of whiskey would be irresistible. He dug a hole, buried it, and rowed back to Manhattan.[4]

McAuley was deeply moved as Gardner told his story. Back in his cell, he picked up a Bible and began searching for a passage that Gardner had recited. He read the whole book twice. "I was resting one night from reading, walking up and down and thinking what a change religion made in Gardner, when I began to have a burning desire to have the same," McAuley said. He knew that he should pray for forgiveness, but he was convinced he had committed too many sins. McAuley was in agony for weeks until he heard a voice say, "Go to God; He will tell you what is right." He fell to his knees on the cold stone floor of his cell, determined to stay there until he found forgiveness. "I was desperate," he said.

> All at once it seemed as if something supernatural was in my room. I was afraid to open my eyes. I was in an agony, and the sweat rolled off my face in great drops. Oh, how I longed for God's mercy! Just then, in the very heart of my distress, it seemed as if a hand was laid upon my head, and these words came to me, "My son, thy sins, which are many, are forgiven." . . . Oh, the precious Christ! How plainly I saw him, lifted on the cross for my sins!

McAuley jumped to his feet and began to pace his cell. "A heavenly light seemed to fill it; a softness and a perfume like the fragrance of the sweetest flowers," he said. He was not sure whether he was living or dead. He began to clap his hands and shout, "Praise God!" A passing guard asked what was the matter. "I've found Christ," McAuley said. "My sins are forgiven. Glory to God!" The guard threatened to report him in the morning for making a ruckus. No punishment followed, but the authorities were skeptical about McAuley's conversion. It was another two years before he was paroled.[5]

McAuley found the streets of New York very lonely when he returned from prison in 1864. "I could not go back to my old haunts and companions, and I knew no others," he said. He no longer believed himself to be a Catholic, but he had never been to a Protestant meeting, and he met no one who might have invited him to attend. "If I had found a single Christian friend at that time, it would have saved me years of misery," he said. He found one friend, but this man introduced him to lager beer, a drink that had recently been imported by German immigrants. McAuley knew he had a problem with alcohol. He had not taken a drink since his release from prison. But he was assured that beer was not like whiskey. "They told me it was a harmless drink, wholesome and good and as simple as root-beer," McAuley said. "I drank it, and then began my downfall. The old appetite was awakened. From that time I drank it every day, and it was not long before I went from that to stronger liquors."[6]

With a ready supply of alcohol to ease a guilty conscience, McAuley returned to the Fourth Ward. The Civil War was in its final bloody year, and the federal government was offering a bounty to volunteers as well as a payment to the men who recruited them. "Rascally business that. I would pick men up wherever I could find them, get them half drunk and coax them to enlist," McAuley said. "I made a great deal of money in this way, which I spent freely. I became a sporting man, went often to the races, and my downward course was greatly quickened." When the war ended, McAuley became a river pirate again and was nearly killed on two occasions. He was so drunk one night that he fell out of his boat and almost drowned.[7]

His conscience finally saved McAuley. It had never stopped bothering him. One day, as he was sitting in his room, he heard a voice in the hallway below ask, "Do you love Jesus?" The voice belonged to a missionary, Henry Little, who had met the landlady on the stairs. "No, indade, do I love Jesus; and who is he?" she asked. McAuley jumped to his feet. "That voice—those words! It seemed like long-forgotten music," he said. Before he could open the door, the missionary had climbed the stairs in search of a tenant at the top of the building. McAuley waited for him on the landing below. He was broke, dressed in dirty clothes, and his head was closely shaved. "I was a frightful looking object," he said. When Little finally appeared, he was afraid that McAuley might attack him but agreed to meet in the street. McAuley hoped Little might help him find an honest job. As they talked, Little led McAuley to a mission on the Bowery. There, Little and another missionary tried to persuade him to sign a pledge to quit drinking. "I told them I shouldn't be likely to keep it, that I had taken it many times before, and broken it," he said. They told him to try again, that God would help him this time. They also promised to help him find work. "Well, to please you I will," he said.[8]

McAuley spent the next two years trying to get sober. In 1870, Julius Chambers, a young reporter for the *New York Herald*, approached McAuley for a story he was writing about river pirates. McAuley was sober and refused Chambers's offer to buy him a drink, saying he would never again touch the "damnable stuff." But he did not look well. "I saw a tall, cadaverous man, with strangely white cheeks," Chambers wrote. "His fine gray eyes had in them a look of hopelessness and lament I could not resist." He was also terribly thin. When Chambers bought him dinner, McAuley admitted he had not eaten in twenty-four hours.[9]

Slowly, McAuley's life began to improve as he found steady work and a sober girlfriend. But he was seeking more than a paycheck and a happy marriage. At work one day, he had a vision in which he saw himself bringing people to God in his old neighborhood by the docks. He persuaded a wealthy friend to give him the use of a former saloon that he owned at 316 Water Street. With money he solicited at religious camp meetings, he cleaned and repaired the space, hung a sign, "Helping Hand for Men," and opened for business in October 1872.

Once the door was thrown open, the needy flooded into the mission. "Such a sight I never saw," McAuley said. "Sinners crying, 'God have mercy on me!' 'Lord help me!' and while I was on my knees the

Lord said, 'You had better open the door every evening.' And so I did."
The mission was a sanctuary for the homeless. Fifty to sixty men slept
there overnight. McAuley said:

> They would be stretched out on the benches and then on the floor
> until there was not room to put your foot down without stepping
> on them. They were a terribly degraded set, hungry and alive with
> vermin, but we looked beyond all that and saw only souls for whom
> Christ died and whom He desired to save, and every now and then
> God found a real jewel among them.

The jewels were several dozen men and women who were converted in
the mission and joined in helping others. Their goal was to lead them to
salvation by accepting Christ as their savior and learning to live a moral
life. The example was set by McAuley, who used the details of his life
to demonstrate that no sinner was beyond redemption.[10]

The nightly meetings at the Water Street Mission were unique. There
were no fire-and-brimstone sermons urging people to repent or face
eternal damnation. The people who came to the mission were already in
hell. The service started with hymns and a reading from the Bible. Then
McAuley rose from his wooden armchair to make a brief statement:

> Why do you come to this prayer meeting? Is it to thank God be-
> cause you're happy? No. You come here because you're wretched
> and miserable. You know you're living in the gutter and you know
> it's your own fault. God didn't put you in the gutter. You went there
> of your own accord.

McAuley did not dwell on the sinfulness of his listeners. He had been a
sinner himself. "I've been a thief; I've been in jail. . . . I've been as low as
any man or woman in this room," he said. He focused on the solution:

> I crawled up out of the gutter at last, with God's help, and now
> I want to get you out. You feel that you're sinners. You feel, deep
> down in your hearts that you're low, miserable and degraded and I
> tell you that you'll never feel any better or be any better until you
> stop sinning and come to Christ.

He would then invite anyone who was ready to stop sinning to stand and speak.[11]

For the next thirty to forty minutes, men and women spoke from the heart. Some simply testified to the power of their conversion. "God spake peace to my soul one day at four o'clock in the afternoon on board the ship *George Peabody* at Pier 14," a sailor said. Others wanted to describe their struggles at length, forcing McAuley to impose a restriction. "SPEAKERS ARE STRICTLY LIMITED TO ONE MINUTE," said signs posted around the room. One minute was long enough to ask for help. "I am a confirmed drunkard. I have lain out all night in the gutter," a man said. "Help me. Pray for me. I'm afraid I can't hold out." "God will help and we will help," McAuley responded. "Let us first ask the pity and the help of God." At the end of the testimonies, McAuley rose again:

> We're going to have prayers now. Don't you want to be saved tonight? Who'll stand up for prayers? There's one, there's two, three, there's another. Don't be afraid to stand up. It don't make any difference what kind of clothes you have on. . . . You've got to cry to God for help if you want to get rid of your bad habits.

McAuley would then walk along the line of people kneeling, placing his hand on the shoulder of each man and woman and helping those who were having trouble forming their words. "I can't pray," one man said. "I'm too bad. I'm afraid to." "You can't be too bad," McAuley replied. "Just say, 'God be merciful to me a sinner.'"[12]

McAuley knew that most of those who experienced conversion would not remain saved, especially the drunks. The converts were surrounded by misery, and whiskey was only three cents a drink. "If you lived in this place, you would ask for whiskey instead of milk," a woman told a missionary as they stood in the rear court of a tenement. McAuley kept his converts busy:

> I'd have fallen again if I hadn't been so busy holding on to others. And that's the way to keep men. Start them to pull in somebody else. When your soul is on fire, longing to get hold of every poor wretch you see, there's no time for your old tricks nor any wanting to try them again.

Each convert contributed what he or she could. Some of the women visited the sick and sewed clothing for children.[13]

The drunks took care of their own. "Happy Charlie" Anderson was in charge of the new men, even before they had finished giving testimony, helping steady them as they spoke. He and the other reformed men made sure that the new recruits were fed and clothed, helped them find jobs, and strengthened their resolve when they were tempted to drink. The sober men were models for the newcomers, living proof that recovery was possible. "I saw men who had come into the mission sodden with drink turn into quiet steady workers," wrote Helen Stuart Campbell, a writer and social reformer who was introduced to the mission in 1878. "Now and then one fell—in one case permanently—but the prodigals commonly returned confessing their weakness and laboring earnestly to prove their penitence."[14]

McAuley died of tuberculosis in September 1884. Not many of New York's numerous newspapers mentioned his death. The few reporters who covered the funeral were probably surprised to discover a large crowd outside the Broadway Tabernacle, one of the biggest churches in the city. It had been full for hours, and people were packed into every approach, forcing the police to push and shout to get the minister in the door. It was one of the largest funerals for a private person that had ever been held in New York. Eminent businessmen and ministers took turns praising McAuley. There were "many gentlemen and ladies" present, but the reporters were watching everyone else:

> "old women, wrinkled and seamed" . . . "here and there sprinkled through the crowd the painted face of the scarlet woman showed itself." . . . "the straw hats of a few homeless tramps" . . . "a great many Negroes of both sexes" . . . "the young shop girl who has been saved from temptation" . . . "gamblers and confidence men who seemed very ill at ease."

These were the lost souls who had found relief at one of McAuley's missions: drunks, prostitutes, former slaves who had fled the South, the homeless, and the working poor. A shabby man asked a reporter to carry a small bunch of flowers inside. "It ain't any great shakes," he admitted.[15]

✦   ✦   ✦

McAuley was not alone in showing kindness to alcoholics and other outcasts in the postwar era. In 1873, the year after the opening of the Water Street Mission, women around the country took to the streets in an effort to halt the sale of alcohol. In just a few months, they demonstrated in nine hundred small towns in thirty-one states. They entered saloons and drugstores that sold liquor. If their request to banish liquor was refused, they knelt in prayer or began singing, driving customers out the door. Some owners agreed to close their business. Others responded with curses and threats or went to court for injunctions barring the women from their establishments. What became known as the Woman's Crusade for Temperance reportedly closed thirty thousand saloons.

The soldiers of the Woman's Crusade believed that they could accomplish their goal through spiritual renewal. The movement started with prayers to change the hearts of saloon keepers and broadened into a campaign to help drinkers. They accepted the fact that some people were incapable of quitting alcohol. Many of them had husbands or family members who were alcoholics. Whether they were morally weak or suffered from an illness, they believed the help needed could only come from God. This was the philosophy of the Woman's Christian Temperance Union (WCTU), which was organized in 1874 to channel the energy unleashed by the Woman's Crusade.

The WCTU's attitude toward drunks would change after it became a pillar of the prohibition movement, but in its early years, it launched a "gospel temperance" crusade that carried the promise of sobriety to drinkers wherever they could be found. The chapter in Newark, New Jersey, was particularly active. A member reported:

> We might speak of our gospel temperance work in the jail: how the prisoners sought and found the Savior, the Lord giving us a trophy the first meeting; of our bands of hope and young ladies' league; cottage prayer-meetings, saloon visiting, etc. But time will not permit....A true record of it is kept on high. It is a blessed work. Unto Him be all the praise and glory forever.

WCTU chapters created "reading rooms, coffee houses, and friendly inns" where men could find sober recreation. Members offered help in literature distributed through Sunday school classes. When a potential convert stepped forward, they stayed after him until he saw the light. In Newark, they visited one man for eighteen months. Finally, he was given suitable clothes so that he could go to church. "He was deeply convicted of sin, and sought the Savior, whom he found able to save, even to the uttermost," the WCTU reported. The convert had been sober for six months when this report was made. He had become the chaplain for a club of reformed men and had spoken of his experience several times in New Jersey and New York.[16]

Another Newark man, a "Mr. Jones," was discovered during a visit to his home, which had received several temperance tracts. His wife greeted the crusaders with evident relief and related the story of her husband's sad decline. His family, including a brother who was a minister, had been praying for him for years, but it hadn't stopped his drinking. Once the owner of two houses, he was unemployed; the family was living in rented rooms and had almost exhausted their savings. Still Mrs. Jones was hopeful because her husband had been reading the temperance pamphlets and wanted to speak with the visitors. "He listened with joy to the 'good news' of redemption through Jesus' blood. How Jesus came to seek and save the lost," one of the visitors recalled. "We felt God's presence there." Everyone knelt in prayer. When they rose, Jones agreed to accompany his guests to their church, where he took the pledge.[17]

When the news of Mr. Jones's conversion got around the neighborhood, a number of women asked the WCTU to visit their homes. Another ten men were converted. Meanwhile, Jones honored his pledge. "Two years have rolled away since that memorable 3rd day of September, and he is one of our most consistent Christian men, a good citizen, and an earnest temperance worker," the WCTU reported.[18]

The Woman's Crusade was at its peak in the winter of 1874 when it discovered one of its most important converts in Bangor, Maine. Dr. Henry A. Reynolds had once been full of promise. He had graduated from Harvard Medical School during the Civil War and spent two years as a surgeon in an artillery unit. On his return, he opened a successful practice and was named the city physician. However, he soon began drinking alcoholically, binging for six weeks at a time. "I have walked my father's house night after night for seven nights and days, a raving, crazy madman, as the result of intoxicating beverages," Reynolds said. He even suffered delirium tremens. He tried different ways to stop, but nothing worked. "I had 'drunk my last drink'; I had broken my bottle; I had sworn off 'before a justice of the peace'; I had tried to 'taper off,'" he said. Finally, he tried the only thing he believed he had left:

> I threw myself on my knees in my office, and asked of my God to save me, and promised him that if he would save me from such sufferings as I had once been through, with his assistance I would be true to myself and to him, and do what I could for the salvation of others.

Soon after, Reynolds attended a prayer meeting organized by the woman crusaders. Some doubted the sincerity of the town's notorious doctor, wondering whether his taking the pledge wasn't a joke. But Reynolds would express his gratitude to the crusaders for the rest of his life.[19]

Reynolds was determined to keep the promise that he made to God to work for the salvation of other alcoholics. He believed that drunks were misunderstood:

> No nobler class of men walk the earth than some who are drinking men. They are naturally generous, whole-souled, genial, jolly; but by intemperance their minds become diseased. They become scorned and degraded outcasts in the ditch, kept there by thoughtless people, less generous and honorable by nature than themselves. But for rum, these might be on the throne instead of in the gutter.

Reynolds was convinced that many could be saved if someone was willing to make an effort to help them. But his own experience convinced him that few were willing. "I am compelled to give the same painful testimony that so many do, that no one asked me to turn over a new leaf, or said an encouraging word to me in the way or urging me to try and live a sober life," he said. "Had some kind friend shown me the way out of it, and whispered in my ear that I could be a better man, I might have been so."[20]

Reynolds decided that he would establish a club for drinkers who wanted to reform. During his first sober months, he had belonged to a Young Men's Crusade Club, whose members included teetotalers, moderate drinkers, and drunks. "The result was constant quarreling and strife. The organization died," Reynolds said. He began to think about a new club that would be closed to nondrinkers, "a society composed entirely of reformed men." "There is a bond of sympathy between reformed men which binds them together," he said. He paid for an ad in the Bangor newspapers, inviting men who wanted to stop drinking to a meeting on September 10, 1874. The men of Bangor had a reputation as the biggest drinkers in a hard-drinking state. Eleven appeared at the meeting.[21]

Reynolds was not a powerful speaker. "It takes me about an hour and a quarter to make a 25-minute speech," he admitted. But what he lacked in eloquence he made up in his commitment to building his organization. His method was to travel to a town and hold meetings that addressed a general audience, collecting pledges from everyone who wanted to sign. But most of the pledge makers were people who did not drink much. It was the drunks he wanted to reach:

> [A]t the close of a series of meetings I get together what of the above-named material I can, and organize a club. These men really become self-constituted missionaries and go to work, which helps to save themselves and others.

Although most reformed men eagerly embraced the missionary role, others needed a kick in the pants. Reynolds was not slow in delivering it to the members he thought were underperforming:

> You are to blame for not having a larger and more effective club. . . . Out of gratitude to God for your deliverance you ought to be the first to go out into the byways and hedges, and compel others to come in. I know what it is to have a pleasant home and a lucrative practice; but I have abandoned both that I may be the means, under God, of saving others from the depth of sorrow and suffering from which I have been extricated. I could not rest. Don't leave a stone unturned to reform others.

He expected his supporters to be as deeply committed to rescuing drunks as he was.[22]

Reynolds's focus on the needs of alcoholics led him to part company with prohibitionists. This was probably not easy for him. "I attribute my salvation from a drunkard's grave to the Woman's Temperance Crusade," he said. "I consider myself as a brand plucked from the burning through the prayers of the Christian women of America." But he refused to lead his troops into the battle for legal restrictions on the sale of alcohol. While he may have favored them personally, he believed that involvement in politics of any kind would distract reformed men. "Let everything else alone. You reformed men have enough business on your hands to take care of yourselves, without being made cat's-paws for politicians to pull their chestnuts out of the fire," he advised. This single-mindedness meant that all their energy went into recruiting, which enlisted fifty-one thousand men in the first twenty-one months.[23]

It certainly helped that Reynolds had a knack for publicity. He developed a catchphrase by continually urging drinkers to "dare to do right" by signing the pledge. But he came up with his greatest innovation as he prepared for the first convention of club members in Bangor in the spring of 1875. Thinking it would be useful for the reformed drunks to recognize one another on the street, he sent his office boy to the dry goods store to buy several yards of red ribbon. He cut the ribbon into six-inch pieces and greeted the arriving delegates by tying a ribbon into the buttonhole of their jacket lapels. The ribbon was more than a tool for promoting group solidarity. It showed the world that they were new men. "I was not ashamed to drink," Reynolds said. "Why should I be ashamed to acknowledge that I don't drink? . . . I want to be known as a man who dares to do right." The red ribbon was also a way of encouraging drinkers to quit. "[I]f every man who reforms wears a Red Ribbon, it won't be long before the absence of the ribbon will be noticeable," he explained. Wearing the red ribbon might even help a man resist a moment of temptation:

> A man with any decency in his makeup would want to take off his ribbon if he was tempted to drink; but while he was taking it off God would be at work at his conscience to save him from falling.

If the man entered the bar still wearing the ribbon, there was always the possibility that the bartender would refuse to serve him. This may have happened occasionally, but there were rumors that some saloon keepers sought to discredit the reform movement by serving liquor to men who had never reformed, tying ribbons on them, and sending them reeling into the street.[24]

Reynolds began to establish clubs at the invitation of a WCTU chapter in Gloucester, Massachusetts. A year later, there were fifty Red Ribbon Clubs with twenty thousand members. Next he traveled to Michigan, where he had even greater success. Seven months later, the Red Ribbon Clubs had enrolled eighty thousand; the Detroit chapter alone had thirty-seven hundred members. The Michigan legislature approved a resolution praising the Red Ribbon Clubs for creating a significant decline in crime, although there are no available statistics to prove this. Some of the enthusiasm for the reform clubs spread into Indiana as well. It was reported that every third man walking the streets of Indianapolis was wearing a red ribbon.

At the same time that Reynolds was launching his movement in Michigan, another reformed drunk, Francis Murphy, was taking Pennsylvania by storm. Murphy was a forty-year-old Irish immigrant who had been a saloon keeper in Portland, Maine, before drink got the better of him. He got sober following a religious conversion in jail and organized a club of reformed men there several years before Reynolds got started. Like Reynolds, Murphy got a boost from the WCTU after his speaking gifts were discovered at a temperance convention. Frances Willard, the WCTU corresponding secretary, invited him to Chicago, where he quickly organized eleven clubs. Also like Reynolds, he differed with the WCTU. He refused to support prohibition or to condemn men who were engaged in the liquor business. He also expressed annoyance at nondrinkers who attended his meetings only to be entertained by hearing drunks tell their stories. His meetings were for "the reclamation of men addicted to drink, and not for the amusement of sober people," he said.[25]

In 1876, Murphy formed a club in the First Methodist Church in Pittsburgh. Some of the church trustees wanted to throw him out when they discovered that he was drawing a rough crowd. "The reform crowd broke windows, spit tobacco juice on the floor, disordered the pews, and did various other obnoxious things," they complained. However, there was no argument over Murphy's success. In the first month, five thousand people signed the abstinence pledge. Churches began to open their doors to new meetings, and Murphy found himself dashing from one meeting to another to address the swelling ranks of reformed men. By the time his campaign was ten weeks old, thirty churches were hosting temperance meetings, and a newly sober man could attend a different one every night of the week. An estimated forty thousand had signed the pledge. Clearly, most of these people were not alcoholics. The enthusiasm generated by Murphy's campaign was sweeping the city.[26]

Some of the meetings drew up to two thousand people. Like Jerry McAuley, Murphy asked them to testify to the blessings of sobriety. "Brother George Magoffin will now tell us how good he feels," Murphy said. "Brother George, tell the people how happy your wife and little ones are since you signed the pledge." Each of the men told his story in his own way:

> The speeches are of every kind, from grave to humorous. Some touching, pathetic recital of past struggles and sorrows, with the names of loved ones, of wife, mother or children, connected with it, elicits tears; while following this may come some quaint reminiscences of services in the tanglefoot battalion, which causes a broad smile, which frequently deepens into a ripple of laughter, among the audience.

Once the new men had gotten used to telling their stories, they were sent to speak at other meetings. They also helped minister to the drunks who were walking through the door for the first time. On Christmas Day, Murphy hosted a dinner for twelve hundred of Pittsburgh's poor. Drunks were helped to find clothing, temporary housing, and jobs.[27]

News of Murphy's success in Pittsburgh soon spread, and he began to receive requests to speak from communities throughout western Pennsylvania. Emulating the success of the Red Ribbon Clubs, Murphy adopted blue ribbons and sent his converts north along the Allegheny Valley to Erie, where one reformed man was said to have obtained pledges from nearly a third of the population. Others worked their way east through southern New York. By early 1877, the blue ribbon movement was becoming a national phenomenon. Murphy became the president of a new organization, the National Christian Temperance Union, which was organized in Pittsburgh in February. At a convention in October, it was reported that members were active in Indiana, Illinois, Kentucky, Kansas, and Nebraska. They claimed to have taken twenty thousand pledges in Missouri, thirty thousand in Colorado, and as many as three million nationwide. Murphy's followers were particularly strong in Ohio, where the state corresponding secretary reported in late 1877 that one hundred forty thousand men had stopped drinking in the Columbus area alone.

God was not the only higher power in the late nineteenth century. A rival, science, was on the rise, as new discoveries began to change daily life, bringing electric light to dark city streets and making possible the rise of buildings to seemingly impossible heights. Frederick B. Hargreaves celebrated science in 1880 in language that was common to the age:

> The march of progress has been … onward; intellect has been making rapid strides. … . Invention has succeeded invention, discovery followed discovery, till the miracle has ceased to be a marvel, and the elements nature and science, have become tributary to the masterly powers of man.

In such an age, it was easy to believe that science would one day cure alcoholism. The men who belonged to the AACI were skeptical, but miracle drugs were being discovered all the time. The public craved new cures, and the purpose of Hargreaves's pamphlet was to deliver the good news to alcoholics. Its title was *Gold as a Cure for Drunkenness, Being an Account of the Double Chloride of Gold Discovery Recently Made by L.E. Keeley of Dwight, Illinois*.[28]

Hargreaves was a twenty-five-year-old English minister who emigrated in 1872 to assume a post at a Presbyterian church in a small rural community south of Chicago. He led his new congregation for only fifteen months before moving on. He secured a job in another church but left after three months. He found one more pastoral position but was fired because of his drinking. He scraped by doing legal work for several years until the rise of the gospel temperance movement gave him a new lease on life. He became a lecturer for the Illinois State Temperance League and traveled around the state addressing members of the ribbon clubs.

During these years, Hargreaves lived in Dwight, a town of eighteen hundred that lay along the line of the Chicago and Alton Railroad, seventy miles south of Chicago. There he became friends with the town's physician, Dr. Leslie E. Keeley, a veteran of the Civil War who had moved to Dwight after graduating from Rush Medical College in Chicago. According to Hargreaves, one day, after returning from a lecture tour, he and Keeley discussed the plight of a mutual friend with alcoholism. They had both heard of a drug that was supposed to help a person stop drinking. It was probably a nauseant like ipecac that could be added to whiskey as Albert Day had done, causing a drinker to vomit so violently that he would become nauseated if he even smelled alcohol again. They decided to experiment with it, using a local saloon keeper, Pat Conafry, as the test subject:

> [Keeley] said Pat would take anything he asked him to take, so he fixed up a bottle and gave it to Conafry; and in a few days he lost his desire for liquor, and could not drink any at the end of about a week. He, however, made strong efforts, and one Sunday got a drink to stick and got gloriously drunk and would not take any more medicine.

Hargreaves and Keeley were delighted with the result of their experiment and believed that they had made an important discovery. They used the medicine to help a second man, John P. Campbell, and began to discuss how to market the product as their own. Campbell joined the venture as a partner.[29]

The only detailed account of the origin of the "Keeley Cure" comes from a deposition given by Hargreaves in a lawsuit that was filed against him by the Keeley Institute in 1902, two years after Keeley's death. Keeley forced out Hargreaves as a partner in 1886, depriving him of a share of the enormous profits generated by the cure a few years later. Hargreaves started marketing his own cure and, after Keeley's death, was sued by his heirs who feared Hargreaves was about to reveal the Keeley formula to help create a new business that would undercut the Keeley Institute. Much of what Hargreaves said about Keeley during his deposition was extremely unflattering, perhaps even defamatory. But there is no question that he worked closely with Keeley in launching his business. His account, which was given under oath, provides details about the discovery of the Keeley Cure that are unavailable elsewhere.

According to Hargreaves, Keeley was initially reluctant to become publicly identified with the sale of a cure for alcoholism. Doctors were seeking to establish their expertise as healers at the time, and one of the ways they emphasized their superiority was by condemning the patent medicines that promised to cure virtually every illness. Keeley feared that being associated with the cure might damage his reputation. He was supplementing his income by serving as a doctor for the railroad and thought he might lose his job. As a first step, they agreed that Hargreaves and Campbell would rent a hotel room in Bloomington, Illinois, and begin advertising for patients. They spent a month in Bloomington, but it was hard going. "It was a new thing, you understand, and people were skeptical," Hargreaves explained. The failure in Bloomington convinced Keeley that he had to vouch for his product publicly. "He took the position that . . . it would give more tone and prestige to the business if his name was used . . . and so we decided to call the firm name 'Leslie E. Keeley, M.D.'"[30]

Meanwhile, Hargreaves and Keeley had decided that they needed to make changes in their medicine. They called it a "tonic" that could help a man stop drinking, but it was effective only in the early days of the sobering-up process. They continued to experiment in the hope that they would find a drug that would permanently eliminate the desire for alcohol. One possibility was gold. Gold salts had been used for medicinal purposes since ancient times. In Keeley's day, the use of gold chloride was declining because of the danger of kidney damage and poisoning by the mercury used in gold extraction. However, some doctors still prescribed it for skin and venereal diseases. It was also thought to stimulate the brain and nervous system. Keeley was not the first doctor to suggest that it might be useful in fighting addiction.

According to Hargreaves, Keeley almost killed the first drunk he treated with gold chloride. A sewing machine salesman named Dalliba, the only patient that they had been able to recruit in Bloomington, had a bad reaction to the gold pills that Keeley had given him. "We had a bad time with him. Keeley had to come down two or three times, and we finally had to stop it," Hargreaves said. But it was only a brief setback, Hargreaves said.

> [W]e hit on another remedy that did all we ever expected the gold to do; and it was a far more valuable specific for drunkenness than gold; and we used that in place of gold. Keeley has often said to me: "What a lucky thing we happened to hit on that drug," as it saved further experiments and was not dangerous.

Hargreaves asserted that Keeley stopped using gold within months of launching the business. Nevertheless, he insisted on advertising his medicine as the "Double Chloride of Gold Cure." "It was an awful good name, and Keeley hated to part with the name," Hargreaves said. He justified it by saying there are particles of gold in everything. "Keeley would often say, 'There is a trace of gold anyway in it, and that is enough.'"[31]

Hargreaves said Keeley bent the truth frequently in the early months of his enterprise. The business was started on a shoestring. None of the partners was wealthy, and they sold very little medicine during the first six months of 1880. They found it hard to raise twenty-three dollars to publish *Gold as a Cure for Drunkenness*. It contained an introductory letter from Hargreaves in his capacity as vice president of the Illinois State Temperance League and several articles purportedly written by Keeley. Hargreaves claimed to have written almost everything published under Keeley's name. "[N]o one ever accused him of being able to [write]," he said.[32]

According to Hargreaves, the only pieces that Keeley contributed to the pamphlet were fictionalized testimonials. Although the business was in its infancy, the pamphlet consisted of dozens of statements from doctors, lawyers, employers, and other prominent men. Hargreaves said he wrote most of them, signing the names of Keeley's friends and associates, even giving one the title of General. Hargreaves said that Keeley wrote the patients' testimonials himself. A little dishonesty was necessary, Hargreaves explained. Times were hard. "We were not 'lying on flowery beds of ease,'" he said.[33]

Slowly, the Keeley Company began to grow. At first, the gold cure was sold by mail. Later, to increase income, patients were encouraged to take their treatment in Dwight under Dr. Keeley's supervision at a cost of a hundred dollars for four weeks. One of the first patients at the Keeley Institute was a newspaper editor from Missouri Valley, a small town in western Iowa. Robert Harris arrived in Dwight in 1889 after more than a decade of heavy drinking. Harris recalled that he was one of only four patients and that the group followed a strict treatment regimen. They received injections of the newly formulated double chloride of gold at 8 a.m., noon, 5 p.m., and 7:30 p.m., and were required to drink several ounces of tonic every two hours. After three weeks of treatment, Harris left Dwight convinced that he could stay sober. "It was the cure I was after . . . and every day since that time I have thanked God that there was such a man on earth as Dr. Keeley," Harris said. Back in Missouri Valley, Harris used his newspaper, the *Times*, to broadcast the news of the liquor cure. He persuaded eight of his friends to depart for Dwight. "[I]n every case, the cure has been as perfect and successful as it was in my case," he reported in 1891.[34]

Missouri Valley was only the first Iowa town to embrace the Keeley Cure. A woman in Boone read one of Harris's articles and showed it to her husband, William Marsh, a prominent businessman who was unable to stop drinking. When Marsh returned from Dwight, he persuaded the son of the town's wealthiest man to go. Over the next eighteen months, the two newly sober men preached the Keeley Cure to every drunk they knew, and helped pay for those who couldn't afford the train fare, treatment charges, and room and board. F. M. Havens, a close observer of the Boone experiment, described the outcome in a letter to a friend:

> The net results in Boone and immediate vicinity are, that 41 men— good men—who 18 months ago were down—many of them to the very worst condition, physically, to which alcohol can drag a human being, are today bright, fresh-faced men, with nothing in their appearance or actions to indicate that they were ever victims of the alcohol habit.

The effect of forty-one sober men returning to a small community must have been dramatic, particularly when they displayed absolute confidence in their ability to stay sober. "If I had the feeling that I am using the least little bit of will power to refrain from drinking, I would be afraid of myself," one man told Havens. "[B]ut on the contrary, I never think of it—no more than if I never tasted whiskey."[35]

The year 1890 was a turning point for the Keeley Company. Keeley and his partners believed that most of the profit from their business would come from the sale of franchises to men who would open Keeley clinics around the country. The franchisees would make a large initial payment for the right to use the Keeley name and become a steady source for the sale of the cure. The dream began to come true with the opening of a Keeley Institute in Des Moines in early 1890. The number of patients was beginning to grow exponentially as graduates shared the good news. Robert Harris, the Missouri Valley editor, explained:

> [I]t is strange what a change comes over the spirit of their dreams within a few days after their arrival at the institute. That fear of the people knowing where they are has gone and they are like a new convert to religion—they have found a good thing and they want the world to know it. That is why every patient cured is a walking advertisement for the cured.

Within a year, more than eighty patients were being treated at Dwight every month, and five more Keeley Institutes had opened around the country.[36]

Keeley's big break came in a letter from Joseph Medill, the publisher of the *Chicago Daily Tribune*. Medill was an important man: he was a founder of the Republican Party, a friend of Abraham Lincoln, and, briefly, the mayor of Chicago. Medill was also a strong temperance man who butted heads with Chicago's Germans by enforcing a ban on the sale of liquor on Sundays. He had been hearing rumors about the Keeley Cure for several years before he finally decided to send a medical student who was "slightly addicted" to alcohol to Dwight. When the man returned and claimed he was cured, Medill wrote Keeley to inquire further. Recognizing his chance, Keeley gambled everything, daring the publisher to send him "half a dozen of the most confirmed inebriates and hopeless wrecks of alcoholism in Chicago." Keeley said that if he failed to cure them, he would publicly confess his failure. Medill was intrigued:

> The challenge was so bold and startling that I at once accepted it. . . . The experimental cases were sent down to Dwight one at a time, extending over a period of several weeks. And in due time they were all returned to me, looking as if a veritable miracle had been wrought upon them. They went away sots and returned gentlemen. It was amazing.

Medill was not convinced until he has sent some of his acquaintances to Keeley. When they returned sober, he pledged to do whatever he could to promote the double chloride of gold. "I felt it to be a duty which I owed to humanity," he said.[37]

The *Chicago Daily Tribune* began covering the Keeley Institute like it was the next Great Chicago Fire. The reporters clearly understood the kind of coverage their publisher wanted. Dwight "is an elysium for inebriates," the first wrote.

> Dr. Keeley has reformed more drunkards than all the temperance lecturers now strutting and fretting before the imbibing public. He is a connoisseur on drunks, plain and frapped. He delights in the drink-addicted and ditch drunkards are his especially weakness.

"[H]e has treated over 5,000 individual cases, coming from every State in the Union and from countries abroad," claimed another *Tribune* reporter, who accepted this grossly exaggerated statistic. The *Tribune* followed up with editorial endorsements, proclaiming that Keeley "appears to be doing a great work in curing the victims of the drink and opium habit." It also featured testimonials from doctors, Keeley graduates, and their grateful families. The *Tribune* promoted the Keeley Cure almost every day for six months, while publishing only a few articles and letters that raised questions about Keeley and his methods. "The town is filled with all the patients it can hold, and every train is surrounded by patients standing ready to welcome the coming and speed the departing," the *Tribune* reported. "Sunshine, quiet, hope, relief—these fill the days at Dwight." The message to drunks was clear. Tens of thousands responded.[38]

Many of the drunks arrived with members of their family. C. S. Clark, a writer and a patient, recalled:

> From a train steps a venerable father or a widowed mother, assisting a wrecked son to reach the platform. Just behind them is a faithful wife, supporting an unsteady husband. Next is evidently a fine business man in the custody of a friend, then a sister accompanying a brother to this place of reformation.

Some arrived alone, drunk and loquacious. Some were unconscious. One man arrived with a tag tied to the lapel of his "ragged, greasy coat":

PLEASE PUT THIS MAN OFF
AT DWIGHT, AND
NOTIFY DR. KEELEY OR ASSISTANTS

Most were middle-class men who could afford to pay a hundred dollars for treatment, plus room and board. A majority of those who got sober at Dwight were farmers, but there were also many professional men. (The drunk with a tag was a doctor.) There were also a few women who were treated in separate facilities, mostly for opium addiction.[39]

The Keeley boom transformed Dwight. Keeley and his partners could now afford to construct a handsome brick building to house their offices and a laboratory. Located just two blocks from the train station, it was impossible to miss, as the steady flow of arriving drunks became a torrent. A year after the publication of the first *Tribune* story, the Dwight institute was treating as many as seven hundred patients per month. Keeley did not provide housing, so the drunks either stayed at the Livingston Hotel next door or boarded with residents. During the day, they strolled along the streets, lounged on the hotel's front porch, and checked their mail at the post office.

But wherever they were, they stopped what they were doing when it was time to take their medicine. Four times a day, they formed lines in the treatment hall to take injections of double chloride of gold. Some rolled up their sleeves; others wore shirts that had been slit to provide easy access. Everyone waited. When Joseph Medill visited Dwight in 1892, he reported that it took six lines to accommodate everyone. The drinking of the tonic, too, was a collective experience. Clark recalled how strangely it struck a newcomer:

> [T]he hour to take it arrives . . . he hesitates and looks around among the hundreds of fellow patients. . . . He notes a sudden graceful, uniform and systematic movement toward perhaps 500 inside pockets; an equal uniform withdrawing of 500 small vials; a grand raising of those bottles toward heaven and then a magnificent lowering to 500 throats! The newcomer looks in profound amazement. Not a smile—not a ripple at this seemingly ludicrous public performance by 500 well-dressed, manly, sensitive men![40]

The new men made friends quickly. Treatment at Dwight encouraged a strong camaraderie among the patients that often began within minutes of their arrival. When the train pulled in, there was always a large crowd of men at the station that included patients who had completed their treatment and the friends who had come to wish them well. The remaining patients were quick to approach the newcomers with offers of advice. Clark was one of two hundred patients at the station one day when a well-known politician arrived. The man appeared stunned as he surveyed the crowd. "Gentlemen of the convention," he said at last. "Is it possible—can such a thing be—that you are all sober?" Amid great laughter, the politician was taken in charge by his fellow drunks.[41]

Many distinguished men went to Dwight for treatment. Clark was in line waiting for an injection one morning when he tried to engage a new man in conversation by asking him something simple. "Damned if I know, sir," the man replied. "I don't know anything; I am simply a fool without sense or reason." He turned out to be one of the most prominent lawyers in Missouri. Patients at Dwight had a lot of time to kill. They spent much of it in conversation with other drunks, exchanging life stories and strengthening their resolve to be better men. The experience created bonds of deep affection. "I have had an opportunity to sit at the feet of men of learning who are an honor to America—men able to instruct the learned, prepared to widen broad mind, and capable of pointing lessons of love and endurance to those already graceful in these accomplishments," Clark said.[42]

What bound the men together even more than their shared history of suffering was the conviction that they were getting better, and not just better—cured. Keeley claimed that 95 percent of his patients got sober and stayed that way. How could the men at Dwight doubt it? They were supplied two-ounce vials of whiskey until they decided that they no longer wanted it. After two or three days, men who had drunk liquor every day for years were revolted by the sight of it.

But this was only a preliminary stage—a reaction to the alcohol antagonist that Keeley and Hargreaves had discovered years before. According to Keeley, the cure—the double chloride of gold—was only beginning to do its work. During his first week at Dwight, John Flavel Mines, a fifty-five-year-old journalist and the author of popular reminiscences of old New York, suffered a kind of depression that normally sent him on a drinking spree. Although Mines had been sober for several months, Keeley prescribed whiskey until the craving passed. When it did, the depression lifted, and Mines experienced a profound sense of release:

> When I saw that it had ceased to make me its victim and slave, I could have cried for joy. I knew from that moment that the bichloride of gold had gotten the upper hand, broken the fetters of my disease, and made me whole. . . . [S]uddenly, as if I had stepped out of the blackness of an African jungle into the quiet sunshine of Central Park, I broke out of my living tomb and knew that I was cured.[43]

In the fall of 1891, the *North American Review* published articles by several doctors who considered Keeley a fraud. But the criticism hardly made a dent in his popularity, even after Mines got drunk and died in a New York charity hospital. Keeley could count on the loyalty of his patients. Two days after Mines's well-publicized death, Keeley returned to Dwight from a European trip. Descending from the train, he found seven hundred patients drawn up in double lines along two blocks of the street leading from the station to the institute. As he passed, the men raised their hats in salute.

Keeley had never claimed that he could save every alcoholic. He estimated that 5 percent of drunks were beyond hope. He acknowledged that he could do nothing for the man who wanted to keep drinking. He told a group of departing patients:

> You must remember that I cannot paralyze the arm that would deliberately raise the fatal glass to the lips. When you all go out into the new life, I will have placed you exactly where you were before taking the first drink. You will look back over the past and then contemplate the future, and you will then choose which path you will follow the balance of your days.

While it was appropriate to warn the drunks that they would face temptation, the warning was undercut by the assertion that they had been fully restored. The promise of the Keeley Cure was that double chloride of gold healed cells that had been poisoned by alcohol, eliminating the craving for drink. The cured drunks were once again like other men.[44]

Not every Keeley graduate felt confidence in the future. Some admitted to nervousness as the train carried them ever closer to home and its temptations. But most expressed confidence in their ability to stay sober. "Yes sir, it is his own fault if he don't [stay cured], and it is not the fault of the treatment," one Keeley graduate said. "If a man wants to behave himself, he can, and he can make a damn fool of himself if he wants to." The feelings of the departing Keeley men were well expressed by Eugene V. Debs in the spring of 1893. In a few years, Debs would help found the Socialist Party and later run for president four times as its candidate, but at the time, he was a thirty-seven-year-old official of a union of locomotive firemen. The remarks he delivered on leaving the Keeley Institute suggest that he had followed the same road as the other drunks:

> I feel this morning as I never felt before, the utter meaningless-[ness] of words to express my gratitude for my deliverance from the fetters that have heretofore bound me, and the privileges I have enjoyed while here, of knowing so many manly men and splendid women. . . . For 20 years I continually indulged in the use of

alcoholic stimulants, and I can see myself this morning, after passing through this magical treatment, as I was, and I feel very grateful
for the great change that has taken place in me.

To the other graduates, too, their sudden deliverance from alcoholism
seemed miraculous.[45]

The growth of the Keeley Institute was breathtaking. Beginning
with one patient in 1889, the Keeley Company reported over $170,000
in profits just two years later. Men who wanted to open franchises
were throwing money at Keeley in 1891. Twenty-five branch institutes opened in that year, and Keeley began to think about expanding
abroad. He dreamed of building a world headquarters in Chicago and
angered the directors of the city's Washingtonian Home by offering to
buy their institution and run it properly. The Keeley juggernaut continued to roll in 1892. It seemed that every city wanted to brag about
their Keeley Institute, and seventy-five new facilities opened. Profits hit
$508,966. In early 1893, Keeley seriously considered selling his com-
pany to a New York syndicate for $2.5 million but was unable to agree
on all the terms of the sale.

As the Keeley Institute spread across the country, its graduates also
established a national presence. In April 1891, when there were still
relatively few patients at Dwight, three of them formed a Bi-Chloride
of Gold Club and began meeting in a blacksmith's shop every morning
after the first shot of the day. New patients were invited to speak, and
men who were departing made farewell remarks. Soon, graduates were
writing to the club about the experience of returning home. "These
letters were always encouraging. Their moral effect on the patients,
still anxious about themselves, is invaluable," a club member recalled.
The men who were writing the letters began to form their own clubs
in Chicago, Pittsburgh, Lafayette, Indiana, and Farmington, Maine.
There were soon fifty clubs in twenty states. Three hundred members
arrived in Dwight in February 1892 to form a national organization.
"With as much pride as if it had been a military decoration," many of
the delegates wore a Bi-Chloride of Gold Club pin, which featured an
upside-down horseshoe bracketing the initial "K." The design became
the emblem of the new Keeley League.[46]

The Keeley League had several goals. It wanted to sustain the camaraderie that existed among Keeley patients as a way of helping them adjust to the difficulties of a sober life. For that reason, membership was limited to drunks who had taken the Keeley Cure. The Keeley League also wanted "to further the cause of temperance among all people by curing the drunkard of the disease of intemperance" and to "extend the knowledge of the Keeley remedies." Its mission was "to bring about a reformation in public sentiment which will close the gates of the prison against the drunkard and open to him the doors of the hospital," a league official said. A weekly newspaper, the *Banner of Gold*, became the voice of the Keeley movement. The most important work of league members was to encourage other drunks to get sober and help pay for men who could not afford treatment. In 1893, it reported that they had referred 2,700 patients and covered the expenses of 574. These numbers would grow as new leagues were established. Two years later, there were more than three hundred branches of the league in forty-two states.[47]

Federal and state governments also supported the Keeley movement. Officials had created veterans' homes to assist men who had been wounded during the Civil War. But boredom was a big problem, and many of the men used their pension checks to buy liquor. The old soldiers' homes were declared to be "in a frightful state of inebricy [*sic*]." Seizing the opportunity to win a federal endorsement, Keeley offered to provide the gold cure at a discount and free training in how to administer it. He won a contract to provide services to the facilities at Forts Leavenworth and Riley. More than a thousand veterans were treated at Leavenworth over the next two years.

State and local governments also promoted Keeleyism. Prodded by constituents who were members of the Keeley League, the legislatures in Minnesota, Louisiana, North Dakota, and Colorado appropriated money to send drunks to local Keeley Institutes. Minneapolis mayor William H. Eustis asked Keeley for advice on dealing with inmates of the city jail who had been repeatedly arrested for drunkenness. Sixty-one men were sent for treatment, including nine who had been arrested more than ten times. Eustis also provided housing for the men until they could find jobs. Fifty-three were still sober five years later.[48]

By 1893, Keeleyism had become a national institution. In July, there were 118 Keeley Institutes in operation across the country. In its annual report, the executive committee of the Keeley League claimed that a hundred forty thousand patients had taken the double chloride of gold cure. Later, Keeley would claim he had treated nearly three hundred thousand, although this figure appears to include mail-order customers. The success of the Keeley Institutes could also be measured in the rapid growth of competing franchises, including the Empire Institutes, the Oppenheimer Institutes, the Gatlin Institutes, and the Neal Institutes. All made the same sweeping claim to be able to cure addiction to alcohol, drugs, and tobacco using products like Dr. Haines Golden Remedy, the Geneva Gold Cure, and the Kelly Bi-Chloride of Gold Cure.

The expansion might have gone on for years if the country hadn't been hit by a deep depression. In 1893, almost five hundred banks and fifteen thousand businesses closed their doors. Unemployment rose to 12 percent in 1894 and remained in double digits for four years. The depression had an immediate impact on the Keeley Institutes. A majority of the drunks who traveled to Dwight were farmers, and farmers were one of the groups hardest hit by the depression. Soon the depression affected almost every American and made it increasingly difficult for men to raise a hundred dollars for treatment. While the Dwight institute was never in danger, five branches closed immediately and twenty-four more by the end of 1894.

Leslie Keeley died at his winter home in Los Angeles on February 21, 1900. The death was widely reported. The *Chicago Tribune*, which had played such an important role in the growth of the institute, published the longest and most respectful obituary. It said that Keeley had built his "palatial residence" two years earlier in the hope that California's sunny climate would ease his bronchial trouble. At sixty-eight, he possessed "a world-wide reputation" and a $1 million fortune. What the *Tribune* didn't say was that Keeley's influence had greatly diminished. His reputation as a doctor had been battered by years of criticism leveled by members of the American Medical Association, who considered the gold cure a fraud. The leaders of the AACI, who shared his concern for alcoholics, were among his severest critics. The profitability of the Keeley Institute had also waned. There were only forty-four institutes still in operation. Profits had fallen nearly 80 percent.[49]

But the Keeley Institute survived. Its fortunes revived when the economy began to grow strongly again in 1897. At that point, the income of the Dwight institute was half of what it had been a few years earlier, but it still treated hundreds of patients every month. The number of branch institutes also stabilized. In January 1900, the Keeley League newspaper, *Banner of Gold*, reported that new institutes had opened in Albuquerque, New Mexico, and Seattle, Washington. H. K. Aiken, the owner of the institute in Waukesha, Wisconsin, told the paper that business was good and growing. A few months later, the Keeley Institute Managers Association held its fourth annual meeting in Dwight. The representatives of twenty-five institutes attended.

The survival of the Keeley Institute owed a great deal to its graduates. According to the *Banner of Gold*, thirteen of the managers who attended the meeting had gotten sober at Dwight or one of the branches. Many of the medical directors were also former drunks. For many of these men, working at the Keeley Institute was more than a job: it was a way of helping other drunks, as well as insurance against a possible relapse.

The depression did kill the national Keeley League, which held its last national convention in 1897. But at least some of the state and local Keeley Leagues continued to operate. The Keeley League of Sewickley, Pennsylvania, reported in 1900 that it raised enough money to send thirty-five drunks to treatment in the previous year.

By 1900, thousands of Keeley graduates had been sober for many years. Most of the former drunks at the managers' meeting had quit between five and ten years earlier. Willard Brown, who was treated in 1891, wrote to the *Banner of Gold* saying that he had recently visited Robert Gibson, class of 1894. Gibson bought and sold livestock, but he had no problem being almost constantly in the company of drinking men as he traveled to Chicago. "[H]e is always thrown among a convivial class of men en route, and when the bottle is passed around the car . . . it is no temptation to him," Brown said. The Sewickley league held a party in 1900 to celebrate the sixth anniversary of the sobriety of its president, George H. Hegner. John R. Heath was seven years sober when he was elected to city office in Joliet, Illinois, by a record majority. Heath was very public about the fact that he was a former drunk, because he hoped it would help others.[50]

Keeley graduates continued to recruit drunks and help pay for their treatment. "Good things are very few and far between in this world, therefore a man ought to take care of them," Heath explained. "I got a good cure at Dwight and why should I not take care of it?" Hegner had a limit on what he was willing to spend to help a man get sober, but it was a generous one. "I have the greatest sympathy for the victim of drunkenness and will do anything possible for him—give him three trials if necessary but not more . . . ," he said. "[I]t is too expensive. Three times is my patience." So many Keeley graduates arrived with drunks in tow that it became part of the daily life in Dwight. The *Banner of Gold* reported:

> There is probably no work in the world so congenial as for a Keeley graduate to place a friend "in line." They are always ready to start on the first trains and to drop everything to accomplish this result. It certainly is an inspiration to the patients taking treatment to see them here, as they always seem well, happy and prosperous.[51]

The Keeley Institute couldn't deliver the miracle it promised for everyone. Most of its graduates would eventually relapse. But many found sobriety for the first time in their lives, and some stayed sober. Even some of those who relapsed kept searching for a miracle, and some would find it. The future held new sources of power for attaining permanent sobriety. One promised a new age.

CHAPTER FIVE

False Dawn

THE MEN IN THE saloon looked fearfully through the makeshift barricade protecting them from the tall woman at the door. In Topeka, Kansas, in 1901, saloons were called "joints" and their owners were "jointists." The woman was Carry Nation. Six feet tall and weighing 175 pounds, "the Kansas cyclone" had been terrorizing jointists for months by smashing their fixtures, first with bricks and stones, then an iron rod, and finally a seven-pound hatchet that had once belonged to the Atchison, Topeka, and Santa Fe Railway. Her enemies considered her a crank. She believed God had sent her on this mission, but she was not without a sense of humor. "Boys, boys, come and let me in," she urged as she stood outside the Topeka saloon in late January. "Your mother would like to talk to you. . . . I'm not mad at you, boys. I'm not hating you a bit, even when I come around with my hatchet." But Mother Nation was also emphatic. "I give you fair warning," she said. "Just you close up and get out of this business. . . . If you don't get out of this, boys, I'll be around in a few days and just break up your wicked little shops for you."[1]

Carry Nation hated alcohol for what it had done to her. At nineteen, while living with her parents in Missouri, she had fallen in love with an alcoholic, Charles Gloyd, a veteran of the Union army who boarded with her family at the end of the Civil War. Her parents warned Carry that Gloyd was a drinker, but the couple carried on a clandestine correspondence and finally married. She realized her mistake almost immediately and left Gloyd, who died two years later. Carry blamed alcohol for the destruction of her marriage, for the ill health of a daughter who was born soon after her separation from Gloyd, and for the seven years of economic hardship that finally forced her to find a new husband, David Nation. She naturally sympathized with the goals of the WCTU and organized a chapter in Medicine Lodge, Kansas. She also became a jail evangelist. Her work with the inmates convinced her "that almost everyone who was in jail was directly or indirectly there from the influence of intoxicating drinks."[2]

Like many Kansas prohibitionists, Nation was also deeply frustrated. They had succeeded in amending the state constitution to ban the sale of alcohol, but the law was not being enforced. Every small town had a saloon operating in the back room of a restaurant or pool hall. In the cities, the bars operated openly, paying a monthly fine into the municipal treasury. Nation began her campaign of civil disobedience in the summer of 1900 by marching into several joints in Medicine Lodge singing,

> Who hath sorrow? Who hath woe?
> They who do not answer no,
> They whose feet to sin incline,
> While they tarry at the wine.

The owner of the first saloon threw her into the street. But most people in the town were on Nation's side, and officials closed all three establishments. Soon after, she traveled to a neighboring town and engaged in her first "smashing," throwing bricks and stones at the mirror behind the bar and the shelf of liquor underneath. She would demolish dozens of businesses in this fashion.

The climax occurred six months later in Topeka, the state capital, when she attacked a saloon favored by legislators. Armed with hatchets, Nation and three other women attempted to rush past a doorkeeper, who grabbed Nation, wrestled away her hatchet, and fired a warning shot into the ceiling. Nation seized another hatchet, demolished the bar, overturned a slot machine, smashed the beer kegs, and threw a heavy iron cash register into the street.

Nation was hailed as a hero by her fellow prohibitionists. "She has aroused the law abiding people of Kansas to the disgrace of law break-ers—partly by her own lawlessness," an editorial in the *Emporia Ga-zette* observed. Even those who deplored her violence were fascinated. Her smashings were front-page news from coast to coast. Later, some would even credit her with drawing national attention to the problem of saloons and leading the country toward Prohibition, which went into effect in January 1920. But the United States was already well along that road. By 1903, prohibitionists had succeeded in drying up many of the rural areas of the country. Thirty-five million people were living in places where it was no longer legal to buy a drink.[3]

The fight for Prohibition was not about curing alcoholism. The ministers who led the temperance movement during most of the nine-teenth century were fighting sin and saving souls. Later, temperance leaders were alarmed by the arrival of hard-drinking immigrants from Ireland and Germany, including millions of Catholics, and by the growth of urban unrest and poverty in the nation's rapidly expanding cities. They wondered how to protect vulnerable women and children, and make improvements in the nation's health. But this did not mean prohibitionists had no hope for saving drunks. They believed that the higher power that alcoholics needed to help them stop drinking would come from the federal government, making alcoholism vanish with the rest of the country's problems. A new, more virtuous age would dawn.

In the early nineteenth century, the temperance movement was will-ing to tolerate some drinking. The pledge not to drink applied only to whiskey and other distilled spirits that contained a lot of alcohol. The temperance societies followed Benjamin Rush in believing that beer and wine were healthful. Rush had actually recommended them as an alternative to people who were trying to give up spirits. But as the movement grew, many activists became dissatisfied with this approach. They argued that if alcohol was addictive, then all alcoholic drinks were dangerous. There was "no safe line of distinction between the *moder-ate* and *immoderate* use of alcohol," a Methodist publication claimed in 1832. It concluded by questioning "whether a man can . . . indulge at all and be considered temperate." In 1836, the national temperance organization began advocating total abstinence from alcoholic drinks.[4]

The rise of the Washingtonians just a few years later helped enshrine total abstinence as the goal of the temperance movement. The transition to teetotalism had cost the movement some support, particularly among upper-class Americans who could afford wine and were sure it was not the problem. The excitement aroused by the Washingtonians quickly made up for all losses and then gave a powerful boost to pledge taking through the country. The drunks who led the Washingtonians believed that their own stories proved that half measures would not work. Their drinking careers had begun innocently enough, but the desire for alcohol grew until they couldn't stop. "Whenever I hear a man say he can regulate *himself*, I say to him—I know *that* man will be a drunkard," William K. Mitchell, a founder of the Washingtonians, said.[5]

But the Washingtonians' experiences as alcoholics also made them skeptical when other reformers began calling for laws banning the sale of alcohol. To the prohibitionists, it seemed clear that voluntary pledges would never eliminate drunkenness. It is "vain to rely alone on self-government and voluntary abstinence," the Reverend Lyman Beecher wrote. "Many may be saved by these means; but with nothing more, many will be lost and the evil will go down to other ages." Most Washingtonians believed that prohibition was bound to fail. They attributed the success of their movement to treating drunks with kindness and appealing to their hearts and minds. "[F]orced obedience, never instills in the mind those feelings of reverence, which the general influence of love causes to spring spontaneously in the erring hearts of the children of men," Charles T. Woodman, a Washingtonian, wrote. It hadn't worked for him. He had been jailed for drunkenness fifteen times. Once, in desperation, he had even had himself locked up. But he always returned to drinking.[6]

Reformed drunks were also concerned that prohibition would distract from the task of helping alcoholics get sober. In January 1842, temperance leaders were excited to learn that Thomas F. Marshall, a congressman from Kentucky, had signed the pledge after experiencing a strong craving for alcohol one day as he entered the House of Representatives. Marshall was an eloquent speaker and a rising political star as well as the nephew of John Marshall, the great chief justice of the Supreme Court who had died a few years earlier. He also strongly opposed prohibition, which he made clear in a speech a few months after he stopped drinking. "Make no statutes . . . on the subject," he told the members of the American Temperance Union at a large meeting in New York. "Let politicians . . . and legislators, *alone*," Marshall said.

> Persecute nobody. Look, rather, with compassion and sympathy on the unfortunate wretches who yet have not power to break their chains; but O! Don't make laws against them! God knows they are under a law hard enough already! This cause is too high for law.

Marshall believed that drunkenness originated in a personal weakness that could only be cured by God.[7]

The reformed men were not unanimous. At least some Washingtonians favored prohibition, and their number grew as the influence of their organization declined and consumption of alcohol began to increase again. In 1847, John H. W. Hawkins expressed alarm over the fact that alcohol-related cases before the police court in Boston had jumped over 20 percent during the previous year. In a letter to the *Mercantile Journal*, he blamed the increase in drunkenness on the rapid proliferation of saloons and demanded city and state officials pass laws so "that the *wicked rum-seller* may feel that he shall not be permitted to grow rich upon the *poor.*"[8]

Maine passed the first statewide ban on the retail sale of alcohol. The victory was achieved by Neal Dow, a Portland businessman, who led a ten-year crusade that culminated in 1851. To make sure that the law would be enforced, he ran for mayor and led the first raid on liquor dealers, dumping $2,000 worth of alcohol into the streets. Hawkins actively supported what became known as "the Maine Law" and was making speeches in the state when it went into effect. He reached the town of Hallowell just as fourteen barrels of liquor that had been confiscated in a raid were being broken open in the street. As soon as the first barrel was empty, Hawkins turned it on end and climbed on top to give a speech. "[I]t was a scene to awaken in his breast a joy beyond the power of his words to express," he told a friend later.[9]

The passage of the Maine Law was a turning point in the fight for prohibition. It inspired temperance advocates throughout the country, and twelve states adopted similar legislation over the next four years. Although opponents succeeded in repealing or gutting all of the laws before the Civil War, the movement began to revive in the 1870s under the leadership of the WCTU. Its president, Frances Willard, was a strong advocate of women's rights, including the right to vote, and the WCTU became involved in a wide range of issues affecting the lives of women besides prohibition. American women responded, and the WCTU became the vehicle through which large numbers of them became involved in politics for the first time. As the number of state and local prohibition laws grew, many critics blamed the rising power of women. Carry Nation saw a close connection between women's rights and prohibition. "If I could vote, I wouldn't smash," she said.[10]

But if prohibition had been just a "women's issue," it would never have won the support of Jack London, America's most popular author in the first years of the twentieth century. Although London was a member of the Socialist Party, which supported equality for women, he opposed women's suffrage until 1911, when California voters gave women the right to vote in state elections. On his return from the polling place, London told his wife, Charmian, that he had voted for the measure because women would support prohibition, and he believed that all saloons should be closed. This puzzled Charmian. London was an alcoholic who had never expressed a desire to stop drinking. He had been drinking all day and was "pleasantly jingled," according to *John Barleycorn*, a memoir that London published two years later. "But I thought you were a friend to John Barleycorn," Charmian said. He replied:

> I am. I was. I am not. I never am. I am never less his friend than when he is with me and when I seem most his friend. He is the king of liars. He is the frankest truth-sayer. He is the august companion with whom one walks with the gods. He is also in league with the Noseless One. His way leads to truth naked, and to death. He gives clear vision, and muddy dreams. He is the enemy of life, and the teacher of wisdom beyond life's vision. He is a red-handed killer, and he slays youth.

London died five years later at the age of thirty-nine.[11]

✦   ✦   ✦

Support for prohibition was growing, but it was only one of several solutions for alcoholism that were being pursued during the first two decades of the twentieth century. This was the most hopeful time for drunks since the rise of the Washingtonians. Historians call this period the Progressive Era because Americans squarely faced a multitude of problems that had been caused by industrialization and confidently set about solving them. The hero of the age was President Theodore Roosevelt, who never met a mountain he couldn't climb. Once again, there was an upsurge of humanitarianism as reformers established settlement houses in urban areas to help impoverished immigrants get a foothold in the new world. Alcoholics became the beneficiaries of the new reform movement when long-discussed plans for establishing government institutions to help them were finally implemented. But it was a program launched by a church that first attracted national attention.

In November 1906, Emmanuel Church, one of the most beautiful in Boston, was in an uproar. Its rector, Elwood Worcester, had launched a bold experiment. A man in his early forties, he had the unusual distinction of holding a PhD in psychology as well as a doctorate in divinity. Worcester had studied in Germany with pioneers in the science of the mind and was fascinated by the potential of curing illness through mental healing. Believing there was an opportunity to combine orthodox religion and modern medicine in a new ministry, he launched a series of weekly lectures in the parish house that featured distinguished doctors talking about the role of the mind in maintaining physical health. Worcester and his assistant, Samuel McComb, who had also studied psychology, lectured later on the nature of religious therapy. At the end of the fourth session, Worcester announced that on the following morning he, McComb, and the doctors would meet with anyone who needed help with a moral or psychological problem.

Two hundred were waiting. There were men and women "suffering from some of the worst diseases known to man, old chronic maladies, rheumatism, paralysis, indigestion." Perhaps as a joke, a local insane asylum sent over some of its patients. But during the next several weeks, the doctors were able to separate applicants with purely physical illnesses from those whose problems were considered strictly psychological, including psychosomatic complaints, phobias, extreme worry, and other neurotic symptoms.[12]

Alcoholics were at the front of the line. "Among all the predisposing causes of nervousness, the first place must be assigned to drunkenness," Worcester wrote. "No other source of mental and nervous disease can be pointed to with anything like the same certainty." Twenty-two of the 178 patients treated during the first year of the program were drunks. The goal of the therapists in the church clinic was ambitious. "The desire for drink should be totally destroyed, the will power strengthened, and new associations built up," Dr. Isador H. Coriat explained.[13]

Psychology was still a new science when Worcester launched his experiment at Emmanuel Church, but interest in it was not limited to PhDs. A clock maker, Phineas Parkhurst Quimby, had launched a thriving popular movement when he opened a clinic in Portland, Maine, back in 1859. "The trouble is in the mind, for the body is only the house for the mind to dwell in. . . . Therefore, if your mind had been deceived by some invisible enemy into a belief, you have put it into the form of a disease, with or without your knowledge . . . ," he wrote. "I correct the wrong impression and establish the Truth, and the Truth is the cure." Quimby used the power of suggestion to counter the false belief that his patients were sick. During therapy sessions, he told them that they possessed the power to feel better and that power would eventually cure them completely.[14]

Quimby often hypnotized his patients before making his suggestions, but this wasn't always necessary. "Instead of telling me that I was not sick, he sat beside me, and explained what my sickness was, how I got into that condition," one patient explained. "The general effect of these quiet sittings with him was to lighten up the mind, so that one came in time to understand the troublesome experiences and problems of the past in the light of his clear and convincing explanations." Suggestion was not going to cure cancer, but Quimby was successful in allaying depression and other mental problems in many people. He claimed that he had treated twelve thousand men, women, and children during his first six years of practice. His ideas were even more successful, launching a mental healing boom that saw the establishments of schools to prepare therapists for a public clamoring for relief.[15]

Soon people were discussing the possibility that "mental therapeutics" might be an effective treatment for alcoholism. One was Henry Wood, a successful businessman who had overcome a severe depression by practicing the precepts of what its followers began to call "New Thought." New Thought was similar to Christian Science in declaring that people could be cured of illness without medical assistance, although it was not as doctrinaire or as hostile to doctors as the religion founded by Mary Baker Eddy in 1879. Wood was just beginning a successful career as an author and advocate of New Thought when Keeleyism took off. In a magazine article, he revealed what he believed to be the real secret of the Keeley Institute. "It is that the so-called bi-chloride of gold cure is in reality *unconscious* MIND CURE," he wrote.[16]

Wood argued that alcoholics were neither evil nor diseased. They were people who had lost their way. He said that the drunk believed his "illusive and sensuous lower personality" was his true self. He did not recognize that the "sensual claimant, which has held him in thraldom, is a falsity and a counterfeit." The Keeley Institute was successful because it made it possible for drunks to recognize the "divine image" in themselves. The gold cure was the key to the process but not because it actually cured. "It is the *belief* in the gold—with other accompanying factors—which produces the result," Wood wrote. The alcoholic "comes full of hope, faith and *positive* expectation of being healed by the mysterious infusion." It was reinforced by the new relationships he forged at the institute:

> He is trusted, and his self-respect is not only preserved, but greatly confirmed. New ideals flash vividly before him. He is a *man*, and no longer a slave. Visions of future usefulness and happiness dawn upon and gradually overspread his mental horizon. The divine "image" in him begins to assert its prerogative, and at length he discovers this as his intrinsic ego.

Gold, he said, was a placebo, but its effect was profound because it made possible a change in the thinking of the alcoholic. "The most radical mental readjustments are below the surface of consciousness, and they are powerful and lasting," Wood said.[17]

Wood observed that there was another type of mental therapeutics that was being used to treat alcoholics. In France and in some places in the United States, doctors and other healers were using hypnosis to curb the appetite for alcohol and other drugs. "Many interesting accounts are given of cases in which, after the use of hypnotic suggestion for a few weeks, the subject acquires a strong aversion to alcoholic liquors so that he not only will not but *cannot* take them," he wrote. Wood believed that the Keeley Cure was vastly superior to hypnosis. "[H]ypnotism implies mental servitude on the part of the subject, and in a deep sense it does not set him *free*," he wrote. Recovery must be achieved from the inside out: the drunk must want to be sober. "The true mind healer must have an overflowing love for his weaker brother, and instead of crowding him up and putting artificial props underneath, must put him upon his own feet," Wood said.[18]

Quimby, Wood, and other advocates of the New Thought were pioneers in developing what Wood described as a "psychological or spiritual science." They were not alone. Sigmund Freud was also frustrated by the efforts of medical men to reduce all forms of illness to physical causes, attributing hysteria and other aberrant behavior to brain lesions and other "somatic" origins. When Wood's article on Keeley appeared, the thirty-six-year-old Freud was establishing himself as a psychoanalyst in Vienna. Like Wood, he recognized the limits of hypnosis. It could be useful to help patients recover memories that might offer a clue to the origin of their problems, from stuttering and facial tics to loss of language, paralyzing fears, and uncontrollable compulsions. But some people couldn't be hypnotized, and Freud had discovered that letting his patients talk freely was more productive. He was already well on his way to developing the theory that would become the basis of modern psychology. He would publish his masterwork, *The Interpretation of Dreams*, in 1900.

At the Emmanuel clinic, there was hope that the use of therapeutic suggestion would be especially effective with alcoholics. A therapist described the steps he took to prepare a patient for his suggestions:

> [T]he patient is seated in the comfortable morris chair before the fire, which I take care by this time to have burning low—is taught by rhythmic breathing and by visual imagery to relax the muscles, and is led into the silence of the mind by tranquilizing suggestion.

Once the patient had been made receptive, the therapist delivered his message. In a 1909 article in *Ladies' Home Journal*, Worcester presented an example of the kind of suggestion he gave alcoholics:

> The habit that has enslaved you so long is beginning to yield and in a short time it will cease to trouble you. The desire for whisky and for every kind of liquor is fading out of your consciousness and soon that appetite will die within you. You do not need liquor and you do not desire it. You do not wish to live a drunkard's life nor to die a drunkard's death. The thought is horrible to you. Henceforth, the sight, smell and taste of whisky will be very disagreeable to you. It will be associated in your mind with sickness, with shame and infirmity, with every sad and miserable experience of your life. . . . You desire now to be the man God wishes you to be, a man your family can love and respect, and on whom your friends can look with satisfaction. . . . You are not fighting this battle alone. God is with you. He will support you and strengthen you and will not let you fail.

The suggestion, delivered in a low, reassuring voice by a trusted minister, must have been enormously encouraging to a shaky and discouraged alcoholic.[19]

Worcester did not depend on words alone. Experience taught him that he could succeed only with drunks who wanted help and were willing to seek total abstinence for life. He also learned that he could only make progress with sober alcoholics, so he made his patients promise not to drink during the first week of treatment. At first, alcoholics were treated like other patients. After their session with the minister, which lasted between fifteen minutes and an hour, the drunks had to get by until their next appointment with the support they received from a weekly health class. The health classes were important: the doctors and ministers gave encouraging lectures on mental, physical, and spiritual health; later, there was a reception for the 250 to 500 members of the audience where people were encouraged to share positive news about themselves and their illnesses.

But the ministers soon realized the drunks needed more support. They began to meet with newcomers on a daily basis, and the length of treatment was extended to one year. They also sat down with members of the drunk's family in an effort to help them understand that alcoholism was an illness that could be cured. The church's social service department helped jobless alcoholics find new employment. By the end of 1908, Worcester and his colleagues had helped forty-four alcoholics get sober. The number of those who remained abstinent is unknown, but "our successes have been far more frequent than our failures," Worcester wrote, looking back over more than twenty years of treating drunks.[20]

One of the most important sources of support for the recovering alcoholics was a new church organization. In the spring of 1910, Worcester announced in the parish newsletter that Ernest Jacoby, a church member who was a successful rubber merchant, had started a club "for men and women who are struggling to escape from the slavery of drunkenness." The goal of the club was to "remind men of their good resolutions" and "to surround them with good influences and to supply them with good motives." The club provided a variety of services to help the drunk get back on his feet. Jacoby explained:

> We go to his home, his friends, his environment. Perhaps his case is one which requires a doctor. His work may be unsuited to him or he may be out of work. We try to get him a new position, or secure work for him.[21]

The Jacoby Club resembled a settlement house by providing the services that helped its members find their place in society. The Jacoby Club also put alcoholics to work helping other drunks. At one level, this was an expression of the Emmanuel movement's spiritual goal. "'Saved thyself, save others,'" Worcester wrote, quoting Buddha. There was also a belief that the sober alcoholic could communicate with a fellow drunk better than others because he had experienced addiction and had overcome it. Most important, however, was the fact that working with drunks helped keep men sober. The Jacoby Club advertised itself as "A Club for Men to Help Themselves by Helping Others." It required every member to take personal responsibility for at least one other person. A newcomer was given a small booklet with the club constitution and a place for his name and the name of his "Special

Brother." The Special Brother or "stepbrother" was expected to "win the confidence of his new charge, be his friend in everything, look after him in man to man fashion, and without any air of patronage, in a word be his chum and his helper." The club membership was not limited to alcoholics and included men like Jacoby who were motivated by their desire to help. As a result, a stepbrother wasn't necessarily an alcoholic. However, all the recovering drunks became Special Brothers.[22]

Beginning with six members in 1909, the Jacoby Club enrolled over five hundred by the end of 1913, a solid majority of whom were alcoholics. The club met at the church on Saturdays, but members were welcome to gather on other nights. In September 1913, the club established a new headquarters in "cozy rooms" with a "cheery" atmosphere. It was furnished with "reading tables, comfortable chairs, books, magazines and musical instruments." During the summer, the group met at a spot on the Charles River that offered "all kinds of sports and games." Club membership nearly doubled over the next several years, partly as a result of newspaper stories and paid advertising. After it incorporated, the club used its annual report as a promotional tool by releasing it as a pamphlet. The 1913–1914 report was titled *The Story of the Lonesome Man*; the next year, it was called *Men Who Have Won*. By the end of 1916, the club claimed to have enrolled fourteen hundred; at least seven hundred were identified as problem drinkers.[23]

Courtenay Baylor joined the Jacoby Club soon after he sought help for his drinking problem. He went on to become one of Emmanuel Church's greatest successes. After working with Worcester for a couple of years, he quit his job as an insurance salesman and became a counselor in the church's social service department. He worked with hundreds of alcoholics and is generally considered the first recovered alcoholic to be paid for it. Baylor did not have a college degree, but he had the benefit of Worcester's education and his own experience. He also possessed a great physical attribute. "He had a soothing, beautiful voice that lulled you but at the same time gave you confidence. It was a voice you could trust," an admirer, Dwight Anderson, recalled. In a photo, Baylor sits confidently with legs crossed, wearing a well-tailored suit. He was far more than a salesman with a golden voice. "[H]e was one of the most illuminating and persuasive personalities I have ever met," Anderson said.[24]

Baylor's confidence grew from his success as a therapist. In 1919, he published a short book, *Remaking a Man: One Successful Method of Mental Retrofitting*. One of his goals was to establish that "the man who has acquired a knowledge of psychology in a practical way has a proper place in the field of psychological work." In the chapters that followed, he proved that he knew more about the alcoholic than most doctors.[25]

Baylor believed that alcoholics were mentally ill. He thought almost everyone who drank exhibited an "alcoholic neurosis" because they felt a need to make excuses for their drinking. In *Remaking a Man*, he wrote:

> [I]t is because the weather is hot or cold, or he is wet or fatigued or depressed or excited, or his foot-ball team has won, or because some one has died. It is almost never that he realizes and frankly states that he wants a drink because it is a drink and that drinking has such a hold on him that he cannot get along without it.

For the alcoholic, this tendency to deny the desire for alcohol became a "philosophy of excuse" that caused him to blame his troubles on external forces:

> He rarely realizes that business, family, friends, and politics seem all wrong largely because of his own fear, depression, irritability, or distorted imagination. He conscientiously believes that he is fearful, depressed or irritable entirely because of negative circumstances or because of the attitudes of other people.

It was not a love for alcohol but a false perception of his problem that drove the compulsion to drink. "[T]he neurotic condition which follows from that drink brings distorted values and as a result false reasoning and wrong impulses," Baylor wrote. Drinking only made his problem worse. "[A]nd so he goes around the circle again and again with ever increasing momentum—fear creating new conditions, and conditions creating new fears."[26]

Baylor did not have an explanation for why drunks were different from other people. He believed they suffered from a temporary but recurrent condition of the brain that he compared to physical tension. He did not speculate why. The important thing was that it was curable.

"I have found that with the release of this 'tenseness' a normal coordination does come about, bringing proper impulses and rational thinking," he said. The first step in therapy was to get the patient's attention. This was accomplished by a number of calming exercises that slowed the alcoholic's fevered thought process, allowing him to escape the circular thinking that kept him reaching for a bottle as his only solution.

Baylor was masterful in his use of suggestion, often asking his patients to imagine themselves in a sailboat traveling toward a tree-covered island on a beautiful summer day. The boat was flying over the waves, overtaking other boats, and finally arrived alone at the island:

> We lower the sail, and the boat is coming slowly in under its own momentum—slower—and slower—and slower—and—now—it—is—barely—moving. We throw over the anchor—the boat slowly comes about, and we are at anchor—and at rest—and at peace—and—we—take—a—long—sigh—of—mental contentment.

Later, Baylor would teach the drunks to use relaxation techniques whenever they felt tenseness returning. "The patient must eventually be re-educated in his whole mental process so as to know how to recognize and to dissolve certain tendencies at their very inception and before they get under way," he explained.[27]

Suggestions were only the beginning. Once the patient was listening, the hard work of reeducation began. "The re-education work is done through logical analysis and explanation and definite instruction," Baylor wrote. "As soon as possible, sometimes at the beginning of treatment, I begin to combine with the personal interviews a line of simple reading which is so chosen that the 'man of the street' may understand and benefit from it." Treatment generally lasted a year, although meetings became less frequent over time. Much of the counseling involved helping the alcoholics think through the situations that would normally drive them to drink.[28]

He discussed the case of one patient with a wife and two children who were almost destitute. The private charity that had supported them for several years was ready to reject them because the husband couldn't stop drinking. The drunk had agreed to work with Baylor, but the landlord was coming for a showdown. "I showed him how it was possible not only to relax the body and the mind but also to relax a tense situation," Baylor explained. He told his patient not to listen to the details of the landlord's complaint but to think of the relaxation he was beginning to achieve through therapy. The drunk's calmness angered the landlord at first, but it allowed the drunk to absorb the anger without becoming angry himself. They were able to discuss the facts of the situation objectively and to come to an agreement. Later, the alcoholic was able to apply the lessons he had learned to his job and was rewarded with a big raise. By 1919, he had been sober for six years.[29]

The title page of *Remaking a Man* identifies Baylor as a representative of the Emmanuel movement. This is certainly true. Baylor, the former patient who became one of its leading therapists, was closely tied to Emmanuel until Worcester retired in 1929. Worcester and Baylor then launched a foundation to continue their work. Both men were strongly influenced by the emergence of the new science of psychology. But there were differences between them. Worcester never lost his faith in the importance of religion in helping men and women recover from illness. But God is not mentioned in *Remaking a Man*. In 1919, Baylor estimated that he had treated over a thousand patients, mostly alcoholics, and claimed to have helped two-thirds of them. There had not been such an effective counselor of drunks since Albert Day of the Washingtonian Home. But the kind of spiritual assistance that Baylor provided did not require belief in a higher power. What was needed were strategies for addressing the alcoholic's serious psychological problems.

The Emmanuel movement started something important. Americans were already fascinated by the idea of the mind cure when Worcester announced his plans in 1906. But the partnership between orthodox ministers and distinguished doctors gave mental healing a legitimacy that it lacked when it was practiced by Christian Scientists, who many considered religious fanatics. Newspapers around the country provided extensive and often sensationalistic coverage. (One claimed that Worcester had brought a woman back to life, when, in fact, she had only fainted.) *Ladies' Home Journal* paid the minister a princely sum to write a series of articles. His book *Religion and Medicine* was an instant best seller that was reprinted eight times in seven months. The United States Surgeon General included it in a list of the three best books on psychiatry. Ministers from around the country traveled to Boston to study Worcester's methods. Similar programs were started by churches in New York, Cleveland, San Francisco, Detroit, Philadelphia, Baltimore, and Seattle. But Worcester could not sustain his movement. He had too many enemies. Doctors didn't like the idea of laymen, even well-intentioned ones, practicing medicine. Many ministers also attacked the Emmanuel experiment, believing that it had nothing to do with religion. The opposition grew so strong that Worcester decided it was pointless to defend his idea and focused on his work in the clinic.

Interest in psychology continued to increase as Freud's ideas revolutionized the practice of psychiatry. Freud was very critical of the Emmanuel movement when he visited the United States in 1909. A reporter asked him to comment on claims by "several psychotherapeutists" that they had cured hundreds of alcoholics "by hypnotism." Freud doubted that the drunks would stay sober for long. Suggestion depended on planting an idea in the patient's unconscious. The goal of Freudian therapy was to discover the underlying cause of neurosis. "The analytic therapy . . . does not wish to inject any thing; but to take away, to get rid of, and for this purpose it concerns itself with the origin and progress of the symptoms of the disease, with the psychic connection of the diseased idea, which it aims to destroy," Freud explained.[30]

Freud may have disagreed with the proponents of mind cure over theory and methods, but his claim to be able to cure illness by destroying "the diseased idea" was no less sweeping—or exciting. Doctors were both shocked and attracted by his theory that neurosis originated in the frustrated sexual desires of children. Many were eager to learn his methods for uncovering and resolving these conflicts, especially the analysis of the hidden meaning of dreams.

It wasn't just doctors who were fascinated. The middle class was growing rapidly in cities of the United States during the first decade of the twentieth century. These men and women hungered for an understanding of the economic, social, and political problems of their day, and they found many of their answers in a new genre of "muckraking" magazine that challenged the platitudes of the previous generation. The muckrakers recognized the revolutionary nature of the new psychology and rushed to explain it to their readers. It provided a new way of looking at the problem of mental illness, including alcoholism. A number of magazines featured articles in which drunks explained how they had been cured through the new Freudian therapy—psychoanalysis.

In September 1917, *McClure's Magazine* published an article, "Is This Why You Drink?," by an anonymous author who claimed he had stopped drinking following several months of psychoanalysis. The author explained that he had been a successful attorney, but in his early thirties, he began to encounter problems. "At pretty regular intervals I drank flagrantly, arrogantly, without regard to the advice of anybody else in the world," he wrote. After eight years of hard drinking, he realized he couldn't stop. He sought advice from doctors, read temperance literature, and tried various "cures." Nothing worked. "[T]here was nothing to indicate why I, an otherwise sensible and industrious man, should inevitably at certain periods, embark on a debauch." Finally, a friend gave him the name of a well-known psychiatrist in another city. He traveled to the doctor's home. The psychiatrist was reassuring. "There are many thousands of others like you," he said. "You are a neurotic. I can straighten you out and set you on your feet if you will give me the required time and will live here in this city."[31]

The lawyer agreed and met with the psychiatrist every day for several months. During one of the first sessions, the doctor told his patient that all drunks shared one quality:

> Every drunkard is a moral coward, because, in getting drunk he runs away from the workaday world with all its problems and burdens and enters into the world of phantasies, a world where the imagination makes things seem the way you want them to be. Drunkenness is flight, a running away from reality.

He analyzed a dream the lawyer had during the previous night. The man was working in his law office, but he was distressed because his secretary, a dark-skinned Hindu man, had left open the transom above the office door. Eventually, the secretary disappeared through the transom, closing it after him. The psychiatrist interpreted the dream as an expression of the lawyer's tendency to be shut up emotionally. Discussion of the Hindu, who was not really his secretary, brought up a painful memory of his mother's rejection of a request he made when he was five. "The long and the short of that dream was that its analysis by the doctor showed me the folly of attempting to live within myself, that I was selfish and that I had become morbid many years before," the author wrote.[32]

The lawyer continued to drink during the early weeks of his therapy. The psychiatrist had never told him that he should stop. "He *knew*, it seemed, that, as the burden of the thing that had troubled me was lightened, the liquor would have less and less attraction for me," the lawyer said. That was what happened. At the end of the first month, he was drinking less. "I had not been really drunk for a week!" He had stopped completely by the end of the third month. By then, his whole attitude toward life had changed. "I was amazed by the degree in which my appreciation of the beautiful things of the world, the flowers, pictures, good books and good plays had taken the place of the 'charm' of whiskey," he said. He moved home full of enthusiasm for his new life and the therapy that had made it possible. He even tried to psychoanalyze five of his acquaintances, four of whom were drunks.[33]

While the lawyer's experience sounded promising, it is not clear whether he was an alcoholic or someone with a drinking problem who found it relatively easy to stop. Whether psychoanalysis could help many drunks was also an open question. The author of "Is This Why You Drink?" could afford to move to another city for several months of intensive therapy. Freud himself had raised doubts about how many people could benefit from psychotherapy. "The psycho-analytical cure . . . makes difficult demands on the patient and on the physician," he told the *Boston Daily Transcript* in 1909. "Of the patient it requires great frankness, occupies a great deal of time, and is therefore expensive." Wealth and education appeared to be prerequisites. Perhaps even more important was a willingness on the part of the patient to explore his or her deepest emotional conflicts. What could it do for those who didn't have the money or the time? Was there any hope for the alcoholic who did not think his drinking was a problem?

Slowly, answers began to emerge. Alcoholism had long been recognized as one of the major problems plaguing urban life, and progressives believed that it was reaching crisis proportions. Bellevue Hospital in New York City treated 6,453 drunks in 1906. A psychiatrist on the hospital staff believed that 40 percent of his insane patients had abused alcohol. Many of these drunks had been repeatedly picked up by the police. The city workhouse became almost home to men and women who returned as often as eighteen times per year. Homer Folks, a leading social worker, saw alcoholism as the root of many social problems:

> The drunkard's family has ever been the insoluble problem in home relief, public and private. The drunkard's children have ever been the despair of child-caring agencies. . . . General hospitals . . . find the alcoholic ward a source of ever recurring trouble. The conscientious almshouse superintendent finds his best plans miscarried. . . . The lower courts are close with habitual drunkards.

Folks believed something had to be done and that it was up to government to do it.[34]

Advocates had been calling for the creation of state institutions for alcoholics since the early nineteenth century, but little had come of it. The New York State Inebriate Asylum was a private institution. There were plans for government-run institutions for drunks in Connecticut and Minnesota in the 1870s, but these were never realized. When the Minnesota legislature passed a tax on liquor sales to pay for a Minnesota Inebriate Asylum in Rochester, angry saloon keepers descended on the state capital, forcing both the repeal of the tax and the cancellation of plans for the asylum.

The political climate during the Progressive Era was more receptive to the idea of a role for government. In 1909, the Minnesota Supreme Court recognized that the attitudes were changing:

> The trend . . . of legislation is to treat habitual drunkenness as a disease of mind and body, analogous to insanity, and to put in motion the power of the state, as the guardian of all of its citizens, to save the inebriate, his family and society from the dire consequences of his pernicious habit.

Homer Folks persuaded the New York legislature to create a New York City Board of Inebriety to investigate cases of public drunkenness and determine how the offenders should be treated. Men and women who had been arrested for the first time were to be released without further court proceedings; repeat offenders would be punished with fines and probationary sentences. If the drunks continued to drink, they could be sent to a proposed state farm for inebriates or, failing that, the work-house or penitentiary. (Workhouses, also known as poorhouses, were established by local governments in the nineteenth century to pro-vide care for those who were unable to support themselves; residents worked in return for their room and board.)[35]

New York City, Minnesota, and Connecticut established inebri-ate farms between 1912 and 1915. Considering the magnitude of the problem they were meant to address, they were all small facilities. The Minnesota Hospital Farm for Inebriates in Willmar had room for only fifty men; the New York farm opened sixty miles outside the city in Warwick with twenty-five beds and eventually housed a hundred drunks; the Connecticut facility had a capacity of sixty. The superin-tendents of the inebriate farms took seriously their responsibility to re-habilitate the men in their charge. Many of the drunks had been locked up in an insane asylum or hospital. Henry M. Pollock, the superinten-dent of the Norwich State Hospital and Farm in Connecticut, made every effort to provide a "normal" environment. The patients were

> subject to simple rules that differ but little from those observed in the usual household, the inmate enters and departs as he pleases. He rises to have breakfast at six-thirty, is employed during the day, and after an evening spent in reading or employed in games or writing goes to bed at nine. On Sunday he attends church in the village where he receives a cordial welcome from both the pastor and people.

The goal of the farms was to help the drunk regain his health and de-velop a skill that would support him once he was released. "As far as possible, he is strengthened physically and morally," Pollock said.[36]

Advocates for a new approach to alcoholism were aided by a ris-ing concern about the public health threat from drunks. Discoveries in the field of genetics led some scientists to sound an alarm about the threat that "defectives," including epileptics, the retarded, the mentally ill, and alcoholics, posed to future generations. The purported science of eugenics claimed that these disabilities were hereditary and called for measures to block their transmission by eliminating the right to beget a tainted offspring. In 1907, Indiana enacted a law providing for the compulsory sterilization of defectives. The US Supreme Court later upheld a Virginia law requiring the sterilization of patients in its mental institutions. By then, most states had adopted similar laws.[37]

The popularity of eugenic ideas provided an impetus for government treatment of alcoholism. In Iowa, Josiah F. Kennedy, the secretary of the state board of health, argued that reformed drunks would father healthy children and urged the creation of a state hospital for alcoholics. The legislature continued to resist the expense of a separate institution, but it approved the creation of a separate ward for alchoholics at two state mental hospitals in 1902.

Sixty-nine alcoholics soon moved into the Mount Pleasant State Hospital, while others were assigned to a second hospital in the northwestern part of the state. The new arrangement proved unworkable. Some of the mental patients thought they were better than the drunks. One of them complained loudly to John Cownie, a state official who was touring the facility. "Mr. Cownie, I want you to know I'm no drunken sot. I'm here for my health," he said. The hospital administrators also had a low opinion of the new patients. "Usually they are dirty and lazy. . . . They won't work. All they do is sit around and spit tobacco juice all over everything, making their rooms dens of filth," one official said.[38]

In 1904, the Iowa legislature finally appropriated $100,000 to renovate an abandoned building in Knoxville that opened two years later as the State Hospital for Inebriates. It was no Garden of Eden. Most of the patients had no desire to get sober. Many had been committed by the courts and were resentful that they were being held against their will. Others were so damaged by drinking that they had lost the ability to recover. Those who could escape did so with the aid of relatives who had been glad to see them locked up briefly but needed their labor during harvesttime.

The drunks were given no good reason to stay. After the initial sobering-up period, treatment mainly consisted of work that was supposed to instill discipline in the men. Rather than teaching skills that might have given them confidence, they were assigned menial tasks. State officials also felt a need to show the voters a return on their investment. They even considered employing the recovering men in local coal mines, producing fuel to heat government buildings. It would also make it harder for the men to escape since they would be underground during the day and too tired to try anything at night. The idea of turning drunks into miners was never implemented. Instead, they were given "the wheelbarrow cure," doing landscape work around the hospital and hired out to neighboring farms. The work was punitive as well as menial. A state official explained:

> Our wheelbarrow cure for dipsomaniacs is working wonderfully well . . . [and] is the best thing we have found yet. . . . I tell you when the men get through with that cure they will hesitate a long time before they touch whisky again and have to go back to the wheelbarrow.

Without any statistics, this is a dubious claim, but the hard physical labor required of drunks certainly helps explain why they escaped at every opportunity.[39]

Massachusetts was having more success with its Hospital for Dipsomaniacs and Inebriates in Foxborough, which treated more than twelve hundred alcoholics by 1919. During the early years, the hospital faced many of the same problems as the Knoxville facility. The staff was deluged by men in the late stages of alcoholism who had been arrested so many times that judges sent them to Foxborough because they didn't know what else to do with them. The hospital became overcrowded, and the escape rate soared. Administrators had tried to provide mental stimulation. Patients had been offered a variety of entertainments, including educational lectures, variety shows, poetry readings, and musical performances. But these were dropped and new restrictions imposed in an effort to reestablish discipline. Wards were locked, and the hours of physical exercise and work were extended.[40]

In 1908, Foxborough made a radical change of course. A thirty-nine-year-old psychiatrist, Irwin H. Neff, took over as superintendent in the spring. Neff was deeply committed to the progressive view that institutions could improve the lives of individuals and create a healthier society. As a result, Foxborough began to focus on the importance of "reeducating" alcoholics. The goal was to help drunks become hard-working, independent citizens. There was no fixed curriculum. "We must appreciate that the personality of the inebriate is an individual personality and cannot be expressed by a composite picture," Neff said. This meant that therapy must be tailored to the individual. Therefore, the relationship between the doctor and his patient became key. Neff demonstrated his commitment to this idea by hiring a business manager to give him more time to work with the men.[41]

Neff recognized that the reeducation process extended beyond the doctor-patient relationship. The recovering drunk had to be reconciled with his family, the community, and the law. To promote this process, he created an outpatient department with offices around the state. When a patient was discharged, his case was referred to a counselor in the office nearest his home. The counselor worked with the alcoholic's family, teaching them about his illness and how to be supportive. The outpatient department also helped the patient find a job and provided food and clothes when necessary. The counselor visited the recovering man periodically to monitor his progress. Foxborough also worked to educate the public about alcoholism. A trustee of the institution published a pamphlet that addressed the misconceptions of probation officers and judges. Neff helped organize one of the earliest state-sponsored conferences about the social and mental problems caused by alcoholism.

Neff believed that staying in touch with former patients was critically important. Hospital statistics showed that two-thirds of them would relapse. Most would not even provide an annual progress report. When they did write, Neff and his staff replied promptly. Neff's letters were full of encouragement. "I want to congratulate you upon your success which I feel sure will be permanent," he wrote one man. "[W]e are ready to do everything we possibly can for your welfare." He also urged his correspondents to help other alcoholics. Neff asked Thomas Rand to write John Rowan, a new patient, because "it offers him considerable encouragement and will be a help to him in the fight which he is now making." When Rowan relapsed and left Foxborough, Neff sent Rand his new address and asked him to let him know how Rowan was getting on.[42]

Neff stayed in touch with his patients for years after they left Foxborough and helped whenever he could. At one point, Rand found himself working at the Water Street Mission, where he discovered "quite a few of the Foxboro [*sic*] boys." When he wanted a new job, Neff put him in touch with a member of the New York City Board of Inebriety. Over the years, Neff also offered Rand advice on dealing with his two alcoholic brothers. When Rand got married, Neff asked his bride to remind Thomas to continue to write to him. Neff's letters were enormously important to Rand. "I was deeply touched by your kind words and the confidence that you have in me that I will never go back to the old life. . . . I mean never to betray that confidence," he wrote. Rand was the son of an alcoholic and the brother of two more. The knowledge that someone believed he could stay sober, and that Neff was both a doctor and a prominent government official, helped Rand make it happen.[43]

In 1908, the same year that Irwin Neff became superintendent of the Foxborough hospital, Quanah Parker, the last great leader of the Comanche people, testified before a committee of the legislature that had just been organized by the new state of Oklahoma. The committee was considering a bill that would reenact a ban on the use of peyote that had been passed in 1899 by the territorial legislature. Parker was famous. Born in 1845, he was the son of a Comanche leader and a white woman, Cynthia Parker, who had been raised by the tribe. He had distinguished himself as a leader of a proud tribe that had heavily resisted white settlement. Following the final surrender of the Comanche, he was appointed the principal chief of the tribe by federal authorities and led his people for the next thirty-six years.

In his testimony, Parker explained that peyote was not just a drug with psychoactive properties. It was the source of a new religion that was changing Indian life from the Mississippi to the Rocky Mountains. Parker told the legislators that banning peyote violated the First Amendment guarantee of freedom of religion. "I do not think this legislature should interfere with a man's religion," he said. There was something else they should know about peyote, he added. "I do think piote beans have helped Indians stop drinking."[44]

Life had not become easier for Indians since the days of Handsome Lake. The misery experienced by the Iroquois and other eastern tribes spread westward until it affected even the remotest natives. The last Indian wars concluded in the Pacific Northwest in 1858. Over the next thirty years, the white population in what is now western Washington State grew from just over one thousand to almost three hundred fifty thousand. Most of the Indians were confined to impoverished and disease-ridden reservations.

The one thing they didn't lack was alcohol, which liquor dealers were more than happy to provide, even though it was against the law. In 1864, a government official observed that one Washington reservation was "surrounded by logging camps, which are occupied by men of very loose and immoral habits, who are continually taking the Indian women and furnishing the men with whiskey." "We all felt blind those times," an Indian leader recalled. "We lost by drowning—our friends drank whiskey and the canoes turn over—we died out in the bay."[45]

The Native Americans needed something to believe in. Their old gods appeared powerless to help them. Peyote became the vehicle of a new religion. The Comanche and the Kiowa, both southern tribes, had discovered it through trade and warfare with Indians living in Mexico. The peyote plant has medicinal properties. Parker was said to have learned this himself when it helped him recover from injuries he suffered when he was attacked by a boar. This quality of the magical power of peyote alone would have impressed the Indians. But the plant also produces mescaline, a psychoactive drug that causes visual and auditory hallucinations that the Indians believed confirmed the mystical power of peyote.

By the early 1870s, the Comanche and Kiowa had created ceremonies during which they ate peyote buttons to achieve spiritual enlightenment. The most common peyote rituals were held in the evenings, when the participants gathered in a tipi and sat in a circle around a small crescent-shaped altar where they placed a large peyote button, "Grandfather Peyote." As the night progressed, several sacred objects were passed around the circle. Each Indian sang four songs before passing the sacred objects to the next man. Small peyote buttons were also passed. The ceremony proceeded until dawn, when the participants joined other members of the tribe for a special meal.

Peyotism connected the Indian directly to his god. "The white man goes into his church and talks *about* Jesus, but the Indian goes into his tipi and talks *to* Jesus," Parker explained. Peyotism also provided an outlet for emotions that could not be expressed in other ways. Followers were encouraged to confess their sins to a Road Man, who presided during the ceremony. When someone called him over, the Road Man would listen to his confession and then raise him to his feet, praying for his redemption. The result was a powerful catharsis that led normally stoic and tight-lipped men to laugh and cry. Many Indians were repelled by such displays of emotion and questioned the manhood of the Peyotists. But the believers felt a new sense of community. They called each other "brother" to indicate their membership in a new family.[46]

Not everyone was happy about the new Indian religion. Many states had banned the use of peyote by 1918 when an Arizona congressman, Carl M. Hayden, introduced federal legislation. During hearings, the bill was supported by Indians who saw the new religion as a threat to their traditional beliefs, government officials who feared that a new Indian religion would encourage opposition to their plans for the assimilation of Native Americans, and white temperance advocates who rejected peyote as a new means of intoxication that might be even worse than alcohol. Others vigorously defended Peyotism as a moral force. Francis LaFlesche described its impact on his tribe, the Omaha:

> At the meetings of this new religion is taught the avoidance of stealing, lying, drunkenness, adultery, assaultism, the making of false and evil reports against neighbors. People are taught to be kind and loving to one another and particularly to the little ones.

LaFlesche said that the many prizes won by Peyotists at tribal fairs showed that they were among the most industrious members of the tribe.[47]

The opponents of the Hayden bill declared that abstinence from alcohol was a key element to the success of the Peyotists. James Mooney, an anthropologist who had made the first detailed study of the peyote movement, testified that sobriety was an absolute among them. "Followers of the peyote rite say that peyote does not like whiskey, and no real peyote user touches whiskey or continues to drink whiskey after he has taken up the peyote religion," he said. Thomas L. Sloane, an

Omaha who would become the first Indian lawyer to argue a case before the US Supreme Court, agreed. "It has changed a large number of men from drunkards to decent people," he testified. A botanist for the Department of Agriculture who had conducted a detailed study of peyote was called as a witness to discuss the charge that peyote was a dangerous drug. "Peyote is undoubtedly a narcotic and if taken in excess it has bad effects," William E. Safford said. However, he added, "in all cases I have investigated I have not found any instance where it was taken to excess." The strong case made for Peyotism did not prevent the House of Representatives from passing the Hayden bill. However, it died in the Senate. By then, there were more than twelve hundred Peyotists in ten states.[48]

Yet even as new forms of assistance were emerging for drunks, the problem of alcoholism appeared to be solving itself. Admissions to Warwick Farm, the new facility for alcoholics outside New York City, began to decline in 1916 following the outbreak of war in Europe. The population of drunks always swelled during hard times and shrank when there were plenty of jobs. During the first years of World War I, the United States maintained its neutrality and experienced strong economic growth while it sold munitions and other goods to both sides. The demand for bodies grew even more when the country entered the war on the side of Britain and France in 1917. Men were drafted into the armed forces, and even those who were not healthy enough to soldier were able to find jobs in the war industries.

The Salvation Army was among the first to notice how this affected drunks. From the time of its founding in 1865, the army had fought to save the souls of the lowest and the poorest. It grew out of the evangelism of General William Booth, who believed that the established churches were failing to reach the working classes in England. He hit on the idea of creating an army of male and female evangelists who would "attack" heathen territory. His soldiers would catch the eyes and ears of the locals by wearing smart red uniforms trimmed in blue and marching to their services, playing drums and musical instruments if they had them and singing loudly if they didn't. By the time the Salvation Army established its first beachhead in the United States in 1880, it had enlisted 1,640 soldiers in 630 "divisions." They were holding more than ten thousand meetings a week.

The Salvation Army had always had a strong interest in recruiting drunks. So it is not surprising that its first American convert was Jimmy Kemp, a well-known drunk and small-time thief on the West Side of Manhattan. A short man with black hair and a mustache that turned up at the ends, he was frequently beaten by larger men. He became known as "Ash-Barrel Jimmy" after falling headfirst into a trash barrel one night. Two policemen had to drag the can to the station house, pulling Kemp by his feet, before he could be extricated. A Salvation Army officer discovered Kemp standing outside the hall where the army was about to hold its first meeting in America and took him inside. The conversion of Ash-Barrel Jimmy became the talk of the neighborhood and helped draw a crowd to the army's meetings. Kemp enlisted in the army and eventually rose to the rank of captain.

The Salvation Army expanded its assistance to the urban poor in the 1890s. Two days before Christmas in 1891, it opened a "Cheap Food and Shelter Depot" in lower Manhattan that provided sixty beds and a restaurant serving hot meals. The cost was eleven cents per day. If a man was broke, he could work for two hours in the shelter or chop wood in the yard. Similar facilities opened in large cities across the country and were later converted to industrial homes where men were employed salvaging and repairing used clothing and furniture that was collected by the army's familiar red, horse-drawn trucks.

In 1909, the Salvation Army launched a Boozers' Convention in New York City to attract drunks to its headquarters on Fourteenth Street. It hired a fleet of buses, and beginning at 4:30 in the morning on Thanksgiving, its soldiers roamed the city, picking up men who could not resist their offer of free food. To draw even more attention, the army organized a nearly mile-long parade in the afternoon that was led by a large water wagon from the city's street-cleaning department. Bums rode the water wagon, which was flanked by army soldiers who pretended to keep them there. Farther back was a reeling drunk chained to a walking whiskey bottle that was ten feet tall; his grieving wife and starving children followed. Five marching bands kept the parade moving.

When they arrived on Fourteenth Street, the guests were led into a large hall. The air quickly grew stale from the smell of over a thousand men, many of whom were homeless. But there was lively entertainment onstage, including a play, *The Trial of John Barleycorn*, which inevitably ended in a conviction and execution. The men also listened to short sermons from army officers and testimonials by sober alcoholics. "Before the Army picked me up . . . I was so lousy that if everything on me could vote I could have been elected president of these United States," one man joked. Several times during the day, the drunks were given an opportunity to come to the penitents' bench at the front of the room where they could pray. Hundreds rushed forward on each occasion. After the meeting, the male converts who were homeless were taken to the army's hotels and industrial homes. There weren't many women, but those who needed shelter were taken to the army's hotel for women on the Bowery.[49]

During the roundup of drunks for the 1910 Boozers' Convention, a Salvation Army "lassie" encountered Henry F. Milans, a drunk who had once been the managing editor of the *New York Daily Mercury*. At forty-nine, Milans was at rock bottom. He had been living on the Bowery for two years, and his drinking had sent him to Bellevue Hospital several times. He had just been released after his latest stay, which had terrified him. Three doctors told him he was incurable. The first two commiserated with Milans, but the last one, a professor from Cornell University, didn't even speak to him. Sitting next to his bed, the doctor addressed himself to the medical students who were following him as he made his rounds:

> "This man," said the professor slowly, as though to give emphasis to his words, "*can never be cured!* . . . He must die as he has lived, a drunkard. Nothing can save him. Before long he will be found dead in one of the human rat-holes that abound in the slums where he will hide away as soon as he leaves the hospital, providing he does not finish here in delirium tremens."[50]

Milans had awakened on Thanksgiving morning nearly frozen after a night of fitful sleep under a warehouse loading platform. He was surprised when a young woman wearing a uniform and blue poke bonnet approached and spoke to him. Still reeling from the death sentence that had been pronounced at Bellevue, Milans poured out his story.

The woman was indignant. "Of course they can't cure you there," she said. "Yours is more than a physical trouble; it is the sort of heart disease that they can't touch. But listen, Jesus can cure you and make you a good man again if you will let him." Milans followed the soldier to army headquarters and was converted a week later.[51]

Even as Milans made a new career in the printing business, he was not afraid to acknowledge the help he had received. He began speaking in churches, Salvation Army halls, prisons, and anywhere else he could find a crowd. He threw the words of the doctors back at them:

> Explain if you can, you who do not profess any belief in the miracle-working power of the Savior. Explain if you can, you wise men of Bellevue, you professors at Cornell, you to whom science has taught so much about these bodies of ours, and who dare to pronounce a man beyond hope because his very vitals demand the poison so insistently that he must dies unless he gets it! . . .
>
> Explain it, if you can. You can't? I can. And in a word—Christ!

During every speech, Milans encouraged his listeners to write to him if they were having a problem with alcohol. His correspondence swelled to the point where he was called "the letter-writing evangelist." He probably joined the United Order of Ex-Boozers, a group of three hundred sober drunks organized by the Salvation Army in 1914 that encouraged its members to help other alcoholics. Milans continued to write letters and make speeches for the rest of his long life.[52]

By the time the United States entered the war in 1917, the Salvation Army had built a thriving business in the sale of used furniture and clothing. Its workshops employed nineteen thousand men. A Salvation Army officer, Colonel William Peart, estimated that 75 percent were drunks:

> Among the vast army of confirmed drinkers were representatives of all trades and professions. We'd get doctors, lawyers, teachers, clock-makers, upholsterers, cabinet-makers, carpenters—all types, in fact, that could turn their hands toward making salable articles out of unsalable ones. . . . In a measure, they were doing to the furniture what we were doing to them.

The war hit the Salvation Army hard. It lost two-thirds of its work-ers, leaving it with a force made up almost entirely of "old men and crip-ples." The change was clearly apparent at the end of 1919. Christmas was normally the busy season in the workshops. "But last Christmas we could hardly corral a handful. And the dead calm in our workrooms and our dormitories has continued," Peart reported in the fall of 1920.[53]

At first, it appeared that Prohibition might finish the job that the war had started, delivering the death blow to alcoholism. The Eighteenth Amendment, which banned the production and sale of "intoxicating liquors," was ratified in January 1919. But many states were already dry, and Congress outlawed the manufacture of liquor during the war. By the time the Eighteenth Amendment took effect in January 1920, Prohibition had already profoundly changed the country and the lives of alcoholics. In October 1921, Evangeline Booth, General Booth's daughter and the "commander" of the Salvation Army in the United States, reported that drunkenness had almost entirely disappeared among the men who were living and working in the army's facilities. Booth acknowledged that liquor was still being sold illegally and "that the task of banishing all intoxicating liquor from the land is a stupen-dous, a lengthy one." But she confidently predicted complete victory. "By the Constitutional Amendment of Prohibition a measure has been enacted that will do more to bring the Kingdom of God upon earth than any other single piece of legislation," she said. It appeared to Booth and many others that the United States was entering an age of joy and prosperity.[54]

Even some drunks were swept away by the promise of Prohibi-tion. "I felt quite safe," Dr. Bob Smith, who would cofound Alcoholics Anonymous in 1935, recalled many years later. His plan was to lay in a supply of alcohol to carry him through the first few months and then quit drinking like the rest of America. On willpower alone, he had managed to stay sober for years at a time during several periods of his life. He expected to do it again. Once the alcohol was gone, he wouldn't have a choice.[55]

Prohibition did significantly decrease drinking in the United States for several years. Estimates vary, but they chart a decline of between

30 and 50 percent in the amount of alcohol consumed. The difficulty of obtaining liquor appears to have improved the health of alcoholics significantly. There were fewer hospitalizations for alcoholism, and the incidence of alcoholism-related diseases like cirrhosis of the liver also declined. A New York psychiatrist who examined the admissions records of New York state hospitals discovered that the number of alcoholics had fallen by more than 80 percent between 1909 and 1920. "With the advent of prohibition the alcoholic psychoses as far as this country is concerned have become a matter of little more than historical interest," he concluded. Even at Bellevue Hospital, the number of drunks admitted daily had fallen to just two or three.[56]

The lives of alcoholics and their families also appeared to improve. The number of arrests for drunkenness declined, and there was evidence that the money that was not being spent on drink was allowing poor families to improve their standard of living. A survey of Salvation Army hotels and industrial homes revealed that men who had formerly been unable to support themselves were saving money. In one hotel, twenty-five men had bank accounts worth between one hundred and five hundred dollars. Evangeline Booth believed that it was children who were benefiting most from these changes. "Better pre-natal care for the mother, more money, and above everything else, the absence of inebriation's brutalities are all in evidence, telling in the life's chances of these infants," she said. These results were confirmed by a more comprehensive survey of social workers.[57]

But the benefits produced by Prohibition did not last. The country's thirst for liquor had never disappeared, and there were many ways to get alcohol. Doctors were allowed to prescribe alcohol as medicine, and Bob Smith was soon writing scripts for fictitious patients that he had filled by pharmacies. By 1925, an illegal industry had been born. Smith stopped drinking pharmacy liquor when bootlegging was well established. His supplier hid the booze near the back steps of the Smith home, more to elude detection by his wife than by the police.

As lawbreaking increased, the attitude of many prohibitionists hardened toward drinkers, who they blamed for undermining reform. Some wanted to make drinking a felony. An extremist proposed confining drunks in concentration camps on islands off the coast of Alaska. These measures were never enacted. However, when bootleggers started stealing millions of gallons of industrial alcohol and turning it into liquor, the federal government responded by adding chemicals to the alcohol. Some merely added an unpleasant taste, but others were toxic.

A decision by the Calvin Coolidge administration in 1926 to require an increase in the amount of one additive, methyl alcohol, had deadly effects. On Christmas Eve, poisoned drinkers began to appear at emergency rooms in hospitals all over New York City. Twenty-five died. There were more than four hundred deaths due to alcohol poisoning in New York that year and the number would grow to seven hundred in 1927. The city's medical examiner, Charles Norris, strongly condemned the government decision to use poison. Most of the victims were poor people "who cannot afford expensive protection and deal in low grade stuff," Norris said. Wayne Wheeler, the head of the Anti-Saloon League, felt no sympathy for the victims. "The person who drinks this alcohol is a deliberate suicide," he said.[58]

Alcoholics were probably among the casualties caused by the poisoned liquor. But even more tragic for drunks was the disappearance of the institutions that had been helping them get sober. Even before the Eighteenth Amendment was ratified, government officials were arguing that there was no need to continue to spend money on drunks. All of the government facilities for treating alcoholism closed in 1919 and 1920. Some had been in operation for only a few years. The Minnesota Hospital Farm for Inebriates opened its doors in 1912 but began adding mentally ill patients in 1917. The inebriate farm in Connecticut closed after five years; the New York farm lasted six. The two largest institutions also shut down. Few patients mourned the loss of the Iowa State Hospital for Inebriates with its wheelbarrow therapy. But the closing of the Norfolk State Hospital in Massachusetts must have been a blow. Norfolk was the successor to the Foxborough facility, where the drunks had been forced to share quarters with mental patients. It was specializing in alcoholism treatment. Irwin Neff was still in charge. The drunks had finally found a home, but their celebration was short-lived.

The end of government support did not mean that treatment disappeared entirely. The number of drunks in state institutions was never large. But most private facilities also closed. They had seen a significant decline in the number of patients during the war years, and they anticipated further losses as Prohibition took hold. Individual therapists still met with their patients. Elwood Worcester and Courtenay Baylor continued to counsel alcoholics. The Jacoby Club remained open. So did four Keeley Institutes. But the start of Prohibition was the end of almost a century of optimism about curing alcoholism. Once again, drunks found themselves in a lonely place. Between 1920 and 1935, Bob Smith sought help more than a dozen times in "rest homes" whose only goal was to put drunks back on their feet until their next binge. Smith remembered these years as "a nightmare."[59]

CHAPTER SIX

Two Drunks

ON A COLD SPRING morning in 1925, Lois Wilson cracked the throttle on her war-surplus Harley Davidson motorcycle and set off on a year-long journey that she hoped would save the life of her husband, Bill. As they pulled away from her parents' home in Brooklyn, New York, Bill's six-foot, two-inch frame was crammed into the sidecar. Stuffed around him were a tent, a mattress, seven army blankets, a gasoline stove, a hamper of food, a small trunk of clothes, a radio, and some large books containing financial statistics. It looked like "we were bound for the Arctic with presents for all the Eskimos," Lois said. The trip was Bill's idea, and Lois had great confidence in Bill and his dreams. She was also desperate to find a way to help him stop drinking.[1]

Bill Wilson had always been ambitious. He once planned to be an engineer but decided to become a lawyer instead. Now that he had completed all of his course work for a law degree, he had changed his mind again. He had his heart set on working on Wall Street, which had become the destination of many ambitious young men as the country experienced the fourth straight year of strong economic growth. Stocks had started what appeared to be an unstoppable rise, and fortunes were being made on "the Street" every day. Bill's dream wasn't wishful thinking. He had a definite plan. He wanted to visit the factories of companies whose stock was traded on Wall Street to find out everything he could about their prospects. Those facts could help stockbrokers invest in unknown companies when their stock was cheap, making themselves and their customers rich when other investors discovered them. Bill was sure of success. All he needed was one sponsor willing to invest a few hundred dollars to cover his travel expenses.

But Bill was in trouble now. From the time of his first drink at age twenty-one, he never drank like other people. That first drink was a Bronx cocktail—a gin martini with a splash of orange juice—a refined cocktail served in 1917 during a reception for Bill and other young army officers at a private home in New Bedford, Massachusetts. The country was at war, and the drink helped Lieutenant Wilson forget his fear of facing enemy fire for the first time. It made him feel as if he deserved the attention of New Bedford's finest citizens and its prettiest young ladies. For an evening, it made him invincible. He quickly lost control. On a visit to her fiancé, Lois found Bill in the barracks, facedown on his bed, a bucket within easy reach on the floor. Bill had become a daily drinker by the time they were married in 1918. He returned safely from the war, only to face a new enemy. When Lois suffered a miscarriage in 1923, Bill was nowhere to be found. He had skipped law school to drink. He was half drunk when he showed up at the hospital.

One morning in March 1925, Bill told Lois he wanted to try his re-search idea on his own. The night before, he had come home so drunk that he couldn't make it to bed. He was badly hung over as he sat with Lois in the kitchen. "Would you take the chance with me, Lo?" he asked. "I finally realized . . . I just can't go on like this anymore." Neither could she. "I was so concerned about Bill's drinking that I wanted to get him away from New York and its bars," Lois said.[2]

William Griffith Wilson was born in 1895 in East Dorset, Ver-mont, a town of three hundred that had complete faith in Protestant religion and the Republican Party. His family was solidly middle class on both sides. His father, Gilman, was a fun-loving man who was su-perintendent at a marble quarry. Gilman married the town's most el-igible girl, Emily Griffith, whose father, Fayette, owned much of the land in town as well as the East Dorset Water Company. A Civil War veteran who had driven an ambulance at Gettysburg, he was an in-dustrious and keen-eyed Yankee who had started life as a farmer and then went into the lumber business. Although he was wealthy by local standards, he believed in hard work and independence. These quali-ties were handed down. Emily studied to become a teacher before her marriage, and Bill and his sister, Dorothy, grew up doing chores on their grandfather's dairy farm.

Bill grew up in a country that believed deeply in its self-made men. John D. Rockefeller, Andrew Carnegie, Thomas Edison, and Henry Ford were changing the face of America. Electricity was beginning to light the nation's cities, and horses were starting to share the road with cars. Bill was imbued with the spirit of his age, but the young man suffered from a severe handicap. At the age of nine, he began to develop a deep sense of inferiority. That was when his father told him that he was leaving Vermont and that it was Bill's responsibility to take care of his mother and sister. It would be nine years before he saw his father again. The next blow fell even before his parents' divorce became final. At a picnic on Dorset Pond the following year, Emily told her children that she was moving to Boston to study medicine. Dorothy would live with her part of the time, but Bill would stay with Fayette in East Dorset. "To this day, I shiver every time I recall that scene on the grass by the lakefront," Wilson said. "I hid the wound, however, and never talked about it with anybody, even my sister."[3]

Bill Wilson grew up believing he had done something to drive his parents away. His insecurity became a driving force in his life as he sought to prove that he could be "the Number One Man." His success only hid his insecurity. He suffered a nervous breakdown at the age of seventeen that only began to lift when he met Lois Burnham.[4]

In the summer of 1913, Lois was twenty-two years old. The daughter of a prosperous doctor with a practice in fashionable Brooklyn Heights, she was a college graduate with a job. She knew Bill Wilson because her family owned a summer home near East Dorset, and he and her brother had become friends. Lois had no romantic interest in the tall and lanky seventeen-year-old. "After all, I was a young lady and he but a teenager," she said. Her opinion of Bill improved as she got to know him better. By the end of the summer, "I thought Bill the most interesting, the most knowledgeable and the finest man I knew," Lois said. "I forgot all about the difference in our ages." They became engaged in the summer of 1915.[5]

Ten years later, Lois was determined to help Bill succeed. A woman who loved the outdoors, she was excited about the prospect of spending as long as a year on the road, sleeping in a tent. Their first stop was the General Electric plant in Schenectady, New York. After setting up camp in a field on a nearby farm, Bill put on his only suit and introduced himself in the office of the GE plant as a small investor seeking a tour. He failed to get the tour, but he discovered that the farm where he was staying was adjacent to GE's radio research laboratory. He made friends with some of the workers, who admitted him to the lab. "I got a preview of the whole radio industry five and ten years away," Wilson said. A month later, Bill and Lois discovered another promising company, Giant Portland Cement, in Egypt, Pennsylvania. Bill's reports on GE and Giant Portland convinced Frank Shaw, a stockbroker with the J. K. Rice Company, that Bill was onto something. The company agreed to help bankroll the rest of the trip, purchasing two thousand dollars of Giant Portland stock for Bill's account and allowing him to borrow against its rising value. When Bill and Lois returned to New York in the spring of 1926, Bill was given a job at fifty dollars per week.[6]

Lois hoped that the trip had been a turning point in Bill's drinking as well. There had been setbacks on the road, but Bill had enjoyed a long period of sobriety for the first time in several years. His drinking was under control until they returned to the road to search for fresh prospects. Driving a used Dodge this time, they revisited Giant Portland and then headed north to Massachusetts and Canada. On their way back to the United States, they stopped on the Canadian side of the International Bridge at Sault Ste. Marie. Bill told Lois that he wanted to buy cigarettes. She was instantly suspicious because cigarettes were more expensive in Canada, but Bill had been sober throughout their trip. She sat in the car in the bridge plaza awaiting his return. Two hours later, Lois began looking for Bill in the local bars. When she found him in the very last saloon, he was almost too drunk to walk. Bill was always quick to apologize when he sobered up. This time he told Lois he would stop drinking, and he put it in writing. "There will be no booze in 1927," he promised.[7]

Back in New York, Bill and Lois created a life for themselves that would have been the envy of most Americans. They had more money than they knew what to do with. Besides Bill's salary, there was an unlimited expense account and a $20,000 line of credit for buying stocks. As the bull market raged, Bill and Lois rented two apartments in one of the toniest buildings in Brooklyn Heights, tearing out the dividing wall to create a large living room that soon boasted a $1,600 grand piano. Prohibition was the law of the land, but New York was a city with a thousand speakeasies. Every day at the ringing of the bell that ended trading at the New York Stock Exchange, Bill began drinking his way uptown. "I'd be pretty much out of commission at 14th Street and completely lose my wits at 59th. Start out with $500 and then have to crawl under a subway gate to get back to Brooklyn," Bill said. On the mornings after, Bill searched for the reason he had once again failed to control his drinking. "I'm halfway to hell now and going strong," he told Lois in late 1927. On October 29, 1929, "Black Tuesday," the stock market collapsed, wiping out the paper fortunes of tens of thousands of Americans, including Bill and Lois.[8]

It was alcohol, not the crash, that ruined the Wilsons. When Bill didn't come home on Black Tuesday, a frantic Lois called his office and learned that he had been fired for his drinking. Eventually, Bill turned up looking worse than Lois had ever seen him: his head was cut, and his jacket and pants were torn. He still enjoyed a reputation as a champion stock picker, and he got another job in Montreal. He drank himself out of that in six months. Lois pleaded with him to quit. She even left him for a week to show that she was serious. Finally, in September 1930, having lost two jobs in less than a year, Bill wrote a pledge not to drink in the family Bible. He had promised before. He had even written his promise in the Bible before. This time, for the first time, he made a real effort to quit. It didn't matter. Three months later, he fell off the wagon and was fired from his job as an assistant bookkeeper after losing the company books in a speakeasy. Lois's mother, Matilda, was dying of cancer at that time. Although he loved his mother-in-law, Bill was drunk when she died and stayed that way for days after.

In desperation, Lois took him to Vermont, where alcohol was less available. The Vermont cure seemed to work as Bill stayed sober through the summer of 1933, but he started drinking again when they returned to New York. It began to seem that Bill might meet the fate of so many alcoholics—confinement in a state mental hospital. There was one place they had not tried—the Charles B. Towns Hospital for the Treatment of Drug and Alcoholic Addictions, which was located on the corner of Eighty-First Street and Central Park West in New York. Founded in 1901 by the forceful Charles Towns, a businessman from Georgia, the Towns Hospital specialized in treating wealthy alcoholics and drug addicts. Towns claimed to have discovered a drug that could cure up to 95 percent of his patients in as few as four or five days. Medical supporters of the Towns treatment acknowledged that the cure rate was much lower—perhaps 20 percent. But they defended the Towns regimen, which included both detoxification and "recuperative treatment" consisting of special diets, exercise, massage, and hydrotherapy, as far more effective than any other methods. Bill and Lois might have turned to Towns sooner if it hadn't been for the cost. But in the fall of 1933, a family member offered to pay, and Bill became a patient.

At Towns, Bill finally found someone who understood him. Dr. William D. Silkworth, the medical superintendent, was a contrarian. The medical profession had turned its back on drunks, but Silkworth believed that alcoholism was an "allergy" that made it impossible for people to have even one drink without triggering uncontrollable cravings. The doctor had to admit that his theory wasn't helping many people get sober. Even an institution like Towns was little more than a place where alcoholics were "purged and puked." Nevertheless, Silkworth's patients loved the short, bald doctor. Silkworth felt deep compassion for their suffering, and he relieved some of their guilt by assuring them that they were not to blame for what was happening to them. He also offered hope. It didn't happen often, but some people did recover. He estimated the cure rate at only 2 percent. When Silkworth delivered this news to Bill and Lois in 1933, they were elated. Now that they understood the nature of Bill's affliction, they were convinced they knew the cure—not to take the first drink. "I left Towns a new man," Bill said.

> Never shall I forget the first courage and joy that surged in me as I opened the door to enter 182 Clinton Street, Brooklyn. I embraced Lois; our union was renewed. . . . Yes, life would begin again, and oh, how deeply we both believed it.

Bill and Lois disagreed about when his drinking started again. Bill said it was four months later. Lois said it was four weeks.[9]

Silkworth was almost as disappointed as Bill and Lois, but he wasn't surprised. His hope had hung on his belief that Bill was strongly motivated. When Bill came back to Towns a few months after his first hospitalization, Silkworth could see his future clearly. Lois tried again to rescue her husband by taking him away to the country, but he got drunk anyway. They returned to Brooklyn. "Not long after we reached Clinton Street, my husband, who had been my daily companion in Vermont, became a drunken sot," Lois said. Bill had not completely given up the fight, but the battles were growing shorter:

> I'd work through hangover after hangover, only to last four or five days, or maybe one or two. In the night hours, I was filled with horror, for snaky things infested the dark. Sometimes by day, queer images danced on the wall.

Bill began to think of suicide. "I swayed dizzily before an open window, or the medicine cabinet where there was poison, cursing myself for a weakling," he said. "Then came the night when the physical and mental torture was so hellish I feared I would burst through the window, sash and all." His mattress was moved to a lower floor. The third time Bill was hospitalized, Lois confronted Silkworth and demanded the truth. The doctor told her that Bill was hopeless and would probably not last another year. Silkworth urged her to commit him to a mental hospital.[10]

Bill stayed sober for a couple of months after leaving Towns in September 1934. He knew his life depended on it, but he had no confidence in his ability to continue. In a bar on Staten Island, he began another spree, surrounded by other veterans of the Great War on Armistice Day, November 11. He had no intention of stopping again. But a few days later, he got a phone call from an old friend, Ebby Thacher, another big drinker. He and Ebby had once humiliated themselves by arriving drunk in a small plane at the airport in Manchester, Vermont. Because the airport was new, a small greeting party approached the plane as it rolled to a stop. When the door of the plane opened, Bill and Ebby fell to the ground, unable to rise.

Bill knew that he and Ebby were on the same road to hell, and he prepared for his friend's arrival by making a pitcher of pineapple juice and gin. (Bill preferred to drink straight gin, but he was afraid Lois might come home.) He was thunderstruck when he opened the door for his old friend and found someone else entirely. He couldn't put his finger on it immediately, but Ebby had stopped drinking. He refused the offer of the pineapple juice. Bill finally asked him what had happened. "I've got religion," Ebby said.[11]

Bill was instantly on his guard. He was not an atheist. He believed that only God could have created a natural world that operated according to natural laws. "With ministers, and the world's religions, I parted right there," Bill said. "When they talked of a God personal to me, who was love, superhuman strength and direction I became irritated and my mind snapped shut against such a theory."[12]

Probably sensing Bill's resistance, Ebby didn't dwell on religion. He brought him up to date on his recent arrest for drunkenly discharging a shotgun in a residential neighborhood. Facing a possible prison term, Ebby was rescued by the friend of a friend, Rowland Hazard, who promised the judge that he would take him in hand. Rowland was an alcoholic who had found sobriety through the Oxford Group, an organization of Protestants of different denominations who were dissatisfied with conventional religion. Rowland took Ebby to New York. He was currently living in a mission on East Twenty-Third Street that was run by the Calvary Episcopal Church, whose rector was a leader in the Oxford Group.

Ebby spoke briefly about the program of the Oxford Group, which was built around the practice of four "absolutes"—absolute honesty, absolute purity, absolute unselfishness, and absolute love. The Oxford Group stressed the importance of taking a complete moral inventory of your life, making restitutions to those you had hurt, and then helping others. "Then, very dangerously, he touched upon the subject of prayer and God," Bill said. Bill did not explode. Whatever Ebby was doing, it obviously was working. It was not just that he had been sober for four months or that he looked good. "I saw that my friend was much more than inwardly reorganized. He was on a different footing. His roots grasped a new soil," Bill said. Ebby was not just sober. He was happy.[13]

One morning, Bill decided he wanted to see the Calvary mission for himself. By the time he had walked the three blocks from the subway to the mission, he was drunk and dragging a new friend, Alec, a homeless Finn who had once been a sailor. The two men made so much noise that they were ejected. Later, Ebby appeared and forced beans and coffee down their throats until they were sober enough to attend the daily service. Still drunk, Bill rose to his feet and swore that he would try to follow Ebby's example. When Lois returned from work that evening, she found Bill sitting at the kitchen table, sober and deep in thought. He told her he was going to give the Oxford Group a try. "I remember how I hugged him and cried in his arms," she said.[14]

For several days, he did try. The sudden withdrawal of alcohol caused Bill to shake so badly that Lois wanted to call the doctor, but he refused. When he did get drunk again, he and Lois had a fight that ended with Bill throwing her sewing machine against a wall. The next day, Bill checked himself into Towns Hospital. He had managed to buy four beers on credit and had consumed them on the way, so he was feeling better when he encountered Silkworth in the hall. Waving a bottle, he told the doctor that he had "found something."[15]

As his detoxification progressed, however, Bill fell into a deep depression. His spirits rose briefly when Ebby visited, then sank again. He knew that death was near. "I again thought of the cancer of alcoholism which had now consumed me in mind and spirit, and soon in body," he said. Ebby had promised that God would save him if he asked for help, but this flew in the face of everything he believed. It would be admitting defeat. At last, in agony, he cried out, "I'll do anything, anything at all. If there be a God, let Him show Himself!"

> Suddenly, my room blazed with an indescribably white light. I was seized with an ecstasy beyond description. Every joy I had known was pale by comparison. The light, the ecstasy—I was conscious of nothing else for a time. Then, seen in the mind's eye, there was a mountain. I stood on the summit, where a great wind blew. A wind, not of air, but of spirit. In great, clean strength, it blew right through me. Then came the blazing thought, "You are a free man." . . . I became acutely conscious of a Presence which seemed like a veritable sea of living spirit. I lay on the shores of a new world. "This," I thought, "must be the great reality. The God of the preachers."

Bill had experienced a spiritual awakening. He was convinced that no matter how wrong things seemed, "there could be no question of the ultimate rightness of God's universe." "For the first time, I felt that I really belonged. I knew that I was loved and could love in return," he said.[16]

Silkworth recognized that something profound had happened and urged Bill not to question what it was. "You are already a different individual," he said. "[W]hatever you've got now, you'd better hold on to. It's so much better than what you had only a couple of hours ago," he said. Lois was also convinced. "The minute I saw him at the hospital, I knew something overwhelming had happened," she said. "His eyes were filled with light. His whole being expressed hope and joy. . . . I walked home on air."[17]

Bill Wilson left Towns Hospital on December 18, 1934, and immediately embarked on a mission to change the world. "I was soon heard to say that I was going to fix up all the drunks in the world, even though the batting average on them had been virtually nil for 5,000 years," he said. It was a crazy idea, but Wilson thought he had discovered the secret of success in the writings of William James, a professor of philosophy and psychology at Harvard College. He had been given a copy of James's best seller, *Varieties of Religious Experience*, and had read how spiritual experiences can transform people:

> Some were sudden brilliant illuminations; others came on very gradually. Some flowed out of religious channels; others did not. But nearly all had the great common denominators of pain, suffering, calamity. Complete hopelessness and deflation at depth were almost always required to make the recipient ready. The significance of this burst upon me. *Deflation at depth*—yes, that was *it*. Exactly that had happened to me.

Later, Bill and the early members of Alcoholics Anonymous would describe "deflation at depth" as the experience of "hitting bottom." Bill was not the first alcoholic to recognize the importance of hitting bottom. Handsome Lake, John H. W. Hawkins, and Jerry McAuley reported that they had been at their lowest point when they discovered a power greater than themselves that made it possible for them to stop drinking.[18]

But it wasn't reading a book that had changed Bill's life. Nor was it Silkworth's wise counsel. It was Ebby's visit to Clinton Street. "[W]hen

Ebby came along and one alcoholic began to talk to another, that clinched it," Bill said. Bill believed he had discovered something new:

> My thoughts began to race as I envisioned a chain reaction among alcoholics, one carrying the message to the next. More than I could ever want anything else, I now knew that I wanted to work with alcoholics.

Bill was hardly the first recovering alcoholic to try to help other drunks. The search for sobriety was over a century old, and many of its leaders were alcoholics who had shown skill in organizing. But something new and important had been added to the quest. Bill would prove to be the greatest leader yet.[19]

Bill and Lois began regularly attending meetings of the Oxford Group at the Calvary Church. The Oxford Group believed strongly in the direct intervention of God in the life of every individual and spent time each day quietly listening for his guidance. For Bill, who had just experienced a spiritual epiphany, this made obvious sense. He was also strongly drawn by the Oxford Group's evangelism. But Bill was only interested in saving alcoholics. There were several sober alcoholics in the group, and they began to meet after the regular meeting at a nearby cafeteria. With Silkworth's support, he spent long hours talking to the alcoholics who could afford to stay at Towns. He also returned to the Calvary mission to try to save the down-and-out. He brought alcoholics back to Clinton Street for a home-cooked meal. Ebby moved in with Bill and Lois, and he joined Bill in trying to convince the dubious drunks that they could stop drinking if they wanted.[20]

After several months, however, Bill's mission was on the verge of failure. No one was getting sober. Lois saw the problem. "He thought a good home-cooked meal plus plenty of inspirational talk about the Oxford Group's principles of honesty, purity, unselfishness, and love would get them sober," she said. Ebby wasn't helping. "[B]etween the two of them, it was obvious to me that all their preaching was only turning off our rather inebriated guests." When Bill took his problem to Silkworth in April, the doctor told him to change his approach. Alcoholics were tough nuts. They had developed inflated egos that prevented them from seeing the damage that their drinking was doing to themselves and their families.[21]

Silkworth urged Bill to start by convincing them that they were suffering from an illness that was going to kill them. "Pour it right into them about the obsession that condemns them to drink and the physical sensitivity or allergy of the body that condemns them to go mad or die if they keep on drinking," Silkworth said. "Coming from another alcoholic, one alcoholic talking to another, maybe that will crack those tough egos down." It was the imminent prospect of his own death that had made Bill willing to ask for help, and there was no reason to think it would work differently for anyone else.[22]

Before Bill had a chance to try this new approach, he had to find a job. Lois had gone to work as a salesclerk in the furniture department at Macy's after Bill was fired in Canada. They lived on Lois's weekly salary of $22.50, facing foreclosure on their Clinton Street home. The only reason they were allowed to stay was that the mortgage company could not find a buyer and was willing to accept a small rent in the interim. Lois and Ebby opposed Bill's decision to look for a job. He had been sober only a few months, and they feared that he would start drinking again if he went back to work too soon. Bill felt guilty about the fact that his wife had been supporting him for almost two years. "I want to get Lois out of that damned department store," he said.[23]

Bill sought out old friends on Wall Street and was invited to lead a group of investors who were attempting to take over a small machine tool company in Akron. It would mean traveling to Ohio in an effort to line up support among the local shareholders. Bill was scared. Years of failure made him wonder whether he could recapture his early success. On the eve of his departure in May 1935, he was irritable and gruff.

As Lois packed his bag, Bill complained that he had only one good suit; that the collar of his dress shirt was frayed, and the heels of his black shoes were worn. His grievances began to mount: he told Lois that he hated his life, that he'd never amount to anything, and that the trip to Akron was a waste of time. Lois was impatient. She told him he should be grateful for his sobriety. "Sober! You call this sober?" Bill asked. "I'm still a drunk who hasn't had a drink yet." When Bill stormed out of the bedroom, Lois was afraid that he would be drunk before he reached Akron.[24]

Five days passed without a word from Bill. Things were not going well in Akron. Bill had joined a team of men from New York, but by the end of the week, there seemed little hope of taking over the company. The rest of the men returned to New York, leaving Bill alone to see if the deal could be salvaged.

On a Saturday afternoon, he found himself standing in the lobby of a hotel in a strange city not knowing what to do next. The new Mayflower Hotel was the best in the city. Prohibition had been repealed, and the lobby bar had become a gathering place for the town's business and social elite. From the sound of voices, Bill could tell that the bar was coming to life in anticipation of another busy Saturday night. "Then I was seized by a thought: I am going to get drunk," Bill said. "Then I panicked."[25]

In New York, Bill had made a full-time job of helping drunks get sober. The focus had always been on them. He suddenly realized what they had been doing for him. "I thought, 'You need another alcoholic to talk to. You need another alcoholic as much as he needs you.'" Bill decided to try to find someone from the Oxford Group in Akron. As Bill later told the story, he picked a name at random from a directory of churches in the lobby: Walter Tunks, an Episcopal minister. Tunks turned out to be a member of the Oxford Group, and he gave Bill a list of ten people he thought might point him in the right direction. The first nine were either unavailable or unable to help.[26]

The last person on the list was someone who knew Henrietta Seiberling, the daughter-in-law of one of Akron's richest men. Bill recognized the name and hesitated to reveal his alcoholism, but he had no choice. "I'm from the Oxford Group, and I'm a rum hound from New York," Bill said. Henrietta knew someone else who needed help badly. "You come right out here," she said.[27]

The next day, May 12, Bill Wilson met Dr. Bob Smith at Henrietta's large home on the Seiberling estate. Smith and his wife, Anne, had been invited for dinner. Bob Smith had no intention of staying. He felt terrible. The previous day, he had arrived home drunk, carrying a large plant as a Mother's Day gift for his wife. After depositing the plant on the dining-room table, he had collapsed, and it had taken all the strength of his wife and two teenage children to get him upstairs to bed. He hadn't wanted to come to Henrietta's at all, but he had been desperately searching for a way to stay sober.

Bob and Anne had joined the Oxford Group in the hope that they might find the answer there, but he was still getting drunk every night two and a half years later. What he had found was a friend—"Henri." When she learned that Bob had a drinking problem, she arranged a special meeting of Oxford Group members with the goal of getting him to acknowledge his alcoholism, which he did. Seiberling was still trying to help him, and she considered Bill Wilson's telephone call a godsend. While Bob couldn't say no when she summoned him, he didn't have to like it. "On the way, I extracted a promise from Anne that 15 minutes of this stuff would be tops," Bob recalled. "I didn't want to talk to this mug or anybody else, and we'd make it real snappy."[28]

"I just loved my grog," Bob said. At first, it was the symbol of his rebellion from the strict morality of the small Vermont town of St. Johnsbury, where he was born in 1879. His parents were leading citizens of the town. His father was not only a lawyer, district attorney, and later a judge, but also the superintendent of schools and a director of two banks. His mother was deeply involved in the activities of the North Congregational Church. Later, Anne Smith would blame her mother-in-law for Bob's alcoholism. She governed her only son with an iron hand, sending him to bed at five every night. What he hated most was church. "From childhood through high school, I was more or less forced to go to church, Sunday school and evening service, Monday-night Christian Endeavor, and sometimes to Wednesday evening prayer meeting," Bob said.[29]

Bob engaged in small acts of protest from his youngest days. After being sent to bed, he often escaped to play outdoors. His failure to make good grades was a continual frustration to his parents. It wasn't until he left for college that he found alcohol. By the time he reached Dartmouth College, the temperance movement had made major strides in drying up the rural sections of the country. Even where the sale of liquor was legal, as it was in Vermont, it was often discouraged.

In St. Johnsbury, it had to be purchased from a merchant licensed by the state, who would sell a pint only if he was convinced it was really needed. Some men avoided prying questions by having their liquor shipped directly from Boston and New York. Everyone knew who they were. They "were looked upon with great distrust and disfavor by most of the good townspeople," Smith said.[30]

Like all freshmen, Bob reveled in the freedom of being on his own. He devoted himself to doing "what I wanted to do, without regard for the rights, wishes or privileges of others." Mostly what he wanted to do was have fun. He became a skilled billiards player and began to develop into a cardsharp. Drinking was what he enjoyed most, and he quickly outstripped the upperclassmen. He amazed his friends by demonstrating the ability to drink a bottle of beer without swallowing. Unlike his friends, he never got sick or suffered a hangover. "Never once in my life have I had a headache," Bob said many years later. The first sign of trouble occurred only after he graduated. He was working as a salesman and drinking heavily on the weekends, when he discovered that he was shaking on some mornings. The "jitters" would only stop after he had a drink. Bob's jitters increased after he enrolled in the University of Michigan Medical School. Many days he turned around on his way to class for fear of disgracing himself if he was called on for an answer. His drinking and his shakes continued to worsen until, in the spring of his second year, he withdrew from medical school and moved to a large farm owned by a friend to recuperate.[31]

After a month of drying out, Bob realized he had made a mistake in quitting school. Although he was given a second chance at Rush University in Chicago, his drinking was out of control. During one of his exams, he submitted three blank examination books because his hands were shaking so badly he couldn't write. However, some alcoholics are capable of functioning without alcohol for long periods before they start drinking again. Unlike Bill Wilson, who could not stop drinking, Bob, under threat of expulsion, remained abstinent for a year, during which he earned grades good enough to help him secure a prestigious internship at City Hospital in Akron.

Bob was able to stay sober for five of the next eight years. He welcomed the long days during his two-year internship because it made it easier not to drink. Soon after he had opened his own office, however, he began drinking again to ease stomach pain. On at least a dozen occasions, he was forced to put himself into private rest homes to dry out. When he collapsed again, his father sent a doctor to bring him back to Vermont. During another period of sobriety, he finally married his longtime sweetheart, Anne. Three sober years followed. But, in 1918, he picked up another drink and kept drinking for seventeen years.

Bob suffered from two major fears. "One was the fear of not sleeping; the other was the fear of running out of liquor," he said. "Not being a man of means, I knew that if I did not stay sober enough to earn money, I would run out of liquor." Since he could not drink in the morning, he started using large doses of sedatives to keep him steady. Anne searched his clothes for bottles when he came home from work. But he had dozens of hiding places. Every morning, Bob would appear at the lunch counter in his office building and order Bromo-Seltzer, tomato juice, and aspirin. A waitress noticed Bob because of his shakes. "Does he have palsy?" she asked the owner. "No, he has a perpetual hangover," the man replied.[32]

Despite Bob's strenuous efforts to keep his alcoholism a secret, it was becoming increasingly apparent to his friends and colleagues. He remained well liked. He struck strangers as gruff and abrupt, but his friends knew that he actually cared deeply about people. Unlike many doctors, he wasn't arrogant or abusive to the staff. Smith naturally sympathized with the underdog and was even willing to accept responsibility for mistakes made by nurses to spare them punishment. He was also popular with his patients. As the nation sank into the Depression, most of his patients became charity cases. "I remember how he'd say, 'Well, I've got three operations this morning—two for the Lord and one for R. H. [Robert Holbrook (Smith)],'" his son remembered. "Not only that but people would come into his office in desperate straits, and he would literally give them his last cent. He might have only 50 cents, but he'd give it to them."[33]

Bill Wilson knew that he had found an alcoholic the moment Bob extended his trembling hand. At fifty-five, the doctor was sixteen years older than Wilson. He was a tall, broad-shouldered man with hands that seemed unusually large for a surgeon. Bob was obviously in bad shape. Bill joked that it looked like he could use a drink. The remark embarrassed the doctor, but Bill thought he seemed to brighten a little. Henrietta took the two men to her small library and left them alone.

As Bill started talking, he was determined to follow Silkworth's advice by steering clear of any discussion of the role that God had played in his recovery. Instead, he spoke about what alcohol had done to him until he was sure that Bob had accepted him as an alcoholic. Then Bill sought to convince Bob of the hopelessness of his condition. He explained Silkworth's theory that alcoholism was an incurable disease.

"What really did hit him hard was the medical business, the verdict of inevitable annihilation . . . ," Bill recalled many years later. "[I]t was not any spiritual teaching of mine, rather it was those twin ogres of madness and death . . . that triggered him into a new life." Bill later saw this as the moment when he found the approach that would guide him in the years ahead.[34]

Bob Smith remembered the encounter differently. He wasn't particularly impressed by the scientific theory that Bill advanced. "It must be remembered that I had read a great deal and talked to everyone who knew, or thought they knew anything about the subject of alcoholism," he wrote. What was new was Bill. Bob explained,

[H]e was the first living human with whom I had ever talked, who knew what he was talking about in regard to alcoholism from actual experience. In other words, he talked my language. He knew all the answers, and certainly not because he had picked them up in his reading.

Bob had always pictured alcoholics as Bowery bums. Bill was no bum. It didn't really matter whether alcoholism was a disease. Bob discovered that he wasn't alone. The two men talked for hours. Back home, for the first time in years, Bob did not drink himself to sleep.[35]

Over the next two weeks, Bill Wilson and the Smiths got better acquainted. Anne invited Bill to move into the Smiths' modest home on Ardmore Avenue. "There I might keep an eye on Dr. Bob and he on me," he explained.

It took the Smiths some time to adjust to their guest. Bill had only been sober for five months, and he was "jittery as hell," he admitted. When he woke early and could not go back to sleep, he would go downstairs to make coffee, sometimes waking the family with a start at

6 a.m. The Smiths would find him in the kitchen, sitting in his bathrobe, "draped around this drip coffeepot."[36]

Bill also insisted that there be liquor in the house. Believing that alcoholics would have to learn to live among people who drank, he bought two large bottles of liquor and placed them on the Smiths' sideboard. "That drove Anne about wild for a while," he said. She was also upset when Bill supported Bob's desire to attend the American Medical Association convention in Atlantic City during the first week of June. The AMA convention had always been an opportunity for a binge, and Anne feared that the temptation would overpower Bob, who had only been sober for two weeks.[37]

They didn't hear from Bob for five days. He had started drinking the moment he got on the train, and he had checked out of his hotel two days later to avoid disgracing himself. He couldn't remember much about the next three days. He had managed to get back on the train and to call his office nurse when he arrived in Akron. She and her husband picked him up and took him to their home, where he finally began to emerge from his blackout.

Now there was another problem. Bob was scheduled to perform surgery three days later, and there was a good chance that he would not be fit to hold a scalpel. Bill took charge. He and Anne drove over to the nurse's home, where Bill gave Bob enough scotch to prevent a rapid withdrawal that could trigger delirium tremens. On their arrival back at Ardmore Avenue, Bob was put to bed. For the next three days, they fed him nothing but tomato juice, sauerkraut, and Karo corn syrup, which Bill believed would give Bob energy and vitamins. Anne and Bill took turns nursing Bob around the clock, sleeping in the second bed in the room.

At 4 a.m. on the day of the operation, Bill noticed that Bob was wide awake. He was still shaking. "I am going through with it," Bob said. "I'm going to do what it takes to get sober and stay that way."[38]

At 9 a.m. Anne and Bill helped Bob dress. As they drove to the hospital where he would perform rectal surgery, Bob kept raising his hand to see if his jitters had subsided. Just before they arrived, Bill gave him a bottle of beer and "one goofball"—a sedative. Terrified that Bob might make a mistake, Anne and Bill returned home to await his call. Several hours later, Bob telephoned to say the operation had gone well, but he did not immediately return home.

As the hours passed, Anne and Bill began to worry again. Bob was sober when he walked in the door. He had been apologizing to his creditors and promising restitution. The Smiths would remain in debt for years to come, but Bob made good on the one promise that mattered most. The beer that Bill gave him to get him through the operation was his last drink. Alcoholics Anonymous, the organization that the two men were about to launch, dates its origin from that day, June 10, 1935.

Bill Wilson and Bob Smith had started searching for another alcoholic to help, even before Bob took his final drink. Wilson had left Towns Hospital following his spiritual experience determined to save alcoholics everywhere. The Oxford Group was also committed to evangelism, although its goal was to convert the world. But Smith had never embraced the Oxford Group's idea of converting others until he met Bill. In their first meeting, Smith had felt the power of one drunk talking to another. He also recognized the truth of Wilson's view that carrying the message of sobriety to alcoholics was essential for the sober drunks, especially for those like him who continued to suffer from strong cravings for alcohol. Wilson and Smith were making little progress in their search to find someone to help when a nurse in the receiving ward at Akron City Hospital told them about a drunk who had been strapped to his bed after assaulting two nurses. It was his eighth admission to the hospital in the last six months.

Smith arranged a meeting with the man's wife, Henrietta D., who was desperately searching for help for her husband. "You aren't reaching him," she had told her pastor. "I'm going to find someone who can if I have to see everyone in Akron." In her first conversation with Smith, Henrietta sensed the compassion behind his rough exterior. "What kind of bird is this egg when he is sober?" he asked. She decided to give him a chance and agreed to move her husband, Bill D., to a private room so that he could confer with Smith and Wilson. She was waiting for him when he was wheeled into his new room. Bill D. was expecting her to say that she was getting a divorce. "You are going to quit," she announced.[39]

Bill D. was relieved that he was still married but skeptical about the rest. After each of his recent hospitalizations, he had emerged with the

Plate 15

Handsome Lake preaching at Tonawanda

From a drawing by Jesse Cornplanter

Wikimedia

Indigenous people were the first to address the problem of alcoholism in America. Here, Handsome Lake preaches abstinence to members of the Seneca nation.

Courtesy of the University of Pennsylvania Art Collection

Dr. Benjamin Rush, a signer of the Declaration of Independence, was the first American doctor to identify alcoholism as a curable disease.

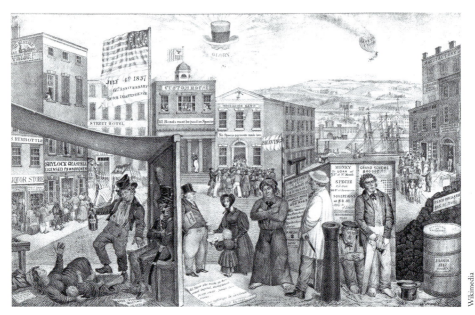

Wikimedia

Alcoholism increased in the 1830s when many men lost their jobs during a severe depression, as depicted in this 1837 cartoon.

Library of Congress (far left); David Harrisson Jr., *A Voice from the Washingtonian Home* (1860) (right)

In 1840, John H. W. Hawkins quit drinking with the assistance of the Washingtonian Temperance Society.

Albert Day treated more than thirty thousand drunks during his forty-year career.

Francis Murphy, an Irish immigrant and saloon keeper, got sober following a religious conversion in jail.

Wikimedia

Wm. H. Daniels, *The Temperance Reform and Its Great Leaders* (1877) (left); courtesy of the Chicago History Museum (far right)

Henry Reynolds launched a campaign to help other drunks through the Red Ribbon Clubs.

Men who have taken the "gold cure" for alcoholism salute their fellow patients as they depart the Keeley Institute in Dwight, Illinois.

INEBRIATE ASYLUM, BINGHAMPTON.

Wikimedia

The New York State Inebriate Asylum opened in Binghamton, New York, after the Civil War.

Wikimedia

Dr. Leslie Keeley's "gold cure" for alcoholism became a national sensation in the 1890s.

Jerry McAuley, a drunk and a thief, founded the Water Street Mission, which aided the destitute, including many drunks.

Wikimedia

Carrie Nation used a hatchet in a series of assaults on Kansas saloons.

Wikimedia

William G. Wilson (Bill W.) (top) and Robert H. Smith (Dr. Bob) (bottom) cofounded Alcoholics Anonymous.

Courtesy of Page 124 Productions

Courtesy of the Illinois Addiction Studies Archive

Courtesy of the AA General Service Office Archives

Sister Mary Ignatia, the admitting nurse at St. Thomas Hospital in Akron, Ohio, conspired with Dr. Bob Smith to secretly admit alcoholics until 1944, when the hospital officially opened its doors to them.

Courtesy of the National Council on Alcoholism and Drug Dependence, Inc. (NCADD), www.ncadd.org

Marty Mann led a national publicity campaign that helped destigmatize alcoholism.

Wikimedia

Betty Ford's decision to speak publicly about her addiction encouraged others to seek help. The rehabilitation boom of the 1980s made alcoholism treatment widely available.

conviction that he would not get drunk again for at least six months. He had lost hope, and he was not pleased to learn that Henrietta had been talking to Smith and Wilson. He felt better when she said these men were drunks themselves who were staying sober by talking to other drunks. "All the other people that had talked to me wanted to help *me*, and my pride prevented me from listening to them . . . ," Bill D. said. "[B]ut I felt as if I would be a real stinker if I did not listen to a couple of fellows for a short time, if that would cure *them*."[40]

A short time later, Bill D. met Wilson and Smith. "I looked up and there were two great big fellows over six foot tall, very likeable looking," Bill D. said. They gained his confidence by talking about their own drinking and then came to the point. Wilson turned to Smith. "Well, I believe he's worth saving and working on," Wilson said. "Do you want to quit drinking?" he asked Bill D.

> It's none of our business about your drinking. We're not up here trying to take any of your rights or privileges away from you, but we have a program whereby we think we can stay sober. . . . Now if you don't want it, we'll not take up your time, and we'll be going and looking for someone else.

"Bill didn't seem too impressed," Wilson recalled. He did agree to see them again.[41]

Over the next five days, Bill D. ate sauerkraut and tomatoes at every meal and met frequently with Wilson and Smith. They told him they were looking for men who recognized that they could not control their drinking and needed God's help to stay sober. The idea of "surrender," or turning one's life over to God's will, was to become enormously important in developing a program of recovery. Wilson would later describe the life of an alcoholic as "self-will run riot." The goal of surrendering to God's will was to reduce the drunk's inflated ego, making it possible for him to recognize that drinking was the cause of his problems and that he needed help to control it.

Wilson had surrendered at Towns Hospital the night he begged for divine intervention. He had discovered that God could do for him what he could not do for himself, and all he had to do was ask for help. Smith, who had been seeking spiritual answers in the Oxford Group for more than two years, had less difficulty accepting this concept. But how would they explain the importance of surrender to others?

Once again, Wilson started with the facts about the incurable disease of alcoholism. If Bill D. accepted the fact that he could not stop on his own, did he believe in a higher power that he could ask for help? "I had no problem there because I had never actually ceased to believe in God, and had tried lots of times to get help but hadn't succeeded," Bill D. said.[42]

One night after Wilson and Smith had left, Bill D. reviewed his life and saw for the first time the damage that alcohol had done. "I finally came to the conclusion that if I didn't want to quit, I certainly ought to want to, and that I was willing to do anything in the world to stop drinking," Bill D. said. The next day, Bill D. announced his decision. "Yes, Doc, I would like to quit, at least for five, six, or eight months," Bill D. said.[43]

Wilson and Smith started laughing. "They said, 'We've got some bad news for you. . . . Whether you quit six days, months, or years, if you go out and take a drink or two you'll end up in this hospital tied down, just like you have been in these past six months.'" But they offered him hope. "'You can quit 24 hours can't you?'" I said, 'Sure, yes, anybody can do that, for 24 hours.' They said, 'That's what we're talking about just 24 hours at a time.'"[44]

They asked Bill D. to kneel by his bed and ask God for help and joined him in prayer. When they finished, Bill D. was ready to leave. "Henrietta, fetch me my clothes. I'm going to get up and get out of here," he said. The partnership of Wilson and Smith had become a group.[45]

Meanwhile, Lois Wilson was growing impatient for her husband to return to Brooklyn. He had been in Akron for over six weeks, and there were no signs that he intended to come home anytime soon. In letters and brief telephone calls, Bill had given Lois status reports on the proxy fight that had carried him to Akron in the first place. He had also explained how he had come to live with the Smiths. Lois pressed for his return. "I was nagging him," she said.[46]

Then Anne wrote Lois, telling her how grateful the Smiths were to Bill and inviting her to visit. In early July, Lois took a vacation from her job at the department store and traveled to Akron. Bill met her at the bus depot. She wouldn't see much of him over the next week. He and

Bob were making daily visits to the drunks at City Hospital. Although Lois was disappointed, she took an instant liking to the Smiths. "[Bob] definitely wanted to help people in trouble. And he was so excited and enthusiastic about this new thing he and Bill had," she said.[47]

Lois spent most of her time with Anne, and although they spoke little about their problems or what was going on, she got a good look at how sobriety had transformed the Smiths. "Mother was a lot less anxious about Dad, and I think he was a lot more satisfied with himself," the Smiths' daughter, Sue, said. "The whole family had good laughs, and it was really a happy time." The change in Bob was particularly important for his teenage son, Smitty. "I never had a chance to know him well during the time he was drinking, but he livened up so much and had such a wonderful time after," he said.[48]

By the time Lois got on the bus back to New York, she had a new worry. If being together was so important for Bill and Bob, what would happen when it was finally time for Bill to go home? Could the men stay sober when they were separated?

In the meantime, the trio of sober alcoholics became a quartet when Ernie G. got sober. A fifth man stopped drinking in the late summer, and the new recruits soon began visiting the alcoholics in City Hospital. Following the example of Bill and Bob, they didn't tell the patients to stop drinking. "They just told me stories for seven days about how they drank," one of the hospitalized drunks remembered.[49]

Once a man announced that he wanted to quit drinking, he was told that he would have to surrender his will to God. If this didn't happen in the hospital, it occurred when he attended his first Wednesday night meeting at the home of T. Henry and Clarace Williams. This was an Oxford Group meeting that Henrietta Seiberling had started to help Smith, and both the drunks and their wives attended. While it included nonalcoholics, the attendees referred to themselves as the "alcoholic squad," and during each meeting, the sober drunks took the newcomers upstairs where they made their surrender. "After about half an hour or so, down would come the new man, shaking, white, serious and grim."[50]

This was a nervous time. "[W]e were people saved from shipwreck," the wife of one drunk recalled. They drew strength from the presence of other survivors. "Do you think your husband is ever going to drink again?" Bill D.'s wife asked Lois. "I know he isn't," Lois said. Bill Wilson had been sober longer than he had ever been in his life—nine months. "We were scared stiff," one of the drunks later explained. "We'd lost everything and were afraid of drinking. Nothing had worked before, and we weren't always so sure that this would."[51]

The truth was that Wilson and Smith were unable to help most of the men they approached, and there was a danger that repeated failures could bring down the whole enterprise. The threat seemed particularly acute in the summer of 1935 when "Lil," the first woman they recruited, fell off the wagon and had sex with another recovering drunk on Smith's examining table. When the man, a former mayor of Akron, tried to take Lil home, she refused, swallowed some pills she had found, and tried to jump out the window. She was finally subdued and taken to the Smiths' house to sleep it off. The drunks and their wives were scandalized. "As drunks I don't know why we should have been," Wilson said. "But we felt that the performance of some of those early people coming in would disrupt us entirely."[52]

It was also a joyous time. The drunks and their wives had found new lives. The men were busy staying sober. Almost none of them had jobs. They had drunk their way into unemployment and had emerged from their alcoholic fog in the middle of an economic depression. Many were flat broke. The Smiths were a little better off than the others, but there were nights when all Anne could afford to serve was milk and bread. The new men clung tightly to the coattails of those who were sober just a few weeks or months longer. "It seems to me as though we just lived together when I first came into the group—me and Paul S. and Harold G.," one man said. "We would go from house to house during the day and wind up one place every night—Bob Smith's." At the Smiths', there was always plenty of strong coffee. Consumption reached nine pounds per week.[53]

The wives were also remaking their lives. Many had lost their old friends, but under Anne's prodding, they started to make new ones within the group. In addition to the Wednesday night meetings, everyone got together at somebody's house on Saturday night. "We had covered-dish suppers and picnics, and later we had a few dances," Henrietta D. remembered. "But for a long time, we just had coffee and tea and crackers. . . . Everybody was so happy to be together."[54]

Wilson returned to New York in August 1935. The proxy fight that had taken him to Akron had finally failed, and he began looking for work again. But his still unnamed group continued to grow. A New York meeting began in the parlor of the Wilson's home at 182 Clinton Street in Brooklyn Heights in the fall. The Akron group started drawing drunks from the neighboring cities of Kent and Canton. People from Cleveland began to drive down for the Wednesday meetings. In November 1937, Wilson visited the Smiths again as he was passing through on his latest job search. When they sat down to take stock of the progress of their enterprise, they began counting group members and were shocked when the number turned out to be forty. Twenty or more had been sober for more than two years. "As we carefully rechecked this score, it suddenly burst upon us that a new light was shining into the dark world of the alcoholic," Bill wrote.

> [A] benign chain reaction, one alcoholic carrying the good news to the next, had started outward from Dr. Bob and me. Conceivably it could one day circle the whole world. What a tremendous thing that realization was! At last we were sure. There would be no more flying totally blind. We actually wept for joy, and Bob and Anne and I bowed our heads in silent thanks.

Wilson and Smith had started a wave of sobriety. There was no way of knowing how large it would grow.[55]

CHAPTER SEVEN

The Birth of Alcoholics Anonymous

BILL WILSON AND BOB SMITH were sure they were onto something. Yet they were making progress "at the snail's pace," Wilson acknowledged. Most of the men they approached rejected their assistance. While many were not ready to stop drinking, others did not want to admit that they were alcoholics. The prejudice against drunks was ancient. It had been challenged briefly by the Washingtonians, the campaigns led by Reynolds and Murphy and later by the Keeley League. But most drunks remained closeted. The stigma of alcoholism may even have worsened in the twentieth century, when most people thought the alcoholic was someone incapable of measuring up to the demands of modern life and pictured a skid-row bum. The little band of drunks who gathered around Wilson and Smith were adamant about protecting their anonymity. Most of them were looking for work, and no one would hire a drunk. But how could a group of anonymous men hope to grow?[1]

Having thanked God for their success, Wilson and Smith began to lay plans for the future. Always the promoter, Wilson made several suggestions. First, it seemed clear that someone would have to be paid to promote the organization. Wilson and Smith were broke: Bill was unemployed and Bob was in danger of losing his home to foreclosure. What were needed were paid missionaries who would travel around the country establishing new groups. In addition, there was a desperate need for medical treatment for alcoholics. Most hospitals had closed their doors to these troublesome patients, who were sometimes violent when they were admitted, resentful and demanding as they sobered up, and too broke or forgetful when it came time to pay their bills. Wilson suggested creating a chain of hospitals that would specialize in drunks. Obviously, this meant there would have to be a large and energetic fund-raising campaign. Finally, he proposed the publication of "a book of experience" that would "carry our message to distant places we could never visit ourselves."[2]

Smith liked the idea of the book, but he was dubious about the rest. He suggested moving slowly. "Why don't we call the Akron boys together," he asked. "Let's try these ideas out on them." Wilson probably didn't welcome the suggestion. Earlier in 1937, he had been offered a paid position at Towns Hospital. Owner Charlie Towns saw a future in this still unnamed group of drunks and believed it might help restore some of the profits his business had lost during the Depression. Wilson wanted desperately to take the job, but the small group of sober alcoholics that had begun meeting at his Clinton Street home was opposed. Everyone agreed that one of the keys to their success was that a sober alcoholic could establish a rapport with someone who was still drinking because he had also suffered. In sharing his story, he offered the hope of recovery. The alcoholics in Wilson's group were convinced that this special bond would be destroyed if drunks suspected they were being recruited as part of a money-making scheme. Wilson turned down the job offer, but now he was preparing to pitch to eighteen members of the Akron group a plan that called for paid missionaries and a chain of hospitals.[3]

Wilson used his considerable powers of persuasion in his presentation. Smith spoke in favor of the plan despite his doubts. "Dr. Bob" was loved and respected by the men whose lives he had helped save. They flatly rejected Wilson's proposal:

> The moment we were through, those alcoholics really did work us over! They rejected the idea of missionaries. Paid workers, they said, would kill our good will with alcoholics; this would be sheer ruin. If we went into the hospital business, everybody would say it was a racket. Many thought we must shun publicity; we would be swamped; we could not handle the traffic. Some turned thumbs down on pamphlets and books. After all, they said, the apostles themselves did not need any printed matter.

Wilson and Smith tried to answer the objections. When a vote was taken, Wilson's plan was approved "by the barest majority." The controversy revealed some of the divisions that would emerge as the small groups of sober alcoholics in Akron and Brooklyn began to grow. The most important part of Wilson's plan would be the publication in 1939 of *Alcoholics Anonymous: The Story of How More Than One Hundred Men Have Recovered from Alcoholism.* Before that could happen, the organization that would take its name from the book would have to resolve its attitude toward religion.[4]

Their membership in a religious group had brought Wilson and Smith together in 1935. The Oxford Group was not organized in the conventional sense. It had no bylaws, members, officers, or dues. Its leader, Dr. Frank Buchman, was a Lutheran minister from Pennsylvania, but the Oxford Group appealed to Protestants of all denominations and sought to maintain good relations with other religions as well. Buchman's goal was ambitious. "The Oxford Group is a Christian revolution for remaking the world," he said.[5]

In the 1920s, Buchman started a religious movement in England by organizing "house parties" at Oxford University and other prestigious locations—wealthy homes, fashionable hotels, resorts, and summer camps. In 1933, five thousand people attended an International House Party at Oxford that filled six of its colleges for seventeen days. The following year, Buchman and a team of twenty-nine led a crusade in Norway that packed the meeting halls of Oslo with more than fourteen thousand eager listeners.[6]

Buchman believed the revolution would come by changing one person at a time. He had served as a missionary in China, giving speeches to large audiences. He was unimpressed with the results. It was "like hunting rabbits with a brass band," he said. Even the most powerful sermons did not produce conversions, because they did not change hearts. Only God could do that.[7]

Buchman's own conversion occurred only after his ordination. Suffering from a deep depression after a dispute with some of his parishioners forced him to resign from his first job as a minister, he traveled to England in search of spiritual guidance. In church one day, Buchman asked God to release him from the anger he felt at members of his congregation. "He told me to put things right with them," Buchman said. "It produced in me a vibrant feeling, as though a strong current of life had suddenly been poured into me."[8]

The experience convinced the minister of the importance of establishing a personal relationship with God. He began to urge others to make time to listen for God to tell them what to do. It became the basis for his successful ministry as a chaplain at Pennsylvania State University, and Buchman was sure that it wouldn't stop there. "The secret lies in that great forgotten truth, that when man listens, God speaks; when man obeys, God acts; when men change, nations change," he said. Buchman was so convinced that listening to the voice of God would produce world peace that he made two unsuccessful attempts to meet with Adolf Hitler in the early 1930s.[9]

While Buchman sometimes appeared childishly naive, there is no doubt that the Oxford Group was helping people, including alcoholics. Buchman had distilled his experience into four practices that he urged his followers to adopt:

1. The sharing of our sins and temptations with another Christian.
2. Surrender of our life past, present and future, into God's keeping and direction.
3. Restitution to all whom we have wronged directly or indirectly.
4. Listening for God's guidance and carrying it out.

Members of the Oxford Group met regularly to help one another fulfill these spiritual goals. A planning committee would meet to choose a speaker to expound on some aspect of the Oxford Group's program, and there was a period in which the members sat in silence listening for God's guidance. Once a newcomer had experienced a spiritual awakening, he or she was encouraged to seek out others who would benefit.[10]

In keeping with the Oxford Group's ambition to change the world, "groupers" were particularly anxious to recruit people of wealth and influence to help them carry their message to the highest echelons of society, business, and government. Drunks were not at the top of their list, but the members of the Oxford Group were confident that their program would work for all kinds of people with problems. Unlike most Americans, they were willing to give alcoholics a chance.

The Oxford Group first came to public attention in Akron when it helped Russell Firestone get sober. His grateful father, Harvey Firestone, the president of the Goodyear Rubber Company, invited Buchman to Akron to lead a crusade in 1933. Launched at a formal banquet in the ballroom of the Mayflower Hotel, Buchman's campaign was hailed as the "dinner-jacket revival" by the local press and drew thousands to its meetings. Several Oxford Group meetings were established at the time, including the group that Bob and Anne Smith began attending.[11]

Although Smith was still leery of religion, he was attracted by the people he met there "because of their seeming poise, health and happiness." "I was self-conscious and ill at ease most of the time, my health was at the breaking point, and I was thoroughly miserable," he said. One of the most striking features of the meetings was the public sharing about personal weaknesses. "These people spoke with great freedom from embarrassment, which I could never do," Smith explained. Although he attended meetings regularly, he continued to conceal his alcoholism. "I at no time sensed that it might be an answer to my liquor problem," he said.[12]

Things began to change the day when Henrietta Seiberling learned from a friend about Smith's problem. "I immediately felt guided that we should have a meeting for Bob Smith," Seiberling said. She asked T. Henry and Clarace Williams whether they would host the meeting in their home. When they agreed, she approached Anne Smith. Seiberling believed that neither Anne nor Bob had ever fully shared their weaknesses during a meeting. While Bob was hiding his drinking problem, Anne was unwilling to discuss feelings or behavior that might be criticized by group members, Seiberling said. Without telling Anne the purpose of the new group, she warned that it would be demanding. "Come prepared to mean business," she said. "There is going to be no pussyfooting around." In the Williams' living room, Seiberling and the other members kicked things off:

> We all shared very deeply our shortcomings and what we had victory over. Then there was a silence, and I waited and thought, "Will Bob say anything?" Sure enough, in that deep, serious tone of his,

he said, "Well, you good people have all shared things that I am sure were very costly to you, and I am going to tell you something which may cost me my profession. I am a secret drinker and I can't stop."

Someone asked if he wanted them to pray for him. He did.[13]

God was very much on their minds as Smith and Wilson began their pursuit of drunks in the summer of 1935. The first dinner at Henrietta's was shortly after Smith's confession at the meeting. Wilson's "white light" moment at Towns Hospital had occurred six months earlier. As soon as a man told them he wanted to stop drinking, they asked whether he believed in God. Clarence Snyder, an alcoholic from Cleveland, learned this when he found himself in Akron City Hospital in 1938. By then, there were more than a dozen alcoholics who had stopped drinking with the assistance of "Dr. Bob," and most of them had visited Snyder. After a week of listening to their stories, Snyder told Smith he was ready to quit. "Young feller, do you believe in God? Not a God, but God!" Smith asked. Snyder was not ready to say that he did but was afraid Smith would walk out of the room if he admitted it. "Well, I guess I do," he replied. Smith stood up, pointing a finger at Snyder. "There's no guessing about it. Either you do or you don't!" he said. Snyder surrendered. "Yeah, I do believe in God," he said.

> That's fine. Now we can get someplace. . . . Get down out of that bed. . . . You're going to pray. . . . You can repeat it after me, and that will do for this time. . . . Jesus! This is Clarence Snyder. He's a drunk. Clarence! This is Jesus. Ask Him to come into your life. Ask Him to remove your drinking problem, and pray that He manage your life because you are unable to manage it yourself.

The two men rose from the concrete floor where they had been praying. "Young feller, you're gonna be all right," Smith promised.[14]

The Oxford Group believed that surrendering to God was essential for spiritual growth. Acknowledging that desires are often selfish and corrupt makes it possible to hear what God desires. It is not surprising that the alcoholic members of the Oxford Group were particularly insistent on the importance of surrender, for they knew only too well that they were in the grip of a force they could not control. They believed that the only path forward was to admit they were unable to control their drinking and that they required divine help to stay sober. The surrender was considered so important that it became a prerequisite. "You couldn't just go to a meeting—you had to go through the program of surrender," recalled Bob E., a drunk who got sober in the Oxford Group in 1937. If a drunk wasn't ready to surrender, he was shown the door. One newcomer who failed to make the grade returned later to try again. "Jeez—when you guys say 'Take it or leave it,' you meant it," he said.[15]

The recovering drunks who met in growing numbers in the Williams's home were proud of their membership in the Oxford Group. Smith was deeply loyal to Henrietta Seiberling and the other members of the group who had helped him get sober, and the alcoholic men he had helped felt the same way toward him. They did not attempt to turn the meeting into something else. Most of the men and women who attended were not alcoholics, and the meetings continued to be conducted like other Oxford Group meetings. There was a heavy emphasis on applying the four absolutes to their everyday lives. Much of the meeting time was devoted to silent reflection as the members sought the guidance of God. It remained a religious meeting.

The Oxford Group could never be the home of a movement that was intent on saving drunks. Buchman was striving for a grander goal. "I'm all for drunks being changed, but we also have drunken nations on our hands," he said. Many of the alcoholics in the Oxford Group recognized that their goals were different from those of the nonalcoholic members of the group. Their priority was getting sober, and while they appreciated the hospitality of the Oxford Group, they had difficulty grasping its principles. Some of its practices drove them crazy. Newly sober, they found it difficult to sit still during the long periods of "quiet time" when others were listening to God and writing down their guidance. "The guidance thing the groupers had never went down well with the drunks," Ernie, an alcoholic, said. He explained:

> It seemed to be getting a little too technical and detailed. Sometimes I felt like they were using a Ouija board. Me and some of the

other alkies felt they put these things down on paper and it was their own personal idea for you.... But out of respect for T. Henry, we didn't kick.

Newly sober drunks found it difficult to tolerate criticism of any kind, but criticism from nonalcoholics, even the constructive kind, was particularly hard to take.[16]

The alcoholic members of the Oxford Group in New York were the first to leave the group. They had been meeting separately for some time. At first, they gathered at a nearby cafeteria following the meetings at the Calvary Church. Later, they met on Tuesday evenings at the Wilsons' home. By then, it was obvious to the nonalcoholic members of the Oxford Group that Wilson was spending all of his time recruiting alcoholics instead of the social leaders whose support would help the group expand. The Reverend Sam Shoemaker, the pastor of the Calvary Church, was a leader of the Oxford Group in America who had become a good friend of Wilson's. But a young priest took advantage of Shoemaker's absence on vacation to preach a sermon condemning the "divergent work" of a "secret, ashamed subgroup." Drunks in the mission were told to stop attending the meetings at Wilson's home. When Shoemaker was unable to repair the damage, Wilson and his friends left the Oxford Group in May 1937 and continued to meet in Brooklyn.[17]

A different problem troubled the Oxford Group meeting in Akron that was home to Bob Smith's "alcoholic squadron." Smith had no idea what a dynamo Clarence Snyder would become. Snyder was a born salesman, and he proved it by quickly making himself the top man at one of the largest Ford and Mercury dealerships in Ohio. No less impressive was his ability to sell drunks on sobriety. His first convert was a man he discovered in an abandoned house in a Polish section of Cleveland that was occupied by more than a dozen drunks. The man, Bill H., was lying paralyzed on the floor, but he told Snyder he wanted to get sober. A couple of drunks helped him get to Snyder's car, and he was driven to Akron City Hospital, where he recovered his health.

Snyder and his wife, Dorothy, drove down to Akron every Wednesday to attend the Oxford Group meetings at T. Henry Williams's home. The car quickly filled with drunks he had recruited in Cleveland. Soon, thirteen people were cramming into two cars. They called themselves the "Cleveland Contingent," and they differed in important ways from the Akron alcoholics. There was a woman alcoholic among them—Sylvia K., who would become a founder of the first Alcoholics Anonymous meeting in Chicago. The Clevelanders also included the first Catholic members of the alcoholic squadron. A majority of them were Irish Americans.

Women alcoholics made the rest of the drunks nervous. The sad story of Lil, the first woman that Wilson and Smith had tried to help, convinced many that mixing the sexes was a threat to their sobriety. But it was the Catholic alcoholics who posed an immediate problem. While the Oxford Group claimed to be an ecumenical movement, its members were overwhelmingly Protestant. Their meetings featured readings from the King James Version of the Bible, which was used only in Protestant churches, and periods of "sharing" during which members were encouraged to admit their sins, which in Catholic churches occurred only in the confessional.

These aspects of the Oxford Group were enough to convince some priests in Cleveland that their alcoholic parishioners were participating in Protestant rituals that threatened their immortal souls. Snyder attempted to intercede with the priests, arguing that membership in the Oxford Group was helping their people stay sober and actually making them better Catholics. "The Church didn't buy this line, not one bit," Snyder said. When he took the problem to Smith, Dr. Bob saw only two alternatives. "Remain with the Oxford Group and probably risk excommunication, or, very simply leave the Church," he said. If the Catholics wanted to stay sober, they had to be prepared to abandon their religion.[18]

Conflict was about to erupt in the Akron and New York groups. Wilson's expansion plans had not made much progress by the spring of 1938. There was no money to pay missionaries, much less to open hospitals. The only project that was making progress was the "book of experience" that would describe how to get sober. Although he had never written a book, Wilson became the principal author. As he finished each chapter, he sent the draft to Smith, who shared it with members of the Akron group. Wilson read the chapters aloud during meetings of the New York group. It was a painful process. Nobody could argue much with Wilson's story in the first chapter, but the New Yorkers had a lot to say about the next three. "[T]he chapters got a real mauling. I redictated them . . . over and over," Wilson said. It took him six months to satisfy everyone.[19]

As he began outlining the fifth chapter, "How It Works," he was dreading the reaction of the other alcoholics. It would be the most consequential part of the book. "[A]t this point we would have to tell how our program for recovery from alcoholism really worked," Wilson said. The "program" would be the steps that Wilson and his friends had taken to get sober. Wilson wasn't sure he could do it. "The hassling over the four chapters already finished had really been terrific. I was exhausted. On many a day I felt like throwing the book out the window," he said.[20]

There was already a "word of mouth program" that was based on the four spiritual practices of the Oxford Group: making a "moral inventory" of your defects of character; sharing these shortcomings with another person; making restitution to those you had been harmed; and praying to God for the power to undertake these tasks. As Wilson lay in bed with a pencil and a pad of paper, these steps did not seem detailed enough for alcoholics. They would have to be clear enough to provide guidance to people in places where there were no members of the group to advise them. They would also need to be unequivocal. "There must not be a single loophole through which the rationalizing alcoholic could wiggle out," Wilson said.[21]

"Finally, I started to write," Wilson recalled. "I relaxed and asked for guidance."

> With a speed that was astonishing, considering my jangling emotions, I completed the first draft. It took perhaps a half an hour. The words kept right on coming. When I reached a stopping point, I numbered the new steps. They added up to 12. Somehow this number seemed significant. Without any special rhyme or reason I connected them with the 12 apostles. Feeling greatly relieved now, I commenced to reread the draft.

Here is Wilson's first draft of the twelve steps:

1. We admitted we were powerless over alcohol—that our lives had become unmanageable.
2. Came to believe that God could restore us to sanity.
3. Made a decision to turn our wills and our lives over to the care and direction of God.
4. Made a searching and fearless moral inventory of ourselves.
5. Admitted to God, to ourselves, and to another human being the exact nature of our wrongs.
6. Were entirely willing that God remove all these defects of character.
7. Humbly on our knees asked Him to remove these shortcomings—holding nothing back.
8. Made a complete list of all persons we had harmed, and became willing to make amends to them all.
9. Made direct amends to such people wherever possible, except when to do so would injure them or others.
10. Continued to take personal inventory and when we were wrong promptly admitted it.
11. Sought through prayer and meditation to improve our contact with God, praying only for knowledge of His will for us and the power to carry that out.
12. Having had a spiritual experience as the result of this course of action, we tried to carry this message to others, especially alcoholics, and to practice these principles in all our affairs.[22]

"I was greatly pleased with what I had written," Wilson said.[23]

For a moment, he allowed himself to believe that he had described a program that was unassailable, if not God given. Wilson's happiness was short-lived. At that moment, he received a visit from Horace C. and another alcoholic who had been sober for only a few months. Wilson read his work to them and waited for their applause. He was shocked by their response:

[Horace] and his friend reacted violently. "Why *twelve* steps?" they demanded. . . ."You've got too much God in these steps; you will scare people away." And, "What do you mean by getting those

drunks down 'on their knees' when they ask to have all their shortcomings removed?" And "Who wants all their shortcomings removed, anyhow?"

Seeing the disappointment in Wilson's face, Horace acknowledged that
"some of this stuff sounds pretty good," but he didn't back down. "Bill,
you've got to tone it down. It's too stiff," he said. "The average alcoholic
just won't buy it the way it stands." Wilson responded with a strenuous
defense, insisting on the importance of every word. The debate went on
for hours. Finally, Lois appeared and suggested they take a coffee break,
which ended the discussion for the night.[24]

The debate over the twelve steps grew during the following weeks.
Horace and his friend were right: Wilson had talked about God a lot.
God was also mentioned frequently in the chapters that Wilson had
already written. While Akron members were generally supportive, the
issue divided the New Yorkers into three groups that Wilson later identified as "conservatives," "liberals," and "radicals." Fitz M., the son of a minister, wanted to go even further in identifying the group as religious. He
believed that the book should declare its allegiance to Christian principles, "using Biblical terms and expression to make this clear," Wilson said.
The liberals had no objection to the use of the word "God" throughout
the book, but they were adamantly opposed to identifying their movement with a particular religion. In their view, the religious missions had
failed because drunks were unwilling to accept their beliefs.[25]

Wilson described the third group as "our radical left wing." At least
one member, James Burwell, was an outspoken atheist. The others were
either agnostics or believers who nevertheless opposed any mention of
God. Henry Parkhurst had been among the first to see the importance
of the book and had developed the fund-raising plan that would make
its publication possible. He was also one of the first to express the view
that religion should be downplayed. In part, this was an expression
of his own religious doubts. But it was also a question of marketing.
In a memo about "sales promotion, possibilities," he expressed concern
about alienating the customers:

> One of the things most talked about . . . among us is religious ex-
> perience. I believe this is incomprehensible to most people. Simple

and meaning [*sic*] words to us—but meaningless to most of the people that we are trying to get this over to. . . . I am fearfully afraid that we are emphasizing religious experience when that is actually something that follows.

Wilson was shocked. "What Henry, Jimmy, and company wanted was a *psychological* book which would lure the alcoholic in. Once in, the prospect could take God or leave him alone," he said.[26]

The debate at the New York meeting continued into 1939. In the meantime, members in both Akron and New York were working to address another criticism of Wilson's draft. There was general agreement that it did not contain enough "evidence in the form of living proof" to convince drunks that they could quit. To meet this need, twenty-eight members contributed short stories describing their experience to a section at the end of the book. The debate over religion was still under way as the final stories were received. To end the impasse, it was agreed that Wilson would be the final judge of what the book said. At the end of January, four hundred copies of the manuscript were sent out for comments from doctors, religious leaders, and others in an effort to identify any problems prior to publication.

The religious debate wasn't over. Shortly before the book was sent to the printer, Parkhurst pushed his argument one last time. He had been sharing his Newark office with Wilson. It was where Wilson had dictated most of the book to a secretary, Ruth Houck. Fitz, who favored a more religious book, was also present. Parkhurst wanted changes in the twelve steps, something Wilson had been refusing to consider. "He argued, he begged, he threatened," Wilson said. "He was positive we would scare off alcoholics by the thousands when they read those 12 Steps." Houck, who was not an alcoholic, was the easiest to persuade. Then, Fitz began to soften. Finally, Wilson agreed to make several changes:

In Step Two we decided to describe God as a "Power greater than ourselves." In Steps Three and Eleven we inserted the words "God *as we understood Him.*" From Step Seven we deleted the expression "on our knees." And, as a lead-in sentence to all the steps we wrote these words: "Here are the steps we took which are suggested as a Program of Recovery." A.A.'s Twelve Steps were to be *suggestions* only.

While the changes made by altering a few words appeared superficial at first, Wilson later acknowledged that the radicals had secured their major objective. "They had widened our gateway so that all who suffer might pass through regardless of their belief or *lack of belief*," he said.[27]

One additional change in the manuscript underlined the commitment to inclusiveness. A psychiatrist who had been asked to comment on the final draft thought the tone was often peremptory, addressing the reader as "you" and telling him what he "must" do. "He suggested that we substitute wherever possible such expression as "we ought" or "we should," Wilson said. He briefly resisted making the change because it would require a lot of editing, but he finally agreed when other outside readers made the same point.[28]

Though Wilson was forced to make a lot of concessions in completing his book, he won a major victory when it was agreed that it would be titled *Alcoholics Anonymous: The Story of How One Hundred Men Have Recovered from Alcoholism*. A majority of the members had initially favored *The Way Out*, but a search of the titles copyrighted by the Library of Congress revealed that there were twelve books by that name. The manuscript was finally sent to the printer and was published in April 1939 by the Works Publishing Company, which had been organized by Wilson and Parkhurst. Five thousand copies of the four-hundred-page book were printed on thick paper to help justify its cost—$3.50. It was the bulkiness of the final product that led members to refer to it as the "Big Book."

The publication of the Big Book had immediate consequences for the Cleveland alcoholics in the Akron group. Snyder had been urging Smith to do something to help the Catholic members. In the days after the release of *Alcoholics Anonymous*, Snyder approached Smith again and got the same answer:

"We're not keeping the Catholics out—the church is keeping them out. . . . We can't do anything about it."

"Yes, we can," Clarence said.

"What do you have in mind?"

"To start a group without all this rigmarole that's offensive to other people. We have a book now, the Steps, the absolutes. Anyone can live by that program. We can start our own meetings."

"We can't abandon these people," Doc replied. "We owe our lives to them."

"So what?" Clarence replied. "I owe my life to them, too. But what about all these others?"

"We can't do anything about them," Doc said.

"Oh, yes, we can. . . . You'll see."

Snyder had recently helped hospitalize a Cleveland patent attorney named Abby G. While Abby was still in the hospital, Snyder told Abby's wife that he was looking for a place to hold a meeting in Cleveland, and she had offered her own large home. In early May, Snyder announced at the Akron meeting that the Clevelanders were leaving the Oxford Group and would begin their own meeting the following week. "Our policy will be mainly this," Snyder wrote Parkhurst a few weeks later. "Not too much stress on spiritual business at meetings."[29]

Some Oxford Group members were outraged at what they saw as a betrayal. They attempted to argue with Snyder after his announcement. When he made the mistake of revealing the location of Abby's home, some of them showed up at the first meeting to continue their protest. "They invaded the house and tried to break up our meeting," Snyder said. "One fellow was going to whip me. All in the name of pure Christian love!"[30]

Smith stayed home. He quickly reconciled himself to the break and began attending the meeting once or twice a month. While he was reluctant to anger his close friends Henrietta Seiberling and T. Henry Williams, he understood the reasons for starting the group in Cleveland, which was soon describing itself as a meeting of Alcoholics Anonymous. By the end of the year, he was convinced that the Akron alcoholics, too, must find a new home. In December, as many as seventy people began cramming into the living room of the Smiths' small home on Wednesday nights. "Have definitely thrown off the shackles of the Oxford Group," he wrote Wilson on January 2, 1940. Alcoholics Anonymous had declared its independence.[31]

✦   ✦   ✦

Free at last, Snyder threw himself into organizing AA in Cleveland. His wife, Dorothy, shared his missionary zeal:

> I felt that nobody in Cleveland should be drunk—or anywhere in the world—as long as there was an A.A. So I was pounding the streets trying to show different bookstores the A.A. book. I went down to the public library and tried to get orders. Nobody would even listen to me, and they looked at me like I was Salvation Nell.

Other members worked on establishing an institutional base in Cleveland. The wife of one of the drunks was a nurse who had many contacts with hospital administrators. She suggested that the head of Deaconess Hospital might be willing to work with AA, providing the private rooms where the AA members could work with alcoholics. Smith and a local doctor who had only been sober for a few weeks persuaded the administrator to take the question to his board of trustees. Despite opposition by the medical staff, the trustees agreed, and Deaconess began accepting alcoholics without any guarantee of payment. The hospital was expecting only a handful of admissions, but in the fall of 1939, a series of stories in the *Cleveland Plain Dealer* produced a sudden boom in AA membership.[32]

It is unknown how *Plain Dealer* reporter Elrick B. Davis became acquainted with AA. Snyder later claimed that he found Davis on a bar stool and helped him get sober. Some AA members accused Snyder of sneaking the reporter into their meeting under the pretense of alcoholism. If Davis wasn't an alcoholic, he must have been a terrific reporter, because the series of five stories that he wrote in late October showed a deep understanding of both alcoholism and Alcoholics Anonymous.

The writing was also remarkable. Because the stories appeared on the editorial page, Davis was freed of the necessity for objectivity. In an informal style flavored by the natural cynicism of a veteran reporter, Davis announced the arrival of something new. "Alcoholics Anonymous has reached the town," he said. "Every Thursday evening at the home of some ex-drunk in Cleveland, 40 or 50 former hopeless rummies meet for a social evening during which they buck each other up." Davis accepted the truth of what he saw. "The basic point about Alcoholics Anonymous is that it is a fellowship of 'cured' alcoholics," he wrote. "Repeat the astounding fact: These are cured. They have cured each other. They have done it by adopting, with each other's aid, what they call a 'spiritual' way of life."[33]

Davis's five short articles appeared on successive days, stressing the simplicity, openness, and disinterestedness of the AA program. In the second article, Davis addressed the religious issue directly. "There is no blinking the fact that Alcoholics Anonymous, the amazing society of ex-drunks who have cured each other of an incurable disease, is religious," he said. But he insisted that this was no barrier. "Every member of Alcoholics Anonymous may define God to suit himself," he said. A drunk did not need to believe in God at all. "[A]s far as the Fellowship of Alcoholics Anonymous is concerned, a pathological drunk can call God 'It' if he wants to, and is willing to accepts Its aid. If he'll do that he can be cured." AA welcomed all kinds:

> The Cleveland chapter includes a number of Catholics and several Jews, and at least one man to whom "God" is "Nature." Some practice family devotions. Some simply cogitate about "It" in the silence of their minds. But that the Great Healer cured them with only the help of their fellow ex-drunks, they all admit.

In the articles that followed, Davis explained the physical and mental aspects of alcoholism. As daunting as these are, AA had discovered that there is really only one obstacle to getting sober. "[I]f you are really willing to 'do anything' to get well . . . you'll have to quit lying to yourself and adopt a spiritual way of life. Are you ready to accept help?" According to Davis, it was that simple. "[T]he miracle is that, for alcoholics brought to agreement by pure desperation, so simple a scheme works," he wrote.[34]

Clevelanders responded instantly. Hundreds asked the *Plain Dealer* to put them in touch with the local group, while others wrote to AA headquarters in New York. In the first month, five hundred requests were forwarded to Snyder, who divided them with the other members of the group. "I would hand them out on Monday mornings like a sales manager—tell them to follow up and to report to me on Wednesday," he said. "Nobody had a job at that time, so it was all right." His wife, Dorothy, remembered being overwhelmed. "Within the space of about two weeks, our meetings grew from 15 to 100," she said. There were only thirteen men who had been sober long enough to call on people who had asked to meet with an AA member. Each was handling as many as eight calls every evening, and the telephone kept ringing. "People couldn't get me on the phone, because the line was busy, so they'd come beating down the doors," Dorothy said.[35]

Snyder welcomed the chaos, but what was happening in Cleveland frightened the earliest members, including Wilson and Smith. "Had it not taken us four whole years, littered with countless failures, to produce even 100 good recoveries," Wilson recalled. "How could they manage?" There seemed to be a better chance that the onslaught of alcoholics would get the Clevelanders drunk than they would get the newcomers sober. A year later, there were thirty groups and several hundred members in Cleveland. AA had proved that it could grow quickly. It was the dawn of the "era of mass production of sobriety."[36]

AA was reaching into new areas of the country. The drunks who had traveled to Akron to put themselves under Smith's care were returning home and starting new groups. There were few overnight successes. It took Earl T. two years to make any progress in Chicago. Archie T. was struggling to reestablish himself in Detroit when a nonalcoholic friend offered to let him hold a meeting in the basement of her home. Some of the most successful AA ambassadors were traveling salesmen. The New York office thought long and hard about whether to turn over a list of contacts in the South to Irwin M., a large and volatile salesman of venetian blinds. But the urgency of answering these calls for help finally persuaded Wilson to give Irwin his chance. "Then we waited— but not for long," Wilson recalled. "Irwin ran them down, every single one, with his home crashing tornado technique. . . . He had cracked the territory wide open and had started or stimulated many a group." A newspaperman known only as Larry J. arrived in Houston from Cleveland and wrote a series of stories about AA for the *Houston Press*. The

Houston group included several members who later helped start new groups: Ed, who launched a meeting in Austin; Army Sergeant Roy, who made a beginning in Tampa and Los Angeles; and Esther, who started a group in Dallas.[37]

In February 1940, John D. Rockefeller Jr. announced his support for AA. He had long had a deep interest in the alcohol problem and had been a strong supporter of Prohibition, until it became clear that it was not the solution. When he had first learned of AA in 1938, he had agreed to contribute $5,000, which was used to provide financial support for Wilson and Smith, who were both nearly insolvent. But he had refused to go further out of concern that a large influx of money would undermine the voluntarism that he believed was AA's greatest asset. He may also have been reluctant to link his name with AA at a time when it was far from clear that the organization would survive.

With AA growing strongly in the wake of the *Plain Dealer* articles, Rockefeller invited four hundred of his business associates to attend a dinner at the Union League Club in New York to hear AA's story. Both Wilson and Smith spoke, as did several eminent nonalcoholics who were familiar with AA. Wilson also made sure that there was an AA member at every table. "What institution are you with?" a banker asked Morgan R. "Well, sir, I am not with any institution at the moment," he answered with a smile. "Nine months ago, however, I was a patient in Greystone Asylum."[38]

The AA members were disappointed when Nelson Rockefeller, who filled in because his father was ill, ended the dinner without making a strong pitch for contributions. A bank had recently foreclosed on the Wilsons' home, and they were living with friends. The Smiths were also facing the possibility of eviction. But Rockefeller announced he was donating only a thousand dollars. Far more important than money, however, was the publicity that followed the Rockefeller dinner. The Rockefellers put Wilson in touch with their public relations firm, which released a statement endorsing Alcoholics Anonymous that was carried in newspapers in the United States and around the world. One headline read "John D. Rockefeller dines toss-pots."[39]

A few weeks later, AA made national headlines again when Rollie Hemsley, a catcher for the Cleveland Indians baseball team, revealed that he was a member of AA. After Hemsley's drinking had led several teams to fire him, he was introduced to Smith in 1939 and had been attending meetings of the Akron group for about a year. When he made his announcement, he was already the focus of national attention as the catcher for the rookie sensation Bob Feller. The effect of the Rockefeller endorsement and the Hemsley revelation became apparent in a jump in the sale of *Alcoholics Anonymous.* There were also hundreds of letters from alcoholics seeking help. Their names were added to the growing list of correspondents who would later become the backbone of a national organization.

But the most important publicity was still ahead. In November 1940, Bill and Lois Wilson were living in a small room in an AA clubhouse in Manhattan when they learned that one of the country's biggest magazines, the *Saturday Evening Post*, was planning a story about AA. The news was tremendously exciting, but they had been disappointed before when a promised story in *Reader's Digest* never came to fruition. There was also a danger that the publicity might be bad. The reporter, Jack Alexander, was very skeptical after his first encounter with AA members. The four men were "good-looking and well-dressed," and he was not sure he believed their "horrendous" drinking stories. "I had a strong suspicion that my leg was being pulled. They had behaved like a bunch of actors sent out by some Broadway casting company."

Alexander didn't know what to make of Wilson's excessive candor as he talked about his drinking and his many errors of judgment since. "We gave him our records, opened the books . . . fixed up interviews with A.A.s of every description, and finally showed him the A.A. sights from New York and Philadelphia all the way to Chicago via Akron and Cleveland," Wilson recalled. At first, Alexander believed that Wilson was "either incredibly naive or a bit stupid." By the time he finished his research, he was convinced that AA was what it purported to be, and his article was set to run as the lead story on March 1, 1941.[40]

The March issue of the *Saturday Evening Post* created a nearly instantaneous response when it became available at newsstands on February 24. The appeals for help exceeded even Wilson's expectations. "By mail and telegram a deluge of pleas for help and orders for the book

Alcoholics Anonymous, first in hundreds and then in thousands, hit Box 658," Wilson wrote.

> Pawing at random through the incoming mass of heartbreaking appeals, we found ourselves crying. What in the world could we do with them? . . . So we rounded up every A.A. woman and every A.A. wife who could use a typewriter. The upper floor of the Twenty-Fourth Street Club was converted into an emergency headquarters.

(At a time when all secretaries were women, it was assumed that no man could type.)

New people started showing up at AA meetings. In New York, the attendance at the clubhouse swelled to 150 just ten days after the Alexander article appeared, and additional meetings were scheduled for the newcomers. The first New Jersey group saw its membership double by the end of March. New groups were forming every day, and every night AA members set out to meet with the men and women who had asked for help. The membership of AA had reached two thousand in early 1941, more than doubling in the previous year. "We thought this was good going," Wilson said. But six thousand alcoholics joined over the next ten months.[41]

There were still important issues to be resolved. The Big Book provided a twelve-step program of recovery, but it did not say how AA would be organized. What it did say seemed to invite chaos: "We are not an organization in the conventional sense of the word. There are no fees or dues whatsoever. The only requirement for membership is a desire to stop drinking." AA was not entirely without structure. To encourage the fund-raising envisioned by Wilson's plans, a nonprofit organization, the Alcoholic Foundation, was organized in 1938. Because a board of trustees made up of alcoholics would not inspire confidence in potential donors, it was agreed that a majority of the board would be nonalcoholics. This decision would cause problems later, when Wilson and Smith decided that AA members must control the future of the organization.[42]

The Alcoholic Foundation played no role in the day-to-day operation of the AA office in New York City. Wilson provided the leadership
there, staying in close contact with Smith. In their view, the business
of the office was to help the people who were organizing groups by
offering advice, not telling them what to do. They eventually developed
a standard response to all requests for guidance. "Of course, you are at
perfect liberty to handle this matter any way you please," it read. "But
the majority experience in A.A. does seem to suggest . . ." The "take it
or leave it" attitude of the early Akron group was transformed into an
invitation to experiment.[43]

Wilson and Smith were well aware that there were dangers to such
an approach. Their members were drunks, and the overwhelming
majority had only just stopped drinking. They were physically shaky
and troubled by emotional problems. "[T]he alcoholic is an extreme
example of self-will run riot," the Big Book observed. In the absence of
central authority, AA members engaged in many bloody battles over
group policies. "A.A. didn't start or grow in unity. A.A. started in riots,"
Snyder said. One of the first fights occurred in the Cleveland group
just a few months after its founding, and Snyder was at the center of
the controversy. The Cleveland group owed its very existence to his
relentless pursuit of new members, but many of the men he had helped
were uncomfortable with his efforts to attract publicity.[44]

Snyder was distributing flyers for his talks at social clubs that read,
"Clarence Snyder of Alcoholics Anonymous will speak on this new
cure for Alcoholism." He was also trying to get a weekly show on a local radio station. His promotional efforts were so aggressive that some
Cleveland AA members believed he was getting paid for his efforts.
Things came to a head in the weeks after the publication of the Elrick
Davis articles in the *Plain Dealer*. A secret ballot was taken, and Snyder was expelled from the membership. The vote was not unanimous,
however. Forty members joined Snyder in founding a second Cleveland meeting. That meeting was only a few weeks old when some of its
members seceded to form a third.[45]

Many groups were also adopting policies that appeared to conflict with AA principles. In its opening pages, the Big Book said, "The
only requirement for membership is an honest desire to stop drinking." When the Alcoholic Foundation asked groups to describe their

"protective" regulations, it compiled a list that was "a mile long" and included many restrictions on membership. "We were resolved to admit nobody to A.A. but that hypothetical class of people we termed 'pure alcoholics,'" an early member explained.

> Except for their guzzling, and the unfortunate results thereof, [pure alcoholics] could have no other complications. So beggars, tramps, asylum inmates, prisoners, queers, plain crackpots, and fallen women were definitely out. Yes sir, we'd cater only to pure and respectable alcoholics!

Early AA members were acutely aware that their lives depended on AA and were prepared to do anything to protect it. "Everybody was scared witless that something or somebody would capsize the boat and dump us all back into the drink," the "old-timer" explained. "We were grim because we felt our lives and homes were threatened. . . . Intolerant, you say? . . . Yes, we were intolerant."[46]

But for every member who trembled at the sight of a newcomer who didn't seem to fit, there was another alcoholic who wanted to save the world. Wilson believed that sober alcoholics were especially prone to crusading:

> How natural that was, since most alcoholics are bankrupt idealists. Nearly every one of us had wished to do great good, perform great deeds, and embody great ideals. We are all perfectionists who, failing perfection, have gone to the other extreme and settled for the bottle and the blackout. Providence, through A.A., had brought us within reach of our highest expectations. So why shouldn't we share our way of life with everyone?

But that passion often brought them to grief. In one town, one of the super-promoters who appear so often in AA history managed to convince his neighbors that they should build "a great big alcoholic center." The promoter created three corporations to run the project, making himself president of all. He promulgated sixty-one rules and regulations to ensure that things ran smoothly. For a while, they did, but eventually the initiative collapsed. The repentant promoter proposed a final rule: "Don't take yourself too damn seriously."[47]

The fears about the survival of AA slowly disappeared. In seven years, its membership grew from a hundred to twenty-four thousand. Group members still fought, but when their differences could not be reconciled, the group didn't die. The minority party started scouting for a location, and a new group opened. Members joked that all you needed to start a group was "a grievance and a coffee pot."

In any other organization, this might have led to disintegration. But the same fear that made early AA members overprotective was also a source of strength. Drunks who wanted to get sober only had one place to go. So few were willing to push their objections to the point where they threatened the organization. As Wilson explained, recognizing the importance of AA in his life, the alcoholic becomes willing to put aside his own views:

> Realization dawns that he is but a small part of a great whole; that no personal sacrifice is too great for preservation of the Fellowship. He learns that the clamor of desires and ambitions within him must be silenced whenever these could damage the group. It becomes plain that the group must survive or the individual will not.

This is the reason that the compromise over the role of religion in AA was reached in only a few months. Unity was a matter of life or death for AA members. "We stay whole, or A.A. dies," Wilson wrote.[48]

As AA's membership grew, its finances improved. Since AA did not collect dues, the New York office urged members to make voluntary donations. The response was disappointing. "We were astounded to find that we were as tight as bark on a tree," Wilson said. But following the publication of the Jack Alexander article in the *Saturday Evening Post* in the spring of 1941, sales of the Big Book began to climb, and it became a reliable source of income for both AA, which had self-published the book, and the cofounders, who were given a share of the royalties. Although Wilson and Smith received only a hundred dollars per month in the beginning, the sales of the book would eliminate their financial woes. AA began to expand its communications. In 1944, six members began publishing a newsletter, the *Grapevine*, to communicate with other AAs around the country, as well as with those who were serving overseas during World War II. It soon became an official publication, *AA Grapevine*.[49]

In April 1946, Wilson used the *AA Grapevine* to outline twelve "traditions" to guide AA. He described them as traditions because they had emerged from seven years of experience in dealing with the conflicts encountered by AA groups and the organization as a whole. "Nobody invented Alcoholics Anonymous. It grew. Trial and error has produced a rich experience. Little by little we have been adopting the lessons of that experience," Wilson said. He emphasized that he was not proposing rules. AA should always be pragmatic:

> Should we ever harden too much the letter might crush the spirit. We could victimize ourselves by petty rules and prohibitions; we could imagine that we had said the last word. We might even be asking alcoholics to accept our rigid ideas or stay away. May we never stifle progress like that!

On the other hand, Wilson thought the development of AA had reached a point where it needed to adopt guiding principles to address issues that would arise in the future. "They involve relations of the A.A. to his group, the relation of his group to Alcoholics Anonymous as a whole, and the place of Alcoholics Anonymous in that troubled sea called Modern Society," he said. "Terribly relevant is the problem of our basic structure and our attitude toward these ever pressing questions of leadership, money and authority." Wilson then presented his suggestions, "An Alcoholics Anonymous Tradition of Relations—Twelve Points to Assure Our Future."[50]

Several years later, Wilson wrote a "short form" of the "twelve traditions":

1. Our common welfare should come first; personal recovery depends upon A.A. unity.
2. For our group purpose there is but one ultimate authority—a loving God as He may express Himself in our group conscience.

3. The only requirement for A.A. membership is a desire to stop drinking.

4. Each group should be autonomous except in matters affecting other groups or A.A. as a whole.

5. Each group has but one primary purpose—to carry its message to the alcoholic who still suffers.

6. An A.A. group ought never to endorse, finance or lend the A.A. name to any related facility or outside enterprise, lest problems of money, property, and prestige divert us from our primary purpose.

7. Every A.A. group ought to be fully self-supporting, declining outside contributions.

8. Alcoholics Anonymous should remain forever non-professional, but our service centers may employ special workers.

9. A.A., as such ought never to be organized; but we may create service boards or committees directly responsible to those they serve.

10. Alcoholics Anonymous has no opinion on outside issues; hence the A.A. name ought never to be drawn into public controversy.

11. Our public relations policy is based on attraction rather than promotion; we need always maintain personal anonymity at the level of press, radio and films.

12. Anonymity is the spiritual foundation of all our traditions, ever reminding us to place principles before personalities.[51]

Even as the twelve traditions were published for the first time, one important organizational issue remained. AA was growing quickly in the years after World War II. An average of 17,000 drunks joined annually after 1946, bringing the total to 111,000 members in over 4,000 groups in 1951. But the organization of AA was becoming decrepit and dysfunctional. It was still governed by the Alcoholic Foundation. The board still played an important role: it supervised a growing staff that was soon shipping eight tons of literature monthly, oversaw the *AA Grapevine*, and acted as the voice of AA on the few occasions that it was necessary (usually stating that AA had no opinion).

But the board was not accountable to AA members. It nominated and elected its own members. Although AA members served on the board, its charter provided that they would never be the majority. This was not a serious problem as long as Wilson and Smith continued to lead the organization. But what would happen when they were gone? At times, even the founders had struggled to control their tempestuous membership. Wilson doubted AA members would follow the leadership of nonalcoholics. In 1945, he began to push the idea of creating a General Service Conference consisting of alcoholics chosen by the membership to direct the future of AA.

Wilson's proposal of a General Service Conference precipitated five years of often vitriolic debate among the leaders of AA. Almost no one except Wilson thought changes were necessary. The board members were nearly unanimous in believing they were doing a good job and were capable of meeting the challenges ahead. The alcoholic members were the most adamant in their views. The board was supported by many of the old-timers in the major cities who were still in control of AA affairs there and did not welcome the creation of a conference that they might not be able to influence. Matters were made worse by Wilson's characteristically bullheaded approach, which alienated potential allies. The bitterness between Wilson and his critics grew so great in 1948 that his announcement that he was undertaking a tour of AA groups around the United States led the board and its supporters to suspect he was recruiting for a potential coup d'état. It convened a meeting of old-timers from around the country who reaffirmed their support for the status quo. Even this show of strength would probably not have been enough to stymie Wilson if he had had the support of Smith. But Dr. Bob was dubious about the idea of the conference. He urged Wilson not to force the issue.

A peaceful resolution of the conference issue was finally reached in 1950, when AA held its first convention in Cleveland. More than three thousand sober alcoholics traveled to the city that had played such an important role in the growth of AA. Cleveland was also close to Akron, and Smith, who was suffering from advanced prostate cancer, would have been unable to attend if the convention had been held anywhere else. Cleveland cab drivers sang the praises of the sober conventioneers, and the good feeling carried through the three days of proceedings. On the second day, Wilson presented the Twelve Traditions for a vote of the membership. Although he asked for debate, there was none, and the traditions were adopted by a unanimous standing vote. The next day, both founders delivered addresses. Smith's weakened condition was apparent, and his close friends knew that his short speech would be his last. "There are two or three things that flash into my mind on which it would be fitting to lay a little emphasis," he said.

> Let's not louse it all up with Freudian complexes and things that are interesting to the scientific mind, but have very little to do with our actual A.A. work. Our Twelve Steps, when simmered down to the last, resolve themselves into the words "love" and "service." We understand what love is and we understand what service is. So let's bear those two things in mind.

Exhausted, Smith left the stage and was driven back to Akron, leaving Wilson to close the convention.[52]

It was Bernard Smith, a trustee of the Alcoholic Foundation, who finally persuaded the other members of the board to turn over control of AA to its members. Smith was a businessman who had been quick to see that Wilson's plan incorporated the best principles of corporate governance. His appointment as chair of a board committee to consider the creation of a conference put him in a position to persuade others to adopt it on a trial basis.

One obstacle remained. Wilson knew that Smith's agreement was essential to win support for the conference from AA members. After the Cleveland convention, he traveled to Akron to make a final pitch. He met Smith in the home where he had been a guest during those crucial months in 1935. There had been a lot of sadness there recently. Anne Smith had died a year earlier, and it was obvious to both men that Bob was in his final days. Wilson spoke plainly about the future of AA after the founders were gone. If they died without endorsing the conference, AA members would assume that they wanted the Alcoholic Foundation to run things. The least they could do was call the first conference and let the representatives decide whether they wanted to take over. Bob Smith agreed. "Bill, it *has* to be A.A.'s decision, not ours," Smith said. "Let's call that conference."[53]

In April 1951, AA members who had been elected by their fellow alcoholics at mass meetings around the country gathered in New York as delegates to the first General Service Conference. They were taken on a tour of headquarters and introduced to the trustees of the Alcoholic Foundation. Then, they settled down to business. The conference charter gave the delegates real authority: by a two-thirds vote, they could issue orders to the trustees, and a simple majority could deliver a strong suggestion that would be difficult to ignore. The conference was also given the power to veto nominations to the Alcoholic Foundation. The delegates began to exercise their authority almost immediately, making a number of decisions that were at odds with the views of the trustees and staff. The success of the first conference was reassuring to all. "They were proving as never before that A.A.'s Tradition Two was correct," Wilson wrote. "Our group conscience could safely act as the sole authority and sure guide for Alcoholics Anonymous."[54]

Smith died before the meeting of the General Service Conference. He and Wilson had said their final good-byes in Akron. Wilson wrote:

> I went down the steps and then turned to look back. Bob stood in the doorway, tall and upright as ever. Some color had come back into his cheeks, and he was carefully dressed in a light gray suit. This was my partner, the man with whom I had never had a hard word. The wonderful, old, broad smile was on his face as he said almost jokingly, "Remember, Bill, let's not louse this thing up. Let's keep it simple!"

Smith had wanted AA to decide its own future. Now it had.[55]

CHAPTER EIGHT

Rise of the Sober Drunk

IN THE WINTER OF 1945, director Billy Wilder took a seat in the back of a theater in Santa Barbara, California, and waited to hear how the audience would react during the first preview of his new film, *The Lost Weekend.* The movie was based on a best-selling novel by Charles Jackson that told the story of five days in the life of an alcoholic, Don Birnam. Wilder had bought the book at the Chicago train station and had read it twice by the time he arrived home in Los Angeles. "Not only did I know it was going to make a good picture, I also knew that the guy who was going to play the drunk was going to get the Academy Award," he said later.[1] Wilder, who was just beginning his career as one of Hollywood's leading writers and directors, knew a good story when he saw one. But the movie had been nothing but trouble since its completion. The censorship boards that existed in many states were insisting on cuts to protect the public from what they saw as shocking scenes of alcoholic depravity. Their British counterparts forced Paramount Pictures to delete the film's climax—Birnam's attack of delirium tremens. The liquor industry was so fearful that the movie would fuel a resurgence of prohibitionist sentiment that it offered to buy it for $5 million.[2]

Wilder and producer Charles Brackett, who had cowritten the screenplay, were nevertheless unprepared for what they heard that night in Santa Barbara. In an early scene, Birnam's brother, Wick, discovers that Don has hidden a bottle of whiskey by tying a string around the neck and hanging it outside a window. "How did it get there?" Wick demands. "I suppose it dropped from some cloud. Or someone was bouncing it against this wall and it got stuck?" The audience members burst into laughter. Most departed before the end, leaving comment cards that called the movie "disgusting" and "boring." Sitting in their car later, Wilder told Brackett the film was now his problem—he was moving on. "If they would have given me the five million, I would have burned the negative," Wilder recalled.[3]

That would have been a mistake. The audience was reacting not to the substance of the story but the clash between a temporary score that suggested a lighthearted comedy and the tragedy of the story line. People didn't know whether to laugh or cry. When new music was added that featured the spooky oscillations of the theremin, one of the first electronic musical instruments, the mood of the film changed dramatically. At a preview in San Francisco that ended well after midnight, no one left early and the audience was "positively limp" by the end. The movie opened to rave reviews, and the box office boomed in response to an ad campaign that promised, "The amazing novel you whispered about rocks the screen with its daring!" Several months later at the Academy Awards, actor Ray Milland received the Oscar for best actor. What Wilder had not foreseen was that *Lost Weekend* would also sweep the awards for best picture, best director, and best screenplay.[4]

Lost Weekend appeared at a moment when attitudes toward alcohol and alcoholics were in flux. Americans had abandoned their "noble experiment" of banning the sale of alcohol, but they lacked a clear vision for how to deal with the problems that led to Prohibition. The ancient stigma against alcoholics remained strong in the minds of average Americans as well as those of the scientists and medical professionals whose help drunks desperately needed. There were also glimmers of change. A review of popular literature during the opening decades of the twentieth century shows that there was a steady decline in the number of articles reflecting the view that alcoholism was the result of moral weakness. With the rapid growth of medicine and greater popular acceptance of the importance of science for explaining all aspects of modern life, there was an opportunity to reconsider the plight of the alcoholic.

Lost Weekend contributed to this change. Charles Jackson's novel portrayed the life of an alcoholic with scalding realism. To ensure its accuracy, he had interviewed doctors at Bellevue Hospital. He wouldn't have gone to Bellevue at all if he had been able to remember his two previous visits as a patient in the alcoholism ward. He had been sober for six years when he began writing his novel, and it documented in great detail the depths of alcoholism. In its first five years, the book sold almost a half-million copies and was translated into fourteen languages. The movie reached an even wider audience.

The movie did more than titillate. A poll conducted among New York University students who had seen it revealed that 78 percent believed alcoholism was an illness that required specialized treatment. Two decades later, Selden Bacon, the director of the Rutgers University Center of Alcohol Studies, would look back at the publication of *Lost Weekend* as a turning point. "Since Charles Jackson wrote the book in 1944, a great change has occurred in the attitude of most Americans toward alcoholism—a change that made possible the first really constructive steps toward control of the problem," he wrote. Like Jackson, many of the men and women who were responsible for that change were sober drunks.[5]

Lost Weekend was still flying off the shelves of bookstores on October 3, 1944, when a new organization, the National Committee for Education on Alcoholism (NCEA), announced that it was opening an office in New York City. It was the first step in what would become a far-reaching campaign to sell the public on three key ideas:

1. Alcoholism is a disease and the alcoholic is a sick person.
2. The alcoholic can be helped and is worth helping.
3. This is a public health problem and a public responsibility.

In its initial press release, NCEA acknowledged that it had a mountain to climb. "The alcoholic is a perennial problem-child," it said. "No one knows what ails him or why he acts as he does. He is generally regarded at best as a willful nuisance, at worst as a vicious criminal." But this idea was mistaken. "Actually, he is suffering from a terrible illness: the disease of alcoholism." There were at least three million alcoholics in the United States, the NCEA said. An assistant surgeon general had described it as "America's Public Health Problem No. 4," and the problem was going to grow. The Allies were now marching toward

Berlin, and there was every reason to believe that the disruptions of the postwar period would lead to more drinking. There was a solution. "The phenomenal success of Alcoholics Anonymous, with over 12,000 rehabilitated alcoholics in its membership, proves this point," the NCEA said.[6]

These were bold words for a fledgling organization. Calling alcoholism a disease and pointing to the success of AA, which had been virtually unknown to the public just a few years earlier, was not going to change things. "[P]eople persist in regarding alcoholism as a moral issue rather than as a health problem," the NCEA admitted. But it had a plan. "Our specific program includes: lectures on alcoholism, the distribution of literature, the formation of local committees all over the country, and the establishment by them, with the aid of the National Committee, of information centers or clinics in their communities." It also had institutional support from the Center of Alcohol Studies that had recently been established at Yale University (later at Rutgers) to encourage scientific research into alcohol and the problems that it caused. NCEA boasted an impressive advisory board that included some experienced alcohol researchers, public health officials, religious leaders, and a couple of celebrities—author Dorothy Parker and actress Mary Pickford. "The founder and co-founder of Alcoholics Anonymous" were also listed, although they were not identified. The names of Bill Wilson and Dr. Robert Smith appeared further down the list without affiliations.[7]

The biggest thing the NCEA had going for it was its executive director, Marty Mann. It was somewhat surprising that the new organization was headed by a woman. While women had been leaders in the fight for Prohibition and female suffrage, the prevailing view in American society was still that women should be wives and mothers. It was probably shocking to many reading the NCEA press release to learn that Mann was "a recovered alcoholic and an early member of Alcoholics Anonymous." The prejudice against alcoholics was strong, but society judged women alcoholics more harshly than men. Many assumed they were prostitutes.[8]

One of Mann's greatest qualifications for her job was simply that she was the first-born daughter of a wealthy Chicago family that could trace its roots back to the Puritans. She had attended elite girls' schools, completing her education with a year at Miss Nixon's School in Florence. When she returned, she was introduced to high society at a debutante ball. Her upper-class breeding was apparent during thousands of public appearances over the next twenty-five years:

> Onto the stage strode a tall (five-foot, eight-inch), handsome, elegant, self-assured woman, her carriage erect and graceful. As one reporter said, "Any woman would have known that her gown of soft gray wool combined with knit came straight from an exclusive designer." Wearing a dramatic hat in the fashion of the day, her short blondish hair in a stylish cut, blue-green eyes snapping, Marty stepped to the microphone.

The woman was a lady.[9]

Mann had also been a terrible drunk. She had always been a handful. "Anyone who knew me could testify that I had been afflicted with a little too much of that commodity known as willpower," she said. In her late teens, Mann turned her enormous energies to drinking. Like all alcoholics, she initially enjoyed a high tolerance for alcohol that allowed her to drink her friends under the table and then drive them safely home at the end of the evening. She married and divorced, moved to New York where she started a career in magazine journalism, and two years later, left for London where she opened and ran a successful photography studio.[10]

By 1932, however, Mann was an alcoholic who was drinking up to two quarts of scotch a day when she could afford it. She attempted suicide once and may have been trying again when she fell out of a second-story window onto a stone terrace, suffering injuries to her face and hip that would bother her for the rest of her life. On her return to the United States, she was carried from the *Queen Mary* on a stretcher because she was too drunk to walk. She spent two years in hospitals and sanitariums seeking a cure for her problem before a psychiatrist gave her a manuscript copy of *Alcoholics Anonymous*. On April 11, 1939, at the age of thirty-four, she attended her first AA meeting at the Wilsons' Brooklyn home. Although she wasn't the first woman member of AA and suffered several brief relapses, Mann was the first AA woman to stay sober.

Mann learned a lot about alcoholism over the next two years. Like most AA members, she did not have a job when she got sober. So following her release from the sanitarium, she had a lot of time on her hands. AA newcomers were given a sponsor who guided them through the twelve steps. Later, AA would recommend that sponsors be the same sex as the persons they sponsored. With no woman available to sponsor Mann, Bill Wilson took on the job. Mann spent a lot of time with Wilson and accompanied him on a trip to Akron where she met Bob Smith. She also worked with more than a hundred women alcoholics during her first year of sobriety but failed to help any of them get sober. Mann was not discouraged, but she had fewer hours to give to AA after she finally found a job as a publicist at Macy's in the fall of 1940.

A chance meeting during lunch with her coworkers started Mann thinking about leading a campaign to educate the public about alcoholism. She noticed Grace Allen Bangs of the *New York Herald Tribune* sitting at a table nearby. Bangs had tried to help Mann get a job during her drinking days, but she did not recognize the young woman who walked over to say hello. "What in heaven's name has happened to you?" Bangs asked. "You have lost at least twenty pounds and you look ten years younger."[11]

Bangs listened closely as Mann told her story. Her son was an alcoholic, and she had searched in vain for information about what was wrong with him. "It's fabulous how little I know," Bangs said. "There must be thousands of mothers and wives like me. Marty, you must tell them." Bangs was a woman of considerable influence. As the head of the *Herald Tribune*'s Club Service Bureau, she knew the leaders of all the women's clubs in the city, including women of great wealth and position. "We should have a primer on alcoholism, pamphlets, an information center. We should organize a committee that will find a way to finance it," Bangs said. Mann did not encourage her at first. She was just getting back on her feet and would soon leave Macy's for another job.[12]

As time passed, Mann began to give serious consideration to the idea. She was aware of a number of favorable developments. In 1940, she and Wilson attended a meeting of a new group, the Research Council on Problems of Alcohol (RCPA). Founded five years after the repeal of Prohibition, the original goal of the RCPA was to undertake scientific research on a broad range of problems created by alcohol. By 1940, however, it had narrowed its focus to "the disease of alcoholism and the alcoholic psychoses." At the same time, it indicated that it would advocate solutions as well as conduct research. "The Research Council on Problems of Alcohol hopes to take a place with the public health agencies now combating tuberculosis, syphilis, poliomyelitis, cancer, and other major diseases," the RCPA director Harold H. Moore declared. These words had special meaning for Mann. She had contracted tuberculosis when she was fourteen and knew that prejudice against TB patients was once widespread. Mann was familiar with the important role that the National Tuberculosis Association had played in eliminating the stigma.[13]

Funding problems prevented the RCPA from fulfilling its ambitious mission, but it attracted others with the same goal. One was Dwight Anderson, an expert in the new field of public relations who became a consultant to the RCPA and the head of its committee on publicity. Anderson was an alcoholic who had stopped drinking in 1932. When he was admitted to the psychiatric clinic of New York Hospital, he was fifty and addicted to the barbiturates that he took to keep from drinking. The attending physician described him as "a disheveled man of past 60, with a bad heart and an incurable mental disorder." Only one young psychiatrist, Dr. William B. Cline, believed there was any hope for him. Over the next two months, he helped Anderson identify his psychological problems. Unlike many psychiatrists, however, Cline did not believe that Anderson could begin drinking again. "Sooner or later, you will find yourself on the point of taking a drink," he warned. "Stop for a moment and answer this question, 'Just what do I expect to accomplish by taking this drink?'" The question had helped him stay sober for eighteen years.[14]

In 1942, Anderson wrote an article, "Alcohol and Public Opinion," that looked at the problem of alcoholism from his perspective as a public relations man and alcoholic. From the PR perspective, things couldn't be worse. There was no social group that viewed the drunk with any sympathy. Everyone assumed that alcoholism was incurable, including doctors. But as a sober drunk, Anderson knew that this fatal diagnosis ignored the facts. Since the days of Benjamin Rush, there had been doctors who recognized that alcoholism was treatable. Anderson cited recent statistics showing that as many as half of drunks could quit drinking or at least reduce the amount they drank. Society had reached an impasse. "The expert awaits a changed public; the public awaits a change in the expert. The result is a stalemate," he wrote.[15]

Anderson believed the stalemate could be broken once the public realized that the alcoholic drank because he was sick. Several key propositions followed:

> Sickness implies the possibility of treatment. It also implies that, to some extent at least, the individual is not responsible for his condition. It further implies that it is worth while to try to help the sick one. Lastly, it follow from all this that the problem is a responsibility of the medical profession, of the constituted health authorities, and of the public in general.

The tools for delivering this message were at hand. "When the dissemination of these ideas is begun through the existing media of public information, press, radio and platform, which will consider them as news, a new public attitude can be shaped," Anderson wrote. It had been done before in the fight against other "incurable" illnesses, including TB, cancer, syphilis, and mental illness. He continued, "Once the opposite concepts were established, it became a thrilling adventure to help to save the health, lives or minds of people by participation in these enterprises."[16]

Mann was stirred by Anderson's words, but she hesitated to answer his call to action. She had found a job writing radio scripts for the American Society of Composers, Authors and Publishers and was quickly promoted to director of research. After years of joblessness, she was reluctant to give up security, and it seemed clear that it would be necessary to start a new organization. The prospects of such a group seemed shaky at best considering the RCPA's financial struggles. On the other hand, there was an opportunity to do for alcoholics what Dorothea Dix had done for the mentally ill.

One night in February 1944, Mann found herself unable to sleep. At 3 a.m., she went to her typewriter and wrote the first description of the NCEA. She discussed the plan with Wilson, who was supportive, but told her that obtaining the sponsorship of a scientific organization was crucial. She also consulted a small group of supporters that included Anderson, Bangs, and Dr. Ruth Fox, who had turned to Mann for advice about her alcoholic husband. The committee suggested that she approach the RCPA. The group was willing to hire her as a speaker, but Mann had set her sights higher.

Fox then urged Mann to contact E. M. Jellinek, the director of the new Center of Alcohol Studies at Yale. Jellinek had become interested in alcoholism while working as the director of research for the United Fruit Company in Honduras. Trained as a biometrician, Jellinek's job was to analyze medical statistics, discerning trends and recommending priorities for treatment. When he discovered that alcoholism was rampant among the employees of United Fruit, he began to collect all the information he could about the problem. This led to a job with the RCPA and then to Yale, where he cofounded the Center of Alcohol Studies. The main work of the center in the early years involved research on alcoholism, including physiological, social, psychological, and historical studies. The center had begun publishing a *Quarterly Journal of Studies on Alcohol*, providing a platform for disseminating scientific studies of alcoholism for the first time since the demise of the *Quarterly Journal of Inebriety*. It also launched a monthlong summer school to educate anyone whose work involved alcoholics. In its first seven years, a faculty composed of physicians, physiologists, attorneys, clergy, and AA members delivered lectures to over a thousand students.

The Center of Alcohol Studies provided services directly to alcoholics at clinics in Hartford and New Haven. Patients received individual counseling and were encouraged to attend AA meetings. Ray McCarthy, the executive director of the Yale Plan Clinic, had pioneered a new form of therapy in which patients met in small groups to listen to short talks on some aspect of alcoholism and then discuss the issues among themselves. McCarthy, who was a sober alcoholic, had been trained by Richard Peabody, a drunk who worked as a therapist following his recovery at the Emmanuel Church clinic. McCarthy believed that group therapy helped overcome the alcoholic's isolation and made it possible for him to recognize the nature of his problem. He also believed that sober alcoholics with proper training could play an important role as therapists. The Yale Plan Clinics treated more than five hundred patients in their first two years of operation, a period when government was spending almost nothing on alcoholism.

Jellinek responded enthusiastically when Mann described her plan for an education campaign. He traveled to New York City the next day to meet with Mann, her planning committee, and Wilson. He offered to pay all the expenses of the NCEA for the first two years and to continue to provide support after that. To educate herself about alcoholism, Mann began commuting to New Haven to work with the staff of the Center of Alcohol Studies, living with "Bunky" Jellinek and his wife during the week. In the summer, she joined eighty-eight other students at the second Yale Summer School of Alcohol Studies. Almost half of her classmates were ministers, and not all were sympathetic to alcoholics. Mann overheard a comment by one clergyman during a class trip to an AA meeting in New Haven. "If I had my way, I'd put them all on a boat and sink it," he said. She spent several evenings trying to convince another student, Mrs. D. Leigh Calvin, that alcoholism was a disease. Finally, Mrs. Calvin, president of the WCTU, agreed. Jellinek had hired the right woman.[17]

The press release announcing the creation of the NCEA made a big splash in October 1944. All nine New York City newspapers carried the story, and the three national wire services spread the news throughout the country. Within days, editorials began to appear welcoming "A New Rational Solution" to the problem of alcoholism. The favorable publicity that AA received since the publication of Jack Alexander's 1941 profile in the *Saturday Evening Post* undoubtedly helped draw attention to the new group, which appeared to be a logical next step toward a broader understanding of the problem. The fact that a novel about alcoholism was currently on the best-seller list didn't hurt either. A decision by Mann gave the press release extra impact. Although she had adopted Dwight Anderson's key concepts for a public education campaign, making them the centerpiece of the press release, she believed that his characterization of the alcoholic as a "sick" person was not strong enough. Mann described alcoholism as a "disease" five times in her brief release. She also suggested that there was a consensus among experts supporting this view. "The fact that alcoholism is a disease rather than a moral shortcoming has been known to scientists for years," the release said.[18]

Mann was stretching the truth. Benjamin Rush and other doctors had described alcoholism as a disease in the eighteenth century. It was so regarded by the members of the American Association for the Cure of Inebriety beginning in 1870. But the scientists at the Yale Center of Alcohol Studies were unaware of the AACI and were only beginning their own research into the nature of alcoholism. Even Anderson had called it an illness, not a disease.

Mann believed that describing alcoholism as a disease was essential to countering the stigma against it. She explained later:

> I want to make alcoholism respectable! So that all those uncounted thousands who are hiding or being hidden by their families like the proverbial skeletons in the closet, may realize that they are simply very sick people and come out for help.... The shame of it all is too much for them—they'd literally rather die of this ghastly disease than admit to having it.

One of the goals of the NCEA was to establish clinics where medical professionals could diagnose alcoholism and send patients to treatment. Based on her own experience, Mann believed that AA would be far more effective in getting people sober than doctors or psychiatrists. But she thought drunks would find it easier to take their first step toward sobriety by visiting a doctor. The existence of alcoholism clinics would also be a powerful symbol. "I believe that the very presence of a clinic will emphasize and advertise to the uninitiated that alcoholism *is a disease*," Mann wrote.[19]

To get things started, the NCEA planned to form local affiliates led by prominent citizens. The launch of these groups in cities across the country was expected to generate a lot of publicity about the problem of alcoholism. The affiliates would begin by opening information offices to provide the latest facts about alcoholism to anyone who was interested, from newspaper reporters to students writing term papers. The information offices would also be a resource for alcoholics and their families, educating them about the nature of their affliction and suggesting where they might find more help.

Mann planned to spend most of her time traveling around the country making speeches and organizing local affiliates. In the beginning, she and Grace Bangs believed that socially prominent women would play an important role in her work. A women's organizing committee was formed at the same time as the NCEA to ensure that it connected with the right people in each community.

The club women turned out to be a disappointment, but they were hardly missed. The extensive newspaper coverage of NCEA produced an avalanche of mail. In addition to hundreds of letters seeking help for individuals and requests for information, there were dozens of invitations to speak. During NCEA's first year, Mann traveled 36,000 miles and delivered 106 speeches in 45 cities to 34,000 people. Fourteen of her addresses were broadcast on radio.

When there was enough support, Mann's speeches were used as the occasion to launch a local committee. An organizing committee was formed to plan for Mann's visit, scheduling a press conference soon after her arrival and arranging at least one talk a day. After her speech, Mann met with the organizers and other interested people; a temporary chair was selected and chose an executive committee that then voted to affiliate with NCEA. Five affiliates were organized in the first nine months. Mann began delivering more than two hundred speeches annually, and the number of local committees grew to thirty-nine in 1948, including state affiliates in Utah and Rhode Island. A public opinion survey suggested there had been a significant increase in the number of people who believed alcoholism was a disease. "[O]ur campaign of education of the public has helped change the opinion of more than 30 per cent of the adult population," Mann said.[20]

The NCEA had certainly had a significant impact, but so had the rapid growth of AA. Between 1945 and 1950, AA membership increased from twenty thousand to over a hundred thousand in twenty-five hundred groups. Mann was counting on their help. She was one of the founding editors of the monthly *AA Grapevine*, which began publishing shortly before the launch of NCEA. So it was no coincidence when the same issue that announced the new group also included an interview with Mann. "Why, Marty, what about us A.A.s helping?" the interviewer asked. Mann agreed. "There's no reason why they shouldn't be. It's my hope that they will, either as groups or as individuals. After all, we A.A.s are the people who understand best how misunderstood this whole thing is," she said. Many of the speeches that Mann made every year were delivered to AA groups, and she encouraged AA members to hold open meetings where committees could be formed.[21]

AA members answered Mann's call. Sober drunks played an important role on many of the executive committees that organized local committees, and when committees succeeded in opening an information office, they often hired a recovered alcoholic to run it. There were so many AA volunteers that Mann began to worry they would swamp the boat. NCEA was seeking broad support for its goals, and it promoted the fact that local committees were chaired by judges, college presidents, doctors, religious leaders, and businessmen. One AA volunteer was encouraged to take on the job of organizing an affiliate but also warned about being too prominent in the new organization. "We should have the fullest cooperation and support from A.A. members, but in order to get this with the least trouble and misunderstanding we suggested that A.A. members should be 'on tap and not on top,'" Ralph McComb Henderson, Mann's assistant, explained. There was also a danger that AA and NCEA would become so closely identified in the public mind that it would lead to confusion. Following a controversy over an NCEA fund-raising appeal in 1946, Wilson and Smith removed their names from the NCEA letterhead, and Mann stopped identifying herself publicly as an AA member.[22]

Although their independence had been clearly established, AA and NCEA still shared the goal of helping drunks, and their efforts often overlapped. They both gave the highest priority to breaking down the barriers that prevented alcoholics from receiving medical treatment in the nation's general hospitals. From the beginning, AA's leaders had believed that hospitalization was a necessary first step toward sobriety. Hospitalization was necessary because so many of the early AA members were men who had been drinking for years and were on the verge of physical collapse. They experienced delirium tremens and seizures when they were unable to get alcohol and sometimes died as a result. A hospital could also provide an opportunity for an alcoholic to think. Sober and sore, he had a chance to reflect on his life and to promise himself that he would never drink again.

The problem was that most doctors believed that alcoholism was incurable. Mann consulted eight doctors before she met Harry Tiebout, who had given her the manuscript of *Alcoholics Anonymous*. Anderson, who also consulted many doctors before he found the right one, believed that doctors were hostile to drunks because they had tried to help them and failed. They could help a man recover from a binge, but no matter how much he had suffered, he was soon drunk again. "Physicians like to feel that they have the full cooperation of the patient and are likely to resent the patient who professes one thing and does another," Dr. Dexter M. Bullard explained.[23]

General practitioners did not have the time or the training to care properly for alcoholics. But what about the specialists in the field of psychology, which had grown astronomically in the decades since the days of alienist Joseph Parrish to include thirty-five hundred psychiatrists practicing in the United States? Many were willing to use the word "illness" when writing about alcoholism, but their understanding of alcohol addiction was also superficial. Some hoped to cure the patient through counseling aimed at underlying problems that they believed had driven the man to drink. More were convinced that the alcoholic was beyond help.

Six of the doctors that Mann consulted were psychiatrists who could not find anything wrong with her and refused to accept her as a patient because they did not know what to do with "people like you." "[When] I frankly admitted under questioning that my drinking was out of control—from then on they wanted no part of me," Mann said. The psychiatrists did not have much hope for any methods of recovery. A psychiatric intern had only discouraging words for a woman who had relapsed. "Well, I see you're back here again, despite 'Alcoholics Anonymous,'" he said.[24]

With many doctors either indifferent or actually hostile toward drunks, it was inevitable that hospitals would close their doors to them. According to the NCEA, only ninety-six general hospitals in the United States were willing to treat alcoholics in 1944, and only one accepted them without an argument. "I have long since lost count of the number of times that I myself have been told, on trying to gain admission for a desperately sick alcoholic, 'This place is for sick people, not drunks,'" Mann wrote. Two of the men she was trying to save died for lack of medical care.[25]

An average of twelve thousand people were dying of alcoholism every year, including many who could have been saved if they had made it to an emergency room. Actually, the number was probably much higher because many families begged their physician to spare them the shame of an alcoholic family member by citing some other cause on the death certificate. Deaths "occurred in flop houses, boarding houses, and homes where the physician was either not called or would not respond to the call to treat a drunk," Mann said. Many drunks died in jail. "We, as a nation, are not wont to treat our sick in that fashion. . . . And yet to a great body of very sick human beings we offer only punishment for their illness. We behave as if we are still in the Middle Ages."[26]

As a result, AA and NCEA spent a lot of time trying to get drunks into the hospital. During the early years, Bob Smith succeeded in having drunks admitted to the Akron City Hospital using a diagnosis of "gastric distress." Deaconess Hospital in Cleveland opened its doors to alcoholics only after AA appealed to the trustees, who overruled the medical staff. Clarence Snyder later described the difficulty he had in securing beds at the Post-Shaker Sanitarium, a hundred-bed facility in East Cleveland. The owner, Sara Post, was desperate for patients to replace those who had recently been moved to a new state facility. Snyder promised to pay twice as much as the state, but she was reluctant. Post didn't like alcoholics and worried that they would be difficult patients. Snyder assured her they would be no more trouble than mental patients. "Most of 'em won't eat for the first few days; and if you taper 'em off of booze, they'll stay calmer than the loonies," he said.[27]

Post agreed to accept alcoholics until one day when Snyder brought in a man who was near death. The editor of the *Cleveland Press* had begged Snyder to help find the man, who was a reporter for the paper. He was found in an abandoned warehouse on skid row. It was winter, and the man was lying unconscious on a damp concrete floor, barely breathing. Snyder took him to the sanitarium, but when Post saw who it was she refused to admit him. The reporter had been married to her niece and had ruined her life, she said. Snyder said he pleaded with Post and offered more money, but she refused. Post relented only after Snyder threatened to remove all the alcoholic patients. The reporter eventually recovered and moved to Houston, where he wrote a series of stories for the *Houston Press* that were collected in AA's first educational pamphlet. He cofounded the first Houston AA meeting with an alcoholic minister he had helped rescue from skid row.

The hospitalization campaign received an important boost in 1939. Unable to find a place for one of his patients, Smith sought help from Sister Ignatia, the admitting nurse at St. Thomas Hospital in Akron. A member of the Sisters of Charity, Ignatia was a native of Ireland who had been raised to believe that drunkenness was a sin. But with the assistance of an emergency room intern, she had been helping alcoholics get treatment for several years before Smith approached her. "She was severely criticized by some of the nuns, and most of the doctors were bastards to her," a medical intern, Thomas P. Scuderi, recalled. Overcrowding was a serious problem in American hospitals during the war years, but Ignatia found a place for Smith's patient in a flower room that also served as a temporary mortuary. Although furtive in the beginning, officials at St. Thomas eventually agreed to treat alcoholics, even though most of the drunks were Protestant. A newly remodeled eight-bed ward opened in 1944 to accommodate alcoholics who began traveling to Akron from around the country.[28]

Under the direction of Sister Ignatia and Smith, St. Thomas Hospital pioneered a treatment program in which AA played an important role. New patients were assigned an AA sponsor and required to demonstrate a sincere desire to stop drinking during an interview with Sister Ignatia or another admitting clerk. Each day of the five-day program had a theme. On day two, "Realization," an AA member would guide the alcoholic through the first three steps of the AA program. The next day was devoted to "Moral Inventory." Day four was the "Day of Resolution," when the patient accepted the statement, "I can surely stay sober today"; the last day was devoted to planning for sobriety after discharge. Not many hospitals that agreed to accept alcoholics were willing to do more than detoxify them, but some worked closely with local AA groups, giving them the right to decide who would get treatment. In some large cities, drunks seeking treatment could call an AA "intergroup" for information.[29]

One of the fullest integrations of AA and a hospital recovery program occurred in the Knickerbocker Hospital, a fifty-nine-bed facility on 131st Street in Upper Manhattan. A 1914 directory of New York

City hospitals described the Knickerbocker's mission as assisting the "worthy" poor, but made it clear that alcoholics were not admitted. In 1945, the Knickerbocker dropped its ban, opening part of a nineteen-bed ward for drunks and later turning over the whole ward for that purpose. From the beginning, AA members in New York played a central role in the operation of the ward. Admissions were handled through the AA intergroup office in Manhattan, where the staff provided AA sponsors for all new patients. Even in the final months of World War II when hospitals were short-staffed, the Knickerbocker had no trouble finding sober drunks who were nurses to staff the alcoholic ward. As many as twenty AA volunteers worked as nurse's aides every week.

AA set the rules at the Knickerbocker. "No families, no friends, no business colleagues may visit the wing—unless they happen to be A.A. members," explained Mann, who continued to work closely with AA. "This gives the patient a temporary but complete release from outside worries and irritations, and plenty of time to think over his situation, and to make plans for dealing with his alcoholic problem upon release from the hospital." It also gave him time to talk to his sponsor, fellow patients, and the AA volunteers, many of whom were former patients. Women alcoholics were treated in private rooms attached to the ward, although male and female patients were not permitted to mix. After five days of treatment, the patients were released and immediately joined AA groups. More than three thousand drunks were treated in Knickerbocker Hospital during the first three years of the program.[30]

NCEA also played a significant role in expanding hospitalization. It urged its affiliates "to survey the existing facilities (if any) for the care and treatment of alcoholics" and supplied a questionnaire to be sent to find local doctors who would be willing to treat them. The next step was to determine whether the affiliate had the financial resources to open a clinic like the ones in Hartford and New Haven. NCEA estimated that it would cost approximately $26,000 annually to employ a full-time psychiatrist, a psychiatric social worker, and three support staff. If the affiliate couldn't afford a clinic, it was urged to open an information center staffed by one or two people who could refer alcoholics for treatment at local institutions. By the end of 1948, there were forty-one NCEA affiliates around the country. While none had been able to open a clinic, twenty-nine established information centers.

On the national level, NCEA tried to educate doctors by offering a discount on subscriptions to the *Quarterly Journal of Studies on Alcohol.* In 1954, just ten years after the launch of NCEA, the number of general hospitals providing emergency care to alcoholics had grown from fewer than one hundred to over three thousand. AA groups had been organized in over two hundred of them.[31]

Hospitalization was a critical issue, but there were many pressing problems. What could be done to help alcoholics who were lucky enough to still have jobs? At the time, almost every company in the country considered drunkenness grounds for immediate dismissal. The issue was so important that AA addressed employers directly in the Big Book. A chapter titled "To Employers" urged businessmen to see their alcoholic employees as individuals. While some would have to be fired, "there are many men who want to stop, and with them you can go far. Your understanding treatment of their cases will pay dividends," it said. The Big Book offered detailed instructions for confronting the employee, helping him find medical treatment, and dealing with him after he returned to work, even encouraging patience if a clearly earnest man suffered a relapse. The Big Book also recommended itself as a source of information about alcoholism that could be shared with junior executives, who might be in direct contact with the staff and in a position to help employees before they had been reported for drinking. Finally, the employer was urged to see the recovered alcoholic as a resource. "After your man has gone along without drinking for a few months, you may be able to make use of his services with other employees who are giving you the alcoholic run-around," it said.[32]

The Big Book was right in predicting that sober alcoholics would play a role in helping their coworkers get sober. Several AA members began helping coworkers in the 1940s. David M. was inspecting bullets at the Remington Arms factory in Bridgeport, Connecticut, when he began taking men to AA meetings. Later he secured a job in the personnel department, which gave him an opportunity to talk to employees who were in trouble because of their drinking. His success in saving the jobs of twenty-two alcoholic workers led him to suggest to superiors that they adopt an official policy encouraging heavy drinkers to seek help. When they rejected the idea, he approached the medical director of DuPont, the company that owned Remington Arms. Dr. George H. Gehrmann had been looking for a solution for alcoholic employees for many years and had recently attended several AA meetings. "By God, you're just the man I'm looking for," Gehrmann said. In January 1944, David M. transferred to DuPont, becoming the first person hired by a company specifically to help alcoholics. During the same period, Warren T., an AA member who worked in a shipyard, was also counseling alcoholics full-time, although in an unofficial capacity. In March 1943, he informed the AA national office that in the first four days of his new job in the personnel department, he had met with seventeen men who wanted help with their drinking problem.[33]

The Yale Center of Alcohol Studies gave strong support to these first steps. In a speech to the Economic Club of Detroit in 1946, Jellinek provided statistics to demonstrate the enormous damage that alcoholism was inflicting on industry. He estimated that there were 3 million Americans who were either alcoholics or heavy drinkers in danger of becoming alcoholics. Approximately 510,000 were unemployable, including skid-row "bums." Two million of the others were workingmen, including 1.3 million who were engaged in skilled and unskilled jobs in manufacturing, construction, and public utilities. Because each one missed an average of twenty-two days a year due to illness, the economy was losing nearly 30 million working days to alcoholism annually. Drinking caused more than four thousand accidental deaths every year. Alcoholics died twelve years sooner than nonalcoholics. Jellinek insisted the United States could do better. His most hopeful statistic was that an alcoholic could be rehabilitated for between sixty and a hundred dollars. A program that encompassed every alcoholic would entail less than a third of the social cost of alcoholism.

NCEA also focused on the problem of drunken workers. Its Chicago affiliate sponsored the First Industrial Conference on Alcoholism in 1948. Its greatest contribution to this phase of the alcoholism movement was Ralph McComb Henderson, a field secretary who traveled widely for NCEA before the Yale Center of Alcohol Studies hired him as an industrial consultant. "Lefty" Henderson was uniquely qualified for the job. He was a naturally gregarious man who had developed a successful law practice in his home state of South Dakota.

One acquaintance described him as a "bear-like man, a friendly husky St. Bernard with a twinkle in his eye." Another called him "an unmade bed." A veteran of World War I, he became the state commander of the American Legion and served as the state chairman of the South Dakota delegation to the 1940 Republican National Convention. He had become an alcoholic by then, but he joined AA soon after.[34]

Henderson traveled constantly over the next ten years, speaking to company executives and business groups about the importance of helping their alcoholic employees. He was a charismatic speaker who used his "ham-like" hands to make sweeping gestures. Selden Bacon, Jellinek's successor as head of the Yale School, called him "the most magnificent platform artist I ever saw." In 1950, Henderson and Bacon developed a program called the Yale Plan for Business and Industry that sought to convince businessmen that alcoholism was a problem that could be managed in a cost-efficient way by identifying the few problem drinkers and getting them help. It described nine steps in creating an effective program, including educating top management, assigning responsibility to an existing department, and developing a policy to decide who would be offered treatment and who would be fired. Henderson won a key battle at Allis-Chalmers, an important manufacturer of agricultural and other industrial equipment. In 1950, he and an AA member, George S., helped persuade company officials in Milwaukee to hire an alcoholism counselor who had gotten sober in AA. The company was undeterred when the counselor suffered a relapse and mentioned its program prominently in company publicity.[35]

As companies began to start employee assistance programs, the evidence of their success grew. "For 28 years, I struggled without A.A., and my results were zero. With A.A. over the past five years, I got 65 per cent [sober]," Dr. Gehrmann declared. After the Allis-Chalmers program had been under way for eight months, the company reported that fifty-one of the seventy-one employees who had been identified as alcoholics had been helped. Not all had quit drinking and joined AA, but the others were either sober or had curtailed their drinking to the point where it was not interfering with their work.[36]

✦   ✦   ✦

A sober drunk named William Swegan launched the first employee assistance program in the military in 1948. He was already an alcoholic when he joined the Army Air Force in 1939. He had lost his mother at any early age and was plagued by fear and a sense of worthlessness throughout his childhood. For a few years, drinking had allowed him to escape his problems. At twenty-one, he enlisted in an alcoholic haze, and he continued to drink heavily after he was stationed at Hickam Field in Hawaii. He was badly hung over when he awoke to the drone of airplanes on the morning of December 7, 1941. While the main force of Japanese planes focused on the nearby naval base, three waves of bombers hit Hickam, killing and wounding more than a quarter of the men in his squadron. Swegan himself was nearly killed by a bomb as he and five other men huddled in the corner of a hangar. His five closest friends—all drunks—died in the attack.

After serving in the South Pacific, Swegan returned home. He was sick with dengue fever and malaria, but he was refused admission to a Veterans Administration hospital because he was an alcoholic. His wife left him and wouldn't let him visit his daughter. He was unable to hold a job. He tried AA, but he was half the age of the men at the meeting near his hometown in Ohio, and neither he nor they believed he was old enough to be an alcoholic. Out of options, he reenlisted for the security of a warm bed and regular meals and was assigned to Mitchell Air Force Base on Long Island, New York. Swegan began attending AA meetings again in nearby Valley Stream and was finally able to stop drinking in 1948.

Soon after joining AA, Swegan began thinking about how to carry its message to others. He didn't have to look far to find alcoholic men and women. "There was an ample enough population of alcoholics in the armed forces. . . . And we were often a real problem to the majority of people around us," he wrote later. He was already working with several airmen who were hard drinkers when he approached the squadron commander with the idea of giving a speech about alcoholism. The commander "looked at me like my sanity had left me," Swegan said. Nevertheless, he agreed to the speech.[37]

The nervous airman got off to a rough start as he stood before 159 members of his squadron. "I am an alcoholic and have found a way to live a useful life without having to drink alcoholic beverages," he began.

> The whole room broke out in uproarious laughter on the spot. They knew all about how much I used to drink.... I really wanted to just crawl through the floor and disappear. But something different happened than had ever happened to me before in this kind of situation. I squared my shoulders and kept on talking.

The laughter stopped, and Swegan saw that the men were listening. Later, two quietly asked for help. "In the days that followed, two rapidly became four, and four became six, and six became eight. Something big was off and running, and I had no idea what was going to happen next," he said.[38]

Swegan discovered that his recruits preferred attending AA meetings away from the base, where they did not have to worry about speaking before superior officers. He drove the men to the Valley Stream meeting in his car, until it broke down. The whole enterprise appeared to be at risk until a member of the AA group, Yvelin Gardner, gave him the money to buy another car. Gardner, the deputy director of NCEA, recognized the importance of Swegan's work and used some of Mann's many contacts to have Swegan assigned to the chaplain's office. Swegan, who hadn't graduated from high school, was also given a scholarship to attend the Yale Summer School of Alcohol Studies to help him prepare for his new career.

Swegan was so successful with the alcoholics at Mitchell Air Force Base that he worked himself out of a job. In 1953, he was given another chance at Lackland Air Force Base outside San Antonio, Texas. Lackland was a huge facility where all enlisted personnel underwent basic training. With strong support from the chief of psychiatry, Swegan had all the resources he needed to implement a large-scale rehabilitation program. Antipsychotic drugs were prescribed when necessary, and during early recovery, patients could request Antabuse (disulfiram), the nauseant that had become available only a few years earlier. Some patients received psychotherapy in individual or group sessions. Swegan said the most important component of the program was getting patients to regularly attend AA meetings conducted by civilians off the base.

Swegan believed that the Lackland rehabilitation program was a major breakthrough, and he produced evidence to prove it. He reported the results for the first fifty patients in the *American Journal of Psychiatry*. Half were sober and successfully performing their duties, based on evaluations provided by their superior officers. Another seven had improved. Swegan estimated that it had cost the air force over a million dollars to train these men, money that would have been wasted if they had been discharged for drinking.

Swegan took his story of success on the road, traveling to the many air force bases in Texas. He also established relationships at army and navy installations in the area, and many facilities opened rehabilitation programs. In 1954, Swegan was given an opportunity to make the case for providing alcoholism treatment at air force bases worldwide. Although still a sergeant, he traveled to Washington to appear before a committee of high-ranking officers investigating the problem of alcoholism in the air force. The committee members appeared interested, but he learned later that his proposals had been rejected as "too expensive." Not long afterward, the chief of psychiatry, who had been Swegan's partner, departed, leaving Swegan without the support he needed to maintain his program. Swegan retired from the air force and took a job running a small alcoholism treatment center. By then, the beginning of a movement to help alcoholics in the workforce was apparent. At least fifty companies had stopped firing employees because they were drunks. A few years later, the first permanent military alcoholism treatment facility was established at the Long Beach Naval Station by Dr. Joseph J. Zuska, a navy captain, and Dick Jewell, a recently retired navy commander who was an AA member.

By the early 1950s, sober alcoholics had made great progress. AA had grown to over a hundred thousand members, and many were actively engaged in helping others get sober. No one had done more than Marty Mann. On the tenth anniversary of the NCEA in 1954, she listed its accomplishments in a memo to her executive committee. The word "alcoholism" hadn't even been used in the general press in 1944. Ten years later, "alcoholism [is] now fully and constantly covered in press. Every national magazine has run one or more articles on alcoholism," she wrote. AA was the only group that supported NCEA in the beginning, but now "interest [is] shown by governmental, professional, and lay groups of all sorts." Thirty-one states had established alcoholism programs. The NCEA staff had grown to include eight people working in two offices, distributing forty-two educational titles and answering two hundred pieces of correspondence per week.[39]

The members of the executive committee knew this was not the full story. Mann's organization had been experiencing hard times after it separated from the Yale Center of Alcohol Studies in 1950. Renamed the National Committee on Alcoholism, it was having difficulty replacing the funding it had received from Yale. Also questionable was her claim to have achieved "general acceptance of disease concept . . . including AMA, medical societies, some industries, press, large segments of public, State government . . . U.S. Air Force, N.Y.C. Police Force, etc."[40]

Mann was clearly exaggerating when she said the AMA was endorsing the view that alcoholism was a disease. The AMA had approved a definition of "alcoholism," but that was as far as it was willing to go. There was no agreement on what caused alcoholism. Was it a psychological condition or the manifestation of a physical process that would qualify it as a disease? As late as 1955, Harry Tiebout, Mann's psychiatrist and a strong supporter of AA, worried about the lack of evidence proving alcoholism was a disease:

> I cannot help but feel that the whole field of alcoholism is way out on a limb which any minute will crack and drop us all in a frightful mess. . . . I sometimes tremble to think of how little we have to back up our claims. We are all skating on thin ice.

If the disease concept was discredited, the medical treatment of alcoholism might fall with it.[41]

But scientists were already engaged in research that would support the argument for treating alcoholism as a disease. Jellinek was perhaps the most influential. He had first entered the alcoholism field when he was hired to conduct a survey of all the existing scientific literature on the subject. After he joined the Yale Center of Alcohol Studies, he began his own research. In 1945, an AA group in New

York's Greenwich Village sent him the results of a questionnaire that it had created and distributed through the *AA Grapevine* to determine whether AA members shared characteristics of age, home environment, and drinking histories that might be statistically significant enough to draw some conclusions about the nature of alcoholism. Jellinek's analysis of the data was published in 1946, suggesting the existence of phases in the drinking history of alcoholics. He immediately began revising the questionnaire, and a new survey was sent to every AA group with a request that it be distributed to the members. "[O]ne of the chief hopes and expectancies is that the data . . . will provide a new and still more complete set of warning signals by which potential alcoholics will determine how far along the road they have come," the *AA Grapevine* said.[42]

Two thousand AA members completed the questionnaire, and the new data was published in 1952 by a committee of the World Health Organization (WHO). WHO had established an alcoholism subcommittee of its Expert Committee on Mental Health, and its first act was to recommend that WHO consider classifying alcohol as an addictive drug. Jellinek's new article, "Phases of Alcohol Addiction," provided support for such an investigation and presented the strongest evidence to date that alcoholism was a disease by describing in detail a process by which a normal drinker became an alcoholic.

According to Jellinek, in the pre-alcoholic phase, the incipient drunk was similar to other heavy drinkers, progressing from occasional to constant drinking for relief of anxiety and other personal problems. At the beginning of the second phase, he began to experience blackouts after drinking relatively little. He hid the fact that his drinking was increasing and drank before social engagements where he feared there wouldn't be enough alcohol. He gulped his first few drinks of the day and began to feel guilty about his drinking. He stopped talking about alcohol and didn't mention that his blackouts were increasing.

At the beginning of the "crucial phase," the path of the alcoholic diverged decisively from that of other heavy drinkers. The heavy drinker might continue drinking for thirty or forty years and consume as much or more than the alcoholic, but he could stop and start at will. At the start of the crucial phase, which began from one year to seven years after the start of heavy drinking, the alcoholic lost the ability to stop drinking once he started and would drink until he was too drunk to continue. "The 'loss of control' is a disease condition per se," Jellinek wrote.[43]

The drunk was not completely helpless. Once he was sober again, he could abstain for a time. Then someone offered him a drink, and he got drunk again despite his sincere desire not to. The alcoholic also began to suffer a series of personality changes: he started rationalizing his behavior, first to himself and then to his family, friends, and employer; his self-esteem suffered as he failed again and again to control his drinking, and he compensated with grandiose behavior intended to prove he was a good and important man. He became more aggressive and self-pitying. He was isolated and alone.

In the final, "chronic phase," the alcoholic began to drink in the morning and didn't stop for days at a time. He drank obsessively to obliterate the evidence of impaired thinking, ethical deterioration, indefinable fears, and uncontrollable tremors. He began to experience vague religious desires, but they didn't last long. His system of rationalization finally collapsed. If he was still breathing, he was ready to admit defeat.

Jellinek's article was accompanied by a chart that showed forty-three symptoms that were typical of the four phases of addiction. He emphasized that he was drawing a composite of the average drunk: not every alcoholic experienced every symptom, and the timing of symptoms could differ. Jellinek also acknowledged that he did not know what caused a person to become an alcoholic:

> Whether this . . . process is of a psychopathological nature or whether some physical pathology is involved cannot be stated as yet. . . . Nor is it possible to go beyond conjecture concerning the question whether "loss of control" originates in a predisposing factor (psychological or physical), or whether it is a factor acquired in the course of prolonged excessive drinking.

The fact that so few excessive drinkers became alcoholics led him to guess that there was "a predisposing X factor in the addictive alcoholic." Jellinek insisted that not knowing the cause of alcoholism didn't mean that it wasn't a disease. In his most significant work, *The*

Disease Concept of Alcoholism, published in 1960, Jellinek concluded, "It comes to this, that *a disease is what the medical profession recognizes as such* [his italics]."[44]

Jellinek's 1952 article and, later, his book gave scientific legitimacy to the campaign to recognize alcoholism as a disease. Another important step in the process was the growth of support within the medical community. One of the early leaders was Milton G. Potter, an alcoholic doctor in Buffalo, New York, who got sober in 1945 or 1946. In 1947, he founded an NCEA affiliate and persuaded the Erie County Medical Society to establish a special committee on alcoholism.

Potter also became reacquainted with a classmate from medical school, Marvin Block, another Buffalo doctor. Potter helped Block treat an alcoholic patient and persuaded him to join his alcoholism committee. The two men then persuaded the state medical society and twenty-one county societies to create alcoholism committees. The AMA was unmoved. It rejected a resolution urging the formation of an alcoholism committee twice in 1950. The AMA did create a subcommittee on alcoholism the following year, naming Potter as chair. But it never met because of a lack of funding.

Finally, in 1954, the AMA created a functioning subcommittee that included Block and Selden Bacon of the Center of Alcohol Studies. By then, Block was treating alcoholics exclusively, and he and Bacon developed a long list of objectives for the committee. They decided that the one most likely to win approval was a "Resolution on Hospitalization of Patients with Alcoholism." "[A]lcoholism must be regarded within the purview of medical practice," it declared, adding:

> The Council on Mental Health, its Committee on Alcoholism, and the profession in general recognizes this syndrome of alcoholism as an illness which justifiably should have the attention of physicians.

The resolution was unanimously adopted by the AMA House of Delegates at a meeting in September 1956.

The AMA resolution did not use the word "disease," but Mann and the burgeoning alcoholism movement eagerly claimed it as a vindication of the disease concept. It was also a turning point for the medical community as a whole. Block immediately began pushing for a similar statement by the American Hospital Association, which issued it a year later. After the *Journal of the American Medical Association* published the AMA resolution, it followed up with articles by Block, Bacon, and other members of the Committee on Alcoholism. In 1957, Block persuaded the AMA to distribute the articles in an official publication, *Manual on Alcoholism.*

Harold E. Hughes, a thirty-year-old Iowa truck driver, hit bottom in the same year that Jellinek published "The Phases of Alcohol Addiction." Alcohol had been causing him trouble for many years. He was six feet two and powerfully built, weighing 220 pounds. He had been a member of an all-state high school football team. During the war, he carried a heavy machine gun into battles in North Africa and Italy. He was frequently involved in drunken brawls and was eventually court-martialed for striking an officer. His drinking worsened after his return to his hometown of Ida Grove, and his family started proceedings to have him committed to a state insane asylum. He escaped confinement by promising to stay sober but started drinking again after fourteen months. Feeling hopeless, he took a shotgun into the bathroom of his home and lay down in the tub with the muzzle of the gun in his mouth, touching the trigger with his thumb.

Hughes paused long enough to decide that he owed God an explanation for his suicide. Kneeling by the tub, he began to pray. He broke down in tears and was lying on the floor when he became aware of a new emotion. "A warm peace seemed to settle deep within me, filling the terrible emptiness, driving out the self-hate and condemnation," Hughes wrote in his autobiography. Although he had been raised in the Methodist Church, Hughes had never felt a personal relationship with God. Now he had found "[a] God Who Cared, a God Who loved me. . . . Kneeling on the bathroom floor, I gave Him myself totally. 'Whatever You ask me to do, Father,' I cried through hot tears, 'I will do it.'"[45]

Hughes had wanted no part of AA when he first heard about it. A friend who was a member had invited him to a meeting during the period he was in danger of being committed. Hughes thought he was doing fine on his own. He only considered AA again after he tried to rescue a drunken friend from Florida and ended up drinking himself. He went to his first meeting in a nearby town with another friend, began attending regularly, and established a group in Ida Grove. Once Hughes's sobriety was firmly established, his career took off. He rose from driving a truck to managing a trucking company. He established an association that represented the interest of small truckers and won election to the Iowa Commerce Commission, which he eventually chaired. A columnist for the *Des Moines Register* called him "the most telling and moving orator I've ever heard." A Democrat in a Republican state, Hughes was elected governor in 1962. Among his first guests at the state capitol were members of the small AA group in Ida Grove, who had joked about the day they would hold an AA meeting in the governor's mansion.[46]

The state of Iowa had a commission on alcoholism by the time Hughes took office. Three-quarters of the states had created something similar, often locating a new division within the mental health department. This was a necessary first step, which involved educating state legislatures about the nature of alcoholism, and it provided support for the view that alcoholism was a medical problem that seriously affected public health. But the Salvation Army was still the largest provider of services to alcoholics in 1961. Most states lacked the money for treatment and rehabilitation.

Hughes encouraged the alcoholism commission to apply for a federal demonstration grant to fund an Iowa Comprehensive Alcoholism Program. The grant made it possible to open the first detoxification center in Des Moines and to improve coordination among government agencies, ensuring that alcoholics got access to the same services as other citizens. Iowa also created some of the first halfway houses, giving recovering alcoholics a place to live until they could get on their feet. Hughes insisted that the state government hire sober alcoholics and appointed one to the alcoholism commission.

Hughes was a liberal who was not afraid to take a strong stand on controversial issues. Soon after he became governor, he announced his opposition to capital punishment and succeeded in repealing it several years later. Iowans responded to his strong leadership. In the middle of his reelection campaign in 1964, a national magazine published an interview in which he revealed the fact that he was an alcoholic. His opponent attempted to use it against him, but the voters returned him to office with the largest majority ever given a candidate in Iowa, helping his party capture both houses of the legislature. Four years later, he was elected to the US Senate. By then, he had turned against American participation in the Vietnam War, and he would become a major critic of the policies of the new president, Richard Nixon.

There were many issues facing the new senator, but he had never forgotten the needs of alcoholics. Early in his term, he left Washington to assist a civic leader who had finally admitted his alcoholism. On the return flight, he wondered if he could do more:

> It had been only 17 years since I had made the same admission. I thought of the hundreds of thousands of men, women and youngsters who never seem to find help, who live as derelicts or die tragically. . . . Was this one of the reasons I was brought to Washington, to represent the millions suffering from addiction to alcoholism and drugs?

Hughes was a deeply religious man. If God had given him a mission, he could not turn away.[47]

The federal government had only just begun to pay attention to the problem of alcoholism. In 1966, Lyndon Johnson, whose father was an alcoholic, became the first president to speak about the problem. "The alcoholic suffers from a disease which will yield eventually to scientific research and adequate treatment," he said in an address to Congress. Soon after, the Office for Economic Opportunity, which created programs to fight Johnson's "war on poverty," began to award grants for the establishment of alcohol programs by state and local governments. These programs had made only the barest of beginnings by the time Hughes arrived in Washington. The administration had requested only $4 million for community alcoholism programs in 1969. "This is like trying to stop the Mississippi River in flood stage with a pebble," Hughes said.[48]

Things began to change when Hughes became the chair of the Special Subcommittee on Alcoholism and Narcotics. The new chair scheduled his first hearing in July 1969. Four of the five witnesses on the first day were sober alcoholics, including the actress Mercedes

McCambridge and Ray Harrison, an Iowa attorney who had been thrown into the very jail that he later supervised as a municipal judge.

Bill Wilson and Marty Mann testified on the second day. Before Wilson spoke, Hughes announced, "For the next witness, there will be no television. There will be no pictures taken." Wilson was eighty-four and suffering from emphysema. But he had survived to see the federal government address the problem of alcoholism. "For me, this is an extremely moving and significant occasion. It may well mark the advent of the new era in this old business of alcoholism," he said. The Apollo spacecraft had landed with the first men on the moon only a few days earlier. "This is splashdown day for Apollo. The impossible is happening," Wilson said.[49]

The following spring, the Hughes subcommittee introduced legislation that was nearly as ambitious as the moon shot. Hughes had asked a Washington lawyer, Peter Hutt, to draft the bill. Hutt had led the American Civil Liberties Union's campaign to get the courts to recognize that alcoholism was an illness and to send drunks to treatment instead of jail. He was an expert on alcoholism. When Hughes gave him just a weekend to write the legislation, he closeted himself with young associates of his law firm and met the deadline, presenting Hughes with a bill, the Comprehensive Alcohol Abuse and Alcoholism Prevention, Treatment and Rehabilitation Act.

Hutt and his associates had examined every federal program that could be used to help alcoholics and created an "administrative structure for a greatly expanded, comprehensive and for the first time well-coordinated federal attack on the problem of alcohol abuse and alcoholism." "There was everything in it but the kitchen sink," Hutt said later. The most important feature of the bill was the creation of a new federal agency, the National Institute on Alcohol Abuse and Alcoholism. The Hughes bill also authorized expenditures of $300 million for grants to state and local governments, nonprofit organizations, and individuals providing services to alcoholics over the next three years. Mann called the Hughes bill "an emancipation act for alcoholics."[50]

Hughes and his staff now had the difficult task of moving the bill through Congress. The support of sober alcoholics would be a key to its success. Hundreds of them sought jobs in his office, and one woman,

Nancy Olson, became a key player in the legislative campaign. Olson had been sober several years and was working part-time for a congressman when she became a volunteer in Hughes's Washington office. She had been hired for a full-time position a few months before the Hughes bill was introduced.

Olson wanted to see the bill passed without changes and often pushed her boss to oppose compromise measures. Hughes did not always listen to her, but she acted as a voice for alcoholics at important moments in the fight. During a committee hearing, a senator asked if a provision of the bill that barred discrimination based on a person's drinking history would prevent him from firing an employee who got drunk and punched him in the nose. Hughes turned to Olson. "How do you feel about that, Nancy," he asked.

> I was stunned and flustered. . . . I think I replied something like this, "Well, Senator Dominick, as a U.S. Senator you are exempt from provisions such as this. You can fire anyone you want to for no reason at all. But if the behavior is caused by a drinking problem, we would hope that you would first give your employee an opportunity for treatment and rehabilitation."

Hughes turned back to the senator. "That is how we alcoholics feel about it," he said.[51]

For the most part, the alcoholics had their way, but they did suffer setbacks. The National Institute on Alcohol Abuse and Alcoholism was created within the National Institute of Mental Health, raising concern that the problem of alcoholism might not receive the attention it deserved. A provision requiring the establishment of alcoholism treatment and rehabilitation in the armed services was removed because of a jurisdictional conflict with another Senate committee.

No other significant amendments were made before the bill was brought to the floor of the Senate for a final vote in August 1970. No senator was willing to oppose the bill openly, and it was approved by voice vote. On returning to their office, some members of Hughes's staff pulled bottles of whiskey from their desk drawers to celebrate. Olson didn't object. "Still, it seemed a strange way to celebrate the passage of an alcoholism bill," she said.[52]

The fate of the Hughes bill was still uncertain. The House did not consider the legislation until late in the year, and it was possible that it would not come up for a vote before Congress adjourned. Even if it passed, there was a good chance it would be vetoed. President Richard Nixon was trying to dismantle Johnson's welfare programs by turning over responsibility to the states. Two members of Nixon's cabinet were arguing against adding an institute on alcoholism to the federal bureaucracy.

Sober drunks across the country were convinced that their moment had come. AA does not endorse legislation. But by the early 1970s, there were more than five hundred thousand AA members worldwide, and many in the United States rallied strongly behind the Hughes bill. Calls and letters poured into the House Rules Committee, forcing the bill onto the floor where it was approved by another voice vote. Sober alcoholics in the Republican Party urged Nixon to sign the bill, including Thomas P. Pike, a prominent party member from California who had served in the Eisenhower administration, and James S. Kemper Jr., the president of Kemper Insurance Company.

R. Brinkley Smithers may have played the decisive role. Smithers was the son of an IBM founder who had devoted much of his time and fortune to the alcoholism movement since getting sober at Towns Hospital in 1954. He persuaded Don Kendall, the head of PepsiCo, to call the president, who was a close friend. Although Nixon was not happy about it, he signed the bill.

Passing a bill didn't matter much if there were no funds for implementing it. In 1971, Congress appropriated only $12 million of the $100 million authorized by the Hughes bill. Another $100 million had been earmarked for 1972, but the appropriations committee approved only $25 million. Olson reported that Hughes "blew his stack" and complained so loudly that he was finally invited to address the committee.

During the walk to the hearing room, Olson and her boss were grumbling over the appropriation when Hughes suddenly stopped. "Listen to us, Nancy, son of an alcoholic dirt farmer in Iowa and the daughter of an alcoholic laboring-class man in Pennsylvania, carrying on about a 'lousy $25 million,'" Hughes said. The sound of their laughter echoed in the marble hall.[53]

CHAPTER NINE

Boom and Bust

BETTY FORD WAS IN deep trouble by the time her family recognized there was a problem in the spring of 1978. They were all aware that she took a lot of pills and drank martinis before dinner and highballs later. Her husband, Gerry, the former president of the United States, complained that it took her forever to get dressed. Although she was only fifty-nine, she seemed to be slowing down. "You were in second gear," he said later. Her son Jack didn't like to bring friends home. "I was always kind of peeking around the corner to see what kind of shape Mother was in," he said. In the fall of 1977, after the Fords had left the White House, NBC hired Betty to narrate a performance of the *Nutcracker* ballet that was being televised from Moscow. But not even the embarrassment of bad reviews, including one that called her "sloe-eyed and sleepy tongued," raised the family's concern.[1]

It was an outsider, Chuck Vance, who sounded the alarm. Vance was a Secret Service agent who often accompanied the former First Lady. He was also secretly dating Susan Ford, the youngest of the Ford children and only daughter. "Susan, you've got to do something about your mother, she's slowly destroying herself," Vance said. Susan angrily rejected his advice, but she began to see the problem for herself after dropping out of college and moving in with her parents in Rancho Mirage, California. During this time, her mother fell and chipped a tooth. Susan moved to a place of her own and was soon at odds with Betty, who was hurt when Susan stopped visiting frequently. Susan talked to her father about Betty, but neither of them had a solution.[2]

Susan finally sought professional help from Dr. Joseph Cruse, Betty's gynecologist and a recovering alcoholic. "I said, 'Dr. Cruse, I've got this friend, and she's got a problem,' and he said, 'Susan, your friend is your mother, isn't she?'" Cruse told Susan he could arrange an intervention during which members of the family would confront Betty with examples of how her alcohol and drug abuse was hurting her and everyone around her. Susan discussed it with her father, who agreed to make a decision when he returned from a speaking engagement. While he was away, Susan and Cruse tried to talk to Betty. The doctor spent an hour and a half telling Betty the story of how he got sober, but only succeeded in putting her to sleep. She got angry at the end and insisted she was taking care of the problem herself. "You are all a bunch of monsters," she said. "Get out of here and never come back."[3]

Susan called her father and urged him to return immediately. The four Ford sons were also summoned, and the family gathered in the former president's office in Rancho Mirage on the morning of April 1 to plan the intervention with Dr. Joseph Pursch, who directed the alcoholism program at the US Naval Hospital in Long Beach, California. At 8 a.m., Pursch, Cruse, and the members of the family confronted Betty, who was still in her bathrobe. Gerry held his crying wife as they sat on a couch surrounded by their children. Everyone took turns talking, and when it was over, Betty agreed to go to Long Beach for treatment.

Betty Ford's hospitalization was big news. During her two years as First Lady, she had endeared herself to millions of Americans for her candor and her commitment to issues that mattered to women. She began to establish her reputation less than two months after her husband became president when she was diagnosed with breast cancer. Ford revealed that she had undergone a radical mastectomy, encouraging so many women to begin self-examinations that it created a notable increase in reported cases of breast cancer—"the Betty Ford blip." The press jumped at the announcement that Ford had entered the Long Beach Naval Hospital. One TV station hid a camera in a bread truck so that it could drive onto the hospital grounds to take pictures. Soon

Ford was receiving bags full of mail expressing concern and support. "I . . . was astonished at the amount of newspaper coverage, the editorial commending my heroism, my candor and my courage," she said. "I hadn't rescued anybody from a burning building, I'd simply put my bottles down."[4]

Betty had no intention of being as forthcoming about her addiction as she had been about breast cancer. The first public statement about her hospitalization said only that she was being treated for "overmedication." She did not consider herself an alcoholic when she entered the hospital, and she was still denying it ten days later. Pursch grew concerned. He summoned her to his office, along with her husband, Cruse, and Pat Benedict, a nurse in recovery who had been assigned to Betty after the intervention. Pursch described the scene later:

> I said, "So far, you have only talked about drugs, but you are going to have to make a public statement saying you are also dependent on alcohol." She said, "I can't do that, I don't want to embarrass my husband." I said, "You are hiding behind your husband and if you don't believe it ask him." And she kind of looked over at the President and said, "Well?" And he said, "No, you won't embarrass me." She was hyperventilating, flushing, blanching, flushing, her blood vessels were going crazy.

Betty had cried quiet tears during the intervention, but this time she broke down, sobbing loudly. "I had cried so much my nose and ears were closed up, my head felt like a balloon, all swollen," she said. The next day, she released a second statement. "Due to the excellent treatment I have had here at Long Beach Naval Hospital, I have found that I am not only addicted to the medication I have been taking for my arthritis, but also to alcohol," it said.[5]

The truth is the First Lady was far from happy with her treatment. She was angry at Pursch. Benedict agreed that her boss had been rough, but she had witnessed similar scenes with other patients. "[T]hat's how Pursch does things. . . . It was very hard on her because he isn't tender," she said. Betty was also mad at Gerry for refusing to defend her. She was still convinced that she wasn't an alcoholic. "What I expected—or hoped—was now they'd all get off my back," she said. A short time later, Ford found herself in a group session listening to a young woman deny that her drinking had hurt her family. "I knew her drinking had caused her folks a lot of trouble, and it was my turn to speak next and suddenly I was on my feet, and I said, 'I'm Betty, and I'm an alcoholic, and I *know* my drinking has hurt my family,'" she said. This was a breakthrough not only because she acknowledged her alcoholism but because she had admitted it to her fellow patients. From the beginning, she had admired those who spoke frankly about their alcoholism, but she did not see herself as one of them.[6]

Betty had no intention of saying anything more about it publicly. She had written a memoir, *The Times of My Life*, which was being prepared for publication in the fall, but she told Pursch that she was not going to add a chapter about her addiction. Later, when he offered her a tape of a well-known politician discussing his alcoholism, she handed it back. "You might as well know, I will never do stuff like that, so don't count on my running around the country talking about how I am an alcoholic," she said. Ford's publisher insisted that she acknowledge what the public already knew, and she finally agreed to add a short postscript. "I am glad I *didn't* win the argument," she said later. "Too many people have written to tell me how that brief chapter gave them the courage to go for help." Because of the increase in federal support for alcoholism programs, there was somewhere for them to go. A quarter of a million alcoholics entered treatment in 1978, the year Betty Ford got sober. The number of alcoholism programs had grown from five hundred to twenty-six hundred in just five years. Business was booming.[7]

Betty had been given several options during her intervention: she could remain at home and attend AA meetings, enter Pursch's program at the Long Beach Naval Hospital, or travel to Hazelden, a pioneering rehabilitation center in Minnesota. She chose a rehabilitation program because she was told she would have a quicker recovery, and she selected Long Beach because she wanted to remain close to her family. The hospital was a military facility; reveille sounded in the morning; doctors and nurses wore uniforms, and regular inspections were conducted. Physical exercise was mandatory, and new patients were required to complete a twelve-minute run to test their fitness. Betty was excused from running and volleyball, but she described life in the hospital as "rough." She was the oldest patient. Most of the others were young men and women who were addicted to alcohol, but she was addicted to pills, too. She had a hard time seeing that she shared the same problem as the young man who had started stealing liquor from his parents when he was eight or the young woman who sniffed the fumes from crankcase grease to get high.

Betty probably would have been better off at Hazelden, the largest alcoholism rehabilitation center in the country. Located in Center City, Minnesota, forty miles north of Minneapolis, Hazelden occupied two hundred acres of former farmland. The founders, who were looking for a place where alcoholic clergy and other professionals could get sober, were attracted by its gently rolling fields and woodlands and the white-shingled farmhouse with a red roof that was located on a lake. The house had seventeen spacious rooms, including a large living room and dining room, well-stocked library, and sunporch. New buildings were added in the 1960s, providing accommodations for over 150 patients.

Besides its beauty, what made Hazelden stand out was a highly developed program that met the needs of alcoholics with a wide range of problems. In the mid-1950s, Hazelden began treating alcoholic women and the members of families affected by alcoholism. It developed a program to help the large number of alcoholics who relapsed after treatment, founded a halfway house in St. Paul, and provided extended rehabilitation for those who needed more time than the standard twenty-eight-day treatment. It created programs to train recovering alcoholics and clergy as alcoholism counselors. Its leaders lectured widely on rehabilitation and were key members of the faculty of the Yale Summer School of Alcohol Studies. Visitors came from around the United States and around the world to see it.

The core of Hazelden's program was AA's twelve steps. This is not surprising since most of the founders were alcoholics who had gotten sober in AA. Minnesota was fertile soil for such experiments. The first man to get sober there was a dynamo named Pat Cronin, who had written to AA in 1940, after reading a review of the Big Book, to see if there was a group in Minneapolis. There wasn't, but two AA members from Chicago showed up on his doorstep just as a historic snowstorm was hitting the city. The three men were snowed in for four days, and when they finally emerged, Cronin was ready to join. He founded the first Minneapolis group, which served as a hub for 450 groups in the upper Midwest. One of the most active members of the group was a fifty-year-old lawyer named Lynn Carroll, who led the effort to create a refuge where alcoholic men could stay for a few weeks after they quit drinking.

A few months after Hazelden opened in 1949, Carroll, who had just been hired as director, explained its purpose to a newspaper reporter:

> This is not a hospital but a home. . . . We have no medical staff. . . . We have no attendants keeping tabs on the men here, because we feel that they are entitled to personal privacy. . . . In the life at Hazelden, there is only one restriction—no alcohol—and it is heartening to see the way in which the men live up to it.

As Hazelden developed, a few more rules were added: practice responsible behavior, attend lectures, talk to other patients, and make your bed. AA groups from Minneapolis and St. Paul sent speakers to lead discussions. The residents spent most of the day in informal conversations with each other and in group discussions that sometimes extended deep into the night. For men who might go into convulsions as they withdrew from alcohol, there was a supply of tongue depressors to keep them from choking. Carroll was always available to talk to patients privately, but he eschewed the trappings of a therapist. When a new man arrived and was well enough to talk, Carroll interviewed him, writing a few facts on a note card.[8]

Carroll had some doubts about his ability to lead a treatment program. He had taught some classes at the AA headquarters in Minneapolis, but he was a lawyer, not a doctor. "There were a lot of problems I hadn't learned to work out quite right," he said. But "I got to thinking—what the dickens! I had had psychiatrists and psychologists and they didn't do me any good and I didn't know any other alcoholic that they ever did anything for." The one thing he was sure of was that AA had worked for him, so he began to lecture on the twelve steps. For the first three years of Hazelden's existence, Carroll was the only counselor and lectured almost every day. He took three weeks to complete a lecture cycle, which became a standard for measuring the treatment period. It wasn't enough for the newly sober alcoholic to listen. Carroll emphasized the importance of completing the fourth and fifth steps, which would require the alcoholic to write an inventory of his character defects and the people he had hurt and then read it to another person. Since people were free to leave Hazelden at any time, not everyone achieved this, but many did.[9]

The early results were highly encouraging. Although at the beginning, there were only four or five men in residence at any one time, Hazelden was home to 156 men during its first eighteen months. At the end of that period, 78 percent were still sober or had stopped drinking again after a relapse. Carroll felt confidence in this number because he had followed their progress through contacts with the AA groups that almost all the men had joined after leaving Hazelden. Hazelden still faced many challenges. One of the biggest was persuading residents to stay long enough to absorb the AA program. Most left after three weeks, partly because of the cost. Residents paid a hundred dollars for the first week and eighty-five dollars for subsequent weeks. The board recognized the problem by establishing a scholarship program that paid the expenses for twelve men. They were able to stay for a month, and the extra time made a difference. Carroll reported that only one was still drinking after eighteen months.

As Hazelden was getting started under private auspices, there were exciting developments at a publicly funded institution located 140 miles west of Center City. In 1950, Dr. Nelson Bradley, a young Canadian doctor, was appointed the new superintendent of the state mental hospital in Willmar. It was a daunting assignment. "It's a 1,600 bed hospital, still a snake pit," he wrote to Daniel J. Anderson, a psychologist he had worked with at another mental hospital. Bradley was trying to recruit Anderson. "I think we can fix it up," he said. One of the first items on his agenda was to do something for the hospital's thirty to forty "inebs"—inebriates. The alcoholic patients were miserable. They were locked in wards with the other mental patients, and they responded by escaping whenever they could. Bradley's first step was to move the drunks to unlocked wards. Longtime members of the hospital staff predicted disaster, but the number of escapes plunged.[10]

When Bradley approached Anderson about working at Willmar, he asked him if he knew anything about alcoholics. Anderson admitted that he didn't, but he promised to investigate. It didn't take them long to discover the very active AA group in Minneapolis, and the two men began attending meetings. Anderson was skeptical at first. AA members appeared highly motivated about staying sober, but many of his patients didn't want to quit. He also thought AA might be too religious for some and too rigid for others. But there was no denying that the AA program was working for some people.

When Bradley issued a *Handbook on the Treatment of Alcoholism*, it cited two principles—"provision of as much psychiatric training as possible" and "presentation of the A.A. program." Bradley and Anderson were particularly impressed by the importance of using sober drunks to counsel alcoholics. There was no civil service classification for such a job, so Bradley hired his first alcoholic counselor surreptitiously. Later, he succeeded in persuading the state civil service commission to create the position of counselor on alcoholism and quickly hired two more.

Adding sober alcoholics to the staff was the beginning of a revolution in clinical practice. The hierarchy at Willmar was dominated by doctors who had undergone years of training in their fields of specialization. They were used to running the show. But Bradley and Anderson embraced AA's characterization of alcoholism as a complex disease that affected sufferers on several levels—physical, mental, and spiritual. To address all of these problems, they believed it was necessary to create a multidisciplinary team consisting of doctors, psychologists, psychiatrists, sober alcoholics, and ministers.

At first, the doctors resented working with nonprofessionals. Even Anderson was reluctant to believe that the counselors might know more than he did. He described how he used to argue about patients with one of them, Fred Eiden. Anderson would say, "Fred, this one's a sick one."

> Eiden would say something stupid like: "I don't know, Dan, he seems to be getting the program." That initially did not mean a thing to me because when one is that crazy—what did it mean "to

get the program"? . . . And then on another occasion I would see a guy who was well. I tested him and said to Fred: "Fred, he's in good shape—not crazy." . . . And Fred would say: "He doesn't have the program, though, Dan."

Anderson slowly developed confidence in Eiden's judgment. He learned that it wasn't enough to address psychological problems. "After shrinking their heads, I watched them get well right in front of me. They would thank me. Shake my hand, and say that they were going home—only to wind up back at Willmar," he said. He also listened to the lesson drawn by many of the relapsed men. "This time I think I'd better see what is going on in the A.A. program," they said.[11]

Once the professionals recognized the important role played by the counselors, the staff began to work together to help their patients. The Reverend John Keller, a Lutheran minister who had been sent to Willmar for training, witnessed the change. "I'd sit in a staff meeting at Willmar and see a recovering alcoholic disagree with a physician, but then they'd walk out and still be friends," he said. "People were here to be together and bring their individual and collective knowledge and experience to provide the care the patients needed."[12]

The patients were also impressed. The counselors were living proof that recovery was possible. They dressed and acted like professionals, and they did not hide the fact that at times they disagreed with the physicians. "The frankness of staff promoted a high degree of trust," a former patient said. Disagreements were inevitable in a program that was pioneering an approach to alcoholism treatment. What Bradley recalled was not the arguments, but the excitement of starting something new. "The enthusiasm we had at Willmar was really something—besides the energy—everyone was caught up in this—we ate and slept it. We talked about it in the coffee shop—we never let go of it," he said.[13]

The program that they created by trial and error would combine the best tools of medical science with the insights derived from the experience of AA members. New patients took a standardized test to identify their psychological problems, which became the basis for an individual treatment plan. The plan involved both individual and group counseling, as well as daily lectures on the nature of alcoholism. A patient's progress was closely charted and discussed during staff meetings to determine if any changes were needed.

Yet Bradley and Anderson never lost sight of the important role that the alcoholic plays in his own recovery. AA meetings were held frequently to give patients the opportunity to hear and speak to sober alcoholics. They were also encouraged to hold group meetings of their own, where they talked without a staff member present. Anderson later described the spirit of camaraderie that filled the alcoholic ward:

> Everybody called everybody else, patients and staff alike, by their first names; drinking experiences and alcoholic histories were dramatically revealed at the slightest provocation; advice was freely given based on one's own experiential background of alcoholism and recovery; hope and enthusiasm were openly expressed about the good prospects for recovery; and coffee was consumed extensively throughout the day and night.

Willmar was not the first institution to treat alcoholics humanely. Unlike the Washingtonian Homes and Massachusetts Hospital for Dipsomaniacs and Inebriates, however, its program would be widely imitated.[14]

One of those watching Willmar closely was Patrick Butler, whose family had purchased Hazelden in 1951. The Butlers were Irish Americans who made their fortune in construction and mining. They were also a family with a drinking problem: the patriarch, Emmett, had quit drinking in 1945; his son, Lawrence, had been Hazelden's first patient; Patrick, his brother, followed in 1949 and finally got sober in 1950. Patrick took charge of Hazelden following the sale and was soon traveling from Minneapolis to Willmar to study the progress of its alcoholism program.

Butler was deeply impressed by the success of the multidisciplinary approach and by Dan Anderson, who began lecturing at Hazelden in 1957. He would have gone further in implementing the Willmar program at Hazelden, but he knew that Lynn Carroll, the director, was fiercely opposed to any changes that might dilute its emphasis on the twelve steps. Carroll also didn't believe that psychologists and other experts had anything useful to offer. He refused to let his assistant attend the Yale Summer School of Alcohol Studies. "What the hell do you want to go there for? You know more than all those Easterners," he said. He reacted coolly to Butler's decision to hire Anderson as Hazelden's chief executive officer in 1961. Anderson was given an office in Minneapolis, allowing Carroll to continue to run his program in Center City.[15]

But change was coming. In 1956, Hazelden had purchased a three-hundred-acre estate in a Minneapolis suburb for alcoholic women. (Carroll thought housing men and women at Hazelden would be disruptive. "They did not make bear traps big enough to keep them apart," he reportedly said.) Called Dia Linn, at first the facility followed the same program as Hazelden. Soon after Anderson was hired, he began to implement the Willmar program there. Several years later, following an expansion of Hazelden to accommodate a steadily growing patient population, Anderson finally moved his office to Center City and Carroll left.

Although Anderson proceeded to institute the multidisciplinary model at the main campus, he made a significant change from the staffing at Dia Linn by appointing a sober alcoholic as the head counselor. In doing so, he underlined Hazelden's commitment to the principles that Carroll had pioneered. As Hazelden grew into the largest private rehabilitation center in the country, it inspired the rapid proliferation of new facilities in Minnesota. By 1977, there were more treatment centers there than in any other state. The "Minnesota model" was dominant just as the growth of alcoholism treatment was increasing around the nation.[16]

Once the importance of alcoholism treatment was generally accepted, there remained the problem of getting the drunk to recognize that he needed to stop drinking. In the early years of AA, it was believed that only a man who had lost everything and hit bottom could begin rebuilding his life. Things had changed by 1953. In *Twelve Steps and Twelve Traditions*, Bill Wilson wrote:

> Alcoholics who still had their health, their families, their jobs, and even two cars in the garage, began to recognize their alcoholism. As this trend grew, they were joined by young people who were

scarcely more than potential alcoholics. They were spared that last 10 or 15 years of literal hell the rest of us had gone through.

It was still necessary for alcoholics to confront the painful truth that they were powerless over alcohol, but AA had discovered that it was possible to "raise the bottom."

> By going back in our own drinking histories, we could show that years before we realized it we were out of control, that our drinking even then was no mere habit, that it was indeed the beginning of a fatal progression.

When the newcomer recognized himself in the story, it became easier to accept his problem. It didn't work for everyone. Some continued to drink, but the next time they got in trouble, many remembered what they had heard. "It was then discovered that when one alcoholic had planted in the mind of another the true nature of his malady, that person could never be the same again," Wilson said.[17]

The staff at Willmar also faced the problem of convincing patients that they were alcoholics. Although many had been committed by the courts, they continued to insist that drinking wasn't the problem. Their success in getting sober was not high—27 to 34 percent. What was a surprise was that patients who had entered the hospital voluntarily were not any more successful. "The conclusion we had to draw was simply that almost all alcoholics are probably locked in resistance and that few initially are able to admit and accept their alcoholism," Anderson said. This resistance manifested itself in many types of conscious and unconscious behavior that alcoholics use to preserve their self-esteem. Unable to face the fact that their drinking is causing behavior that violates their deepest moral values, drunks blind themselves to the brutal truth. As alcoholism worsens, their denial of the facts grows, becoming "massive and extremely difficult to penetrate," Anderson said. "The terminal stage alcoholic, for example, may be dying from cirrhosis of the liver yet denying any history of uncontrolled or excessive drinking."[18]

There was good news in the fact that voluntary and involuntary patients at Willmar had the same rate of recovery. If fewer voluntary patients got sober than expected, many of those who initially resisted treatment had changed their minds. Anderson attributed this to Will-mar's success in breaching their defense mechanisms and getting them to recognize their problem with alcohol. The first priority was to convince patients that concern for their welfare was the sole motivation. Their greatest fear was being condemned, so it was essential to convince them that they were in a place where their problem was understood and help was available.

Once this was achieved, it was possible to begin educating them about alcoholism. This was addressed on multiple levels. Anderson had a PhD in psychology, and in his lectures to patients, he explained what science had revealed about alcoholism. In a photo that shows him speaking to patients, he is standing beside a blackboard on which he has written "ambivalence," "ambiguity (conceptual, normative)," "wet vs. dry conflict," "utilitarian stress-relief," and "high risk culture."[19]

It wasn't enough to talk in generalities. It was also necessary to gather the facts of the patient's life history in order to show him that alcoholism was at the root of his self-defeating behavior and then to persuade him to do something about the problem. Staff members could play a key role in this process, but others might contribute. "Even other alcoholic patients who have only partially shed their own denial systems are in a good position to help with this, due to the seeming fact of human nature that we can always see another's problems more clearly than our own," Anderson said.[20]

The discovery that denial was a significant obstacle to getting people sober encouraged a search for new ways to attack the problem of alcoholism. The Reverend Vernon E. Johnson, an Episcopal priest, believed that it was possible to get help for an alcoholic before he set foot in an AA meeting or was admitted to a hospital. Johnson was an alcoholic who entered Hazelden in 1962. When he left treatment, he began working with a church group that included families of alcoholics in a suburb of Minneapolis. Several years later, he founded the Johnson Institute to develop programs for alcoholics based on research that the institute would conduct.

Johnson realized that he needed a laboratory to conduct the research and persuaded a local hospital to admit sixteen alcoholics for that purpose. One of the first surveys circulated sought answers to the question, why do people who have the disease wait so long to get treatment? The results of the first questionnaire were disappointing. "We repeatedly got reports from recovered alcoholics that they had simply seen the light, that a spontaneous insight had brought them to treatment," Johnson said. A second questionnaire that sought more information about the events leading up to the decision to quit was more revealing. "[A]ll these people had suffered a buildup of crises that brought them to a recognition of their condition," Johnson said.[21]

Johnson saw crisis as an opportunity. Family, friends, and even employers normally tried to help the alcoholic avoid the consequences of his drinking. What if people who were affected by the drunk's behavior used these crises to confront him with his drinking problem? The first step was to educate the people who were closest to the alcoholic:

> [They] do not realize how little he knows of himself and his own behavior. He is *not* confronted by his own actions; many of them he is not even aware of, although those around him assume that he is. They believe that he seems himself as they see him. In point of fact, he is increasingly deluded.

Once it was understood that the drunk needed help, their responsibility to do something became clear. "[T]hey must take the initiative if the illness is to be arrested," Johnson said. The Johnson Institute supported strict enforcement of the laws against drunken driving because going to jail was the kind of crisis that would propel drunks into treatment.[22]

Critics began to complain about the use of coercion soon after the Johnson Institute started arranging interventions, like Betty Ford's, in which family members, friends, and coworkers confronted drunks and urged them to seek treatment. Johnson was accused of manufacturing crises. "[O]ur response is that we do not invent crisis," Johnson said. "Every alcoholic is already surrounded by crises. . . . All we have to do is to make those around him knowledgeable enough so that they can start using the crises." Moreover, while pressure was being applied, the participants in the intervention were people who knew the alcoholic best and were able to confront him with specific incidents that occurred as a result of his drinking. It was certainly not a pleasant process for the drunk, who was frequently angered by the confrontation. On the other hand, some alcoholics were grateful to be offered an escape from a situation that had appeared insoluble. Johnson remembered one woman who had spent four hours fighting with her husband and daughter over their demand that she enter treatment. "If that's all either one of you cares, the hell with you," she said. Forty-five minutes later, she surrendered. When Johnson put out his hand to congratulate her, she embraced him. "Thank God, somebody did something," she whispered.[23]

Family intervention was powerful but not always successful. Many family members refused to participate because they were not convinced that their loved one was an alcoholic. In the early years of the Johnson Institute, many of the clients were companies that wanted to help an employee to sober up. Employers also had more power than family members because they could fire the alcoholic if he did not agree to accept treatment. At first, this threat applied mainly to executives and other key employees. By 1980, thousands of companies had created programs, including more than half of the nation's biggest corporations.

At first, there weren't enough places to put everybody. In 1968, there were only 183 programs for treating alcohol and drug addiction in the entire United States. But the passage of the Hughes bill led to a rapid expansion of federal spending, which rose to $386 million in 1973. More than thirty federal agencies and departments were soon playing a role, including the National Institute of Mental Health, the Veterans Administration, the Department of Justice, and the Department of Defense. In 1978, the number of treatment programs had grown to more than 2,400 and 250,000 alcoholics were being admitted to federally supported treatment every year. Much of the federal money was distributed by the National Institute on Alcohol Abuse and Alcoholism in the form of grants to state and local governments as well as nonprofit agencies in the hope that this would encourage them to spend additional funds. The seed grants achieved their purpose. In 1980, there were more than four thousand treatment units with total expenditures of $800 million.

The growth of private treatment centers was explosive. In 1970, there were only a handful, and Hazelden, which had recently expanded to 167 beds, was the largest. A decade later, there were 3,800 residential beds in Minnesota alone. The expansion of private treatment was made possible by insurance companies. Early in the century, these companies had done their best to deny insurance to alcoholics. Those who quit drinking had to prove they had been sober for five years before they could obtain a life insurance policy. This began to change in 1964 when Kemper Insurance Company added alcoholism coverage to group insurance policies at no additional cost. Many of James Kemper's competitors believed he would go broke, but he argued that the industry would actually save money by helping alcoholics get sober, saving the cost of their future care. The Prudential Insurance Company and the Hartford Insurance Group followed Kemper's lead in the early 1970s, and a majority of the companies would follow in the 1980s.

These were exciting days for men and women who were committed to changing the way their communities viewed alcoholics and drug addicts. Suddenly there was money to open halfway houses, clinics, and drop-in centers, and those who ran them were deeply committed to their cause. "Those of us who chose to take on such an upstream battle often brought more commitment than competence, and, as a result, we created work milieus more typical of a social movement than of a service agency," William L. White, a treatment professional and a historian of the recovery movement, has written. Admissions procedures were informal. "Alcoholics and addicts walked in off the streets and could be in a group a few minutes later," White said.[24]

Many of the counselors were alcoholics and addicts who had been in treatment only a short time before. Everyone worked long hours for little pay, but they were driven by the urgent needs of their clients. White quotes another veteran of the period:

> This was a time when alcoholics were hanging themselves in jail cells and dying from withdrawal because they couldn't get adequate medical care. This was an era where every staff member had come face-to-face with alcoholic seizures and had stood over the bed of a dying alcoholic. We knew beyond a shadow of a doubt that, if what we were doing didn't work, the death of many of our clients was not only possible but imminent.

The danger that the counselors would exhaust themselves was very real. The threat was particularly acute for those who were newly sober, and many suffered relapses. But there are always casualties in a great undertaking, and the fight against alcoholism and drug addiction was becoming a major humanitarian movement.[25]

AA flourished in these years. Its twelve-step program was a critical component of the Minnesota model of alcoholism treatment, and almost all of the treatment institutions that opened in these years followed the Minnesota model. Sales of the Big Book jumped because it was given to patients who were expected to complete AA's fourth and fifth steps before they returned home. It had taken thirty-four years to sell the first million copies, which finally occurred in 1973. Another million were sold in the next five years. By 1983, AA was selling 500,000 copies per year. Meetings were overflowing with recent graduates of rehabilitation centers (rehabs). The number of AA groups quadrupled to over 73,000 by 1987. By then, there were 800,000 members in the United States and Canada, and annual sales of the Big Book had risen to over 800,000. AA had also become an international movement with nearly 700,000 members in 109 foreign counties.

While it was growing, AA was also becoming more diverse. In 1970, the overwhelming majority of AA members were middle-aged white men. The number of women had grown significantly from the days when female alcoholics were regarded almost with suspicion, but more than three-quarters of the people at AA meetings were still men. This changed as treatment centers began to focus on the special problems of women alcoholics. Women were a majority of the patients at the Betty Ford Center, which Ford cofounded in 1982 in Rancho Mirage. By the mid-1980s, one in three AA members was a woman. The AA membership had also grown considerably younger. In the early years of AA, young alcoholics were sometimes told that they hadn't suffered enough to join. But the number of young members tripled between 1968 and 1983, reaching 20 percent of the total.

Many of these new members were addicted to another chemical in addition to alcohol. Women alcoholics had always been more likely than male drunks to be addicted to prescription drugs because the stigma of women who drank was greater and pills were easy to hide. Psychoactive drugs had become a prominent part of the youth subculture. The number of AA members reporting dual addiction almost doubled in just six years. By 1983, they were almost one-third of the members.

AA was also becoming more ethnically diverse and accepting of sexual preference. African Americans joined AA soon after its founding. However, the existence of racial segregation during the early decades of AA inhibited the growth of African American membership. AA groups set their own rules, and many groups in the South excluded blacks. William Swegan, who introduced AA to the military, remembered the hostility that greeted him when he brought African American service members to meetings in San Antonio during the 1950s.

African Americans responded by starting their own AA groups; the first opened in Washington, DC; the first New York City group started in Harlem in 1945. Native Americans began joining AA in 1953 and adapted the twelve steps by replacing references to the Christian "God" with "the Creator" or "Great Spirit." There were twenty Indian AA groups in 1966. Spanish-speaking groups proliferated with the rapid growth of the Hispanic population. Gay men and lesbians established special meetings where they would feel comfortable discussing their experiences.

The expansion of AA created many problems. The chief of staff of the General Service Office described some of them in 1978:

> Groups in the vicinity of treatment centers have been inundated with busloads of patients. Young people bring with them other addictions, explicit language, and free discussion of sex. Court-referred drunk-driving offenders wanted attendance slips signed. These and a thousand other problems have strained A.A. unity and rocked the serenity of many an old-timer.

Many AA members were skeptical about the prospects of newcomers who were attending meetings against their will and irritated by the discussion of drugs. AA had dealt with the drug issue for the first time in the 1940s when dual-addicted people began to speak up during meetings. The fear was that allowing people to talk about their drug addictions, particularly those that involved criminal behavior, would alienate drunks who had not had the same experiences. The agreement at the time, and reaffirmed in the 1960s, allowed drug addicts to attend AA meetings as long as they spoke only about their alcoholism. As the number of dual-addicted members grew, however, talk about drugs increased. The use of profanity also became common, which some old-timers blamed on the drug addicts. As a result, many groups began meetings by encouraging members not to talk about drugs. Some banned both drug talk and profanity.[26]

By the early 1980s, the complaints had reached a point where some began to worry that AA would not be able to adapt to new challenges, including the growing diversity of its membership. "[T]here appears to be developing within our Society a rigidity, a perceived need for law and order, a determination to enforce the Traditions to the letter, without any elasticity," the keynote speaker told the AA General Service Board in 1983. "If that attitude became widespread, the Fellowship could not function."[27]

Diversity continued to grow. Hundreds of men's, women's, and LGBT meetings were organized as a result of a decision to allow the formation of special groups; the only requirements were that they promote sobriety and were open to all alcoholics. The AA General Service Board also made a vigorous effort to recruit alcoholics from minorities that were underrepresented in the membership. Pamphlets addressing specific minorities were prepared and distributed through the literature racks of groups around the country. AA also recognized that illiteracy prevented its message from reaching alcoholics who lived in poverty. It created comics for them and expanded the distribution of AA literature on audio cassettes, which were originally created for alcoholics with impaired vision.

As the number of people in recovery grew, new sobriety groups were created to meet their needs. The first, Women for Sobriety, started in 1975. Dr. Jean Kirkpatrick, a sociologist and sober drunk, believed that women alcoholics needed a fundamentally different recovery program than men. AA stressed the importance of accepting powerlessness over alcohol and turning one's will over to a higher power. Kirkpatrick said this might be fine for men, but the biggest problem women alcoholics faced was low self-esteem. They already felt powerless. To empower them, Kirkpatrick created Thirteen Statements of Acceptance that emphasized the importance of self-assertion. Unlike AA, Women for Sobriety encouraged its members to offer encouragement and advice during meetings. It shared AA's commitment to lifetime abstinence and the importance of spiritual reconstruction. A study found that a third of Women for Sobriety members also attended AA meetings.

Many of the new groups were started by alcoholics who didn't feel it was necessary to acknowledge their dependence on a higher power. The first of these agnostic or atheist groups was established within AA in Chicago in 1975. The founder was Don W., an alcoholic who had joined AA in the early 1960s but quit after six months. "I was unable to work it because of the religious language in which the 12 steps were couched," he said. He drank for another ten years but finally returned and worked the steps as they were written.[28]

Four years later, Don W. gave a speech in several Unitarian Universalist churches, "An Agnostic in A.A.: How It Works for Me." One of the ministers invited him to start a group, and the first meeting of Alcoholics Anonymous for Atheists and Agnostics (Quad A) was held in the church basement. AA meetings for nonbelievers were organized in Los Angeles in 1980 and in New York in 1986. Recognized as a special group in AA, the atheists and agnostics adapted the twelve steps by removing references to God and a "Higher Power," while continuing to recognize the need to receive help from others to stay sober.

Two other sobriety groups were organized outside of AA in the 1980s. James Christopher, an alcoholic who got sober in AA despite his frustration with references to a higher power, organized Secular Organizations for Sobriety—Save Our Selves (SOS) in 1985. Unlike the atheists and agnostics who remained in AA, Christopher did not believe spirituality was necessary for sobriety. "S.O.S. credits the individual for achieving and maintaining his or her own sobriety," he wrote. At the same time, SOS shared AA's commitment to lifetime sobriety and emphasized its respect for AA and other organizations that were helping alcoholics. At its peak there were as many as 450 SOS groups in the United States, but the number declined to 47 in 2016, according to its website.[29]

The second group, Rational Recovery, was organized the year after SOS and had a similar philosophy. There were six hundred Rational Recovery groups in 1995, but it was closed by its founder several years later following a split in the organization. In 1994, former Rational Recovery members started SMART Recovery to provide "free, self-empowering, secular and science-based mutual-help groups." In 2013, there were more than 1,000 SMART Recovery meetings around the world, including 470 in the United States.[30]

The search for recovery in the 1980s was not limited to alcoholics. AA's program was adopted by many new groups that were struggling with other problems. The wives of early AA members were the first to discover that they could benefit from the twelve steps. They began to form informal support groups in the 1940s to help them deal with the emotional damage caused by their husbands' drinking, as well as the problems that arose once they were sober. Lois Wilson recognized that she needed help one night when a newly sober Bill made her so angry that she threw a shoe at him. She and a friend, Anne B., established a service office for the family groups, later incorporated as the Al-Anon Family Group Headquarters. Al-Anon grew from 145 groups in 1951 to over 1,500 in 1963. Al-Anon also established Alateen, a program for the children of alcoholics.

The 1950s were also when drug addicts started their own twelve-step organization. In 1953, several members of AA in Los Angeles helped organize Narcotics Anonymous (NA), which emphasized a version of the steps and traditions that had been adapted to apply to drugs as well as alcohol. NA gradually developed its own literature. In 1982, it published *Narcotics Anonymous*, which serves the same purpose for addicts as the Big Book does for alcoholics. While developing its own language and culture, NA remained committed to the twelve-step program as it grew from thirty-eight meetings in 1971 to forty-four thousand in 2008.

In the 1980s, dozens of new groups began adapting the AA program. AA counted eighty-three in 1987. Some groups sought members based on the drug they abused, including Potsmokers Anonymous, Pills Anonymous, and Cocaine Anonymous. Others formed to help people address problems with gambling, overeating, sex, and other kinds of compulsive behavior. As the decade progressed, the concept of addiction broadened to include people who had suffered as a result of dysfunctional relationships. In 1983, psychologist Judith Woititz published a book describing the problems faced by the children of alcoholics. *Adult Children of Alcoholics* sold almost two million copies and helped inspire the creation of an organization that adopted AA's twelve steps with only one change in the first step, applying its admission of powerlessness to "the effects of alcoholism or other family dysfunction." There were fifteen hundred Adult Children of Alcoholics groups by 1990.

Two other media sensations—the 1985 broadcast of a ten-part PBS series, *Bradshaw On: The Family*, featuring John Bradshaw, an educator, a counselor, and a motivational speaker, and the 1987 publication of Melody Beattie's *Codependent No More: How to Stop Controlling Others and Start Caring for Yourself*—lifted the self-help movement into the national limelight. Bradshaw and Beattie argued that people who suffer in destructive relationships were as sick as those causing the problem, which might be alcohol or drug addiction but could include any mental illness. *Codependent No More*, which was copublished by Hazelden, was enormously successful, selling more than eight million copies. It became the Big Book of a new group, Co-Dependents Anonymous, which would join so many others in adopting the twelve steps and traditions. It almost seemed that AA, just a little group of nameless drunks fifty years earlier, was remaking the world.

But the mood of the country was changing. The optimism that had led Lyndon Johnson to declare a war on poverty dissipated as the country struggled to extricate itself from the war in Vietnam. Confidence in government hit bottom as a result of the Watergate scandal, and the economy, which had been robust, was plagued by slow growth, high inflation, and increasing joblessness. Fear was growing over a violent crime wave that began in the 1960s and was still growing. In 1979, President Jimmy Carter acknowledged in a televised speech that the country faced "a crisis of confidence." The next year, the American people replaced Carter with Ronald Reagan, a sunny Californian who promised to restore the country's greatness. The new president said the only thing wrong with America was that government was too big. He wanted to free business of costly regulation and to give state governments control of social welfare programs. Although Reagan said he would provide strong leadership in the "war on drugs," the only significant initiative during his first term was the launch of an educational campaign, led by his wife, Nancy, that told schoolchildren to "Just Say No" to drugs.

Then, in 1984, crack made its first appearance on city streets. A cheap form of cocaine that was smoked, it provided an intense but short-lived intoxication that quickly addicted the user. Crack addiction spread rapidly, destroying lives as well as the neighborhoods where it was sold. Homicide rates among young African American men doubled as gangs fought for control of the trade. Congress responded in 1986 by passing the Anti-Drug Abuse Act, which made possession of five grams of crack punishable by a mandatory five-year prison sentence without the possibility of parole. The law symbolized a shift in federal priorities as the nation confronted a new generation of addicts, providing almost $1.5 billion for law enforcement and only $230 million for drug treatment.

The result was soon apparent in a rapid rise in the prison population, which reached one million in 1994. Sixty-one percent of the inmates had been sentenced for drug offenses, and many of them were addicts. The number of prisoners continued to grow to more than 2.4 million in 2013, four times the prison population in 1980. Surveys of federal and state prisoners indicated that approximately half had a drug or alcohol problem.[31]

At the same time, there were signs that the treatment industry was on financially shaky ground. The rapid expansion of alcoholism treatment that had begun a decade before had reached its peak. There were almost three times as many alcoholism wards in hospitals—1,148—and more than twice as many beds—34,364. The number of private for-profit treatment units more than quadrupled. In many places, there was suddenly too much help available. In 1985, in the East Valley section of Phoenix, there had been only seventy-four beds for alcoholics and drug addicts serving a population of almost a half-million people. By the time the St. Luke's Behavioral Health Center opened an eighty-bed treatment center there two years later, four other companies were making plans to open similar facilities. In 1989, there were over four hundred beds available in the area, and St. Luke's was forced to close its East Valley unit.

The competition among treatment centers quickly turned into a struggle for survival. The leaders of these institutions realized they couldn't sit around waiting for patients to show up. They began advertising and hiring salesmen who courted the managers of employee assistance programs and representatives of the health maintenance organizations. "I've got seven or eight lunches scheduled with people who could send patients here and quite frankly we've never done that before," the vice president of a Milwaukee treatment center said.[32]

In this often desperate hunt for patients, ethical problems began to arise. The focus of many institutions shifted from providing effective treatment to financial sustainability. "There was never any doubt in my mind that my primary, if not my exclusive area of accountability, was filling beds in the hospital," one administrator said. "In the four years I spent at the hospital, I was never asked one question by my superiors about the relative success of our efforts to treat addictions."[33]

William L. White described industry abuses at the time as "widespread and severe." They included "unethical marketing practices, financially motivated and clinically inappropriate admissions, excessive lengths of stay, inappropriate readmissions, excessive fees and the precipitous abandonment of clients when they reached the limits of their financial resources." "In this climate, alcoholics and addicts became less people in need of treatment and more a crop to be harvested for their financial value," he said.[34]

The treatment industry was also under fire for the cost of its services. Almost half of the alcoholics in treatment were enrolled in programs that followed the Minnesota model, which involved four weeks of expensive inpatient treatment. The managed care companies raised questions about the need for prolonged inpatient treatment, and not without reason. Alcoholics and addicts were being treated, were relapsing, and were readmitted repeatedly. Treatment costs ranged from $35 to $2,000 a day for what looked on paper like the same services. "People began to ask, 'My god, what kind of professional field is this?'" recalled Dan Anderson, the former president of Hazelden.[35]

Private industry paid a significant proportion of the $9 billion that was spent on treatment in 1986, and companies were soon adopting measures to control their costs, including hiring managed care companies to review requests for treatment. In the early days of managed care, there was some mutual understanding between the two sides: many treatment professionals agreed that there were patients in twenty-eight-day programs who could be treated just as effectively in outpatient programs, and managed care executives acknowledged that some patients required hospitalization. But the detente between the cost cutters and the caregivers did not last long.

The representatives of the managed care companies began to scrutinize the records of every patient and made decisions that were often at odds with the recommendations of their doctors. "Pardon me if I use some four-letter words," a treatment center administrator apologized. "We just had a patient sent here by his physician. . . . [He] had insurance . . . and some f———b—— on a phone tells us the patient is not appropriate for treatment." Another complained:

> These [patients] are actively suicidal and self-mutilating and have had outpatient treatment and failed, yet they say they don't need inpatient care. At what point do you need inpatient? When you're dead?

The managed care companies held the purse strings and were bound to prevail. The number of approved inpatient days dropped steadily until it reached the several days required for detoxification. The average occupancy of private inpatient programs fell 25 percent in a single year, 1988–1989. Treatment companies began to merge units and lay off staff. Many hospitals closed their addiction units, sending alcoholics and addicts who needed hospitalization back to the psychiatric ward. Most new patients were referred to outpatient programs, although it was harder to keep them sober. A new era had begun. In the future, the only people in a twenty-eight-day program were those who could afford to pay for it themselves.[36]

A period of consolidation in alcoholism treatment was inevitable following such rapid expansion, but many working in the field believed that something worse was happening. They were on the receiving end of a backlash that was ideological as well as economic. A chorus of voices criticized those who had embraced the disease concept to explain the problems in their lives. Many were conservatives who had a long history of insisting that people were to blame for their failures. There was also criticism from the left. "We are a nation of sexaholics, rageholics, shopaholics and rushaholics," Wendy Kaminer wrote in her

1991 book, *I'm Dysfunctional, You're Dysfunctional: The Recovery Movement and Other Self-Help Fashions*. Kaminer had surveyed the burgeoning literature of recovery and emerged with serious concerns about its impact on politics. "Imagine the slogan of recovery—admit that you're powerless and submit—as a political slogan, and what is wrong this movement becomes clear. That is hardly a slogan for a participatory democracy," she wrote. Instead of focusing people on the injustices in the world, the widespread adoption of the twelve-step program was infantilizing them:

> The phenomenal success of the recovery movement reflects two simple truths that emerge in adolescence: all people love to talk about themselves, and most people are mad at their parents. You don't have to be in denial to doubt that truths like these will set us free.

Kaminer's criticism was directed mostly at programs that addressed "codependency," but the disease concept of alcoholism was also under heavy attack.[37]

One of the sharpest critics of the disease concept of alcoholism was Herbert Fingarette, a mild-mannered, semiretired professor at the University of California at Santa Barbara. In the spring of 1988, he won national attention with the publication of a slim volume, *Heavy Drinking*. The circumstances of its release were fortuitous. The US Supreme Court was considering a case in which two alcoholics were suing the Veterans Administration for denying them an extension of the period when they could apply for education benefits. Such extensions were granted to veterans with physical or mental problems, and the men, who had stopped drinking, argued that their alcoholism had caused them to miss the application deadline. The VA said their failure to apply was the result of "willful misconduct." Fingarette's views had been cited by the VA. When the Supreme Court ruled against the alcoholic veterans, it appeared to validate the thesis of his book, which Fingarette was soon repeating in magazine and newspapers articles, TV interviews, and on talk shows.

Fingarette charged those who portrayed alcoholism as a disease with perpetrating a fraud. "Almost everything that the American public believes to be the scientific truth about alcoholism is false," he wrote in *Heavy Drinking*. "[I]n fact, we know that there are *no* decisive physical causes of alcoholism," Fingarette asserted in an article published in the same year. He continued:

> [T]he public has been kept unaware of a mass of scientific evidence accumulated over the past couple of decades, evidence familiar to researchers in the field, which radically challenges each major belief generally associated in the public mind with the phrase, "alcoholism is a disease."

The disease concept declares that at a certain point in an alcoholic's drinking, he loses control and continues to drink until he is so drunk that he passes out. In other words, "one drink—one drunk." Fingarette pointed to experiments that he claimed had shown that alcoholics were capable of moderating their drinking for extended periods. In one hospital experiment, men who were accustomed to drinking a quart of whiskey a day were given a monotonous task to earn credits for liquor. It was easy to earn enough credits to get drunk, but none of them did during the one- to two-month duration of the experiments. "The consensus in the research literature is that even in their normal, everyday settings, chronic heavy drinkers often moderate their drinking or abstain voluntarily, the choice depending on their perceptions of the costs and benefits," Fingarette wrote.[38]

Fingarette did not deny that biology played some role in alcoholism. He acknowledged that studies had shown that the children of alcoholics were three times as likely to become drunks than other children. This meant that as many as 14 percent of alcoholics had a genetic predisposition to heavy drinking. But Fingarette rejected claims that this evidence supported the disease theory. He pointed to the fact that the overwhelming majority of alcoholics did not have an alcoholic parent. Not even a majority of the children of alcoholics became drunks. At most, the studies had proved that genetics was one factor among many in alcoholism, he said.

Potentially more damaging than Fingarette's criticism of the disease concept was his claim that alcoholism treatment didn't work. He acknowledged that this contradicted what people were hearing in ads for treatment and "the heartfelt testimonials of celebrities . . . who write books and appear on talk shows to praise their newfound sobriety." Fingarette said most people who conquer their drinking problem—as many as 30 percent—did it on their own. The majority were young men who "aged out" of their guzzling habit when they got their first job and started raising a family.[39]

Fingarette did not dispute the fact that some people did get sober in treatment, particularly those who were strongly motivated, possessed economic security, and had strong family support. But he asserted that there was no evidence that it was because of treatment. "The current consensus in the research community is that by scientific standards of effectiveness the therapeutic claims of disease-oriented treatment programs are unfounded," he wrote. Fingarette also rejected the idea that AA would ever be a solution for most alcoholics. He cited one study that estimated that 82 percent of AA members relapsed in the first year and a half. This meant that AA was helping only 5 percent of the drunks in the United States and Canada.[40]

Fingarette's sweeping rejection of the disease concept and the effectiveness of treatment infuriated many people, including those who worked with alcoholics and the drunks they had helped. "[H]e swings at those he sees as the enemy with the same vigor that Carry Nation used in swinging her hatchet at bottles of booze," observed William Madsen, a colleague on the faculty of the University of California at Santa Barbara. In *Defending the Disease: From Facts to Fingarette*, Madsen, an anthropology professor, argued that Fingarette's conclusions rested on "misconceptions, fallacies and examples of poor reasoning." He accused Fingarette of an over-reliance on psychological and sociological research while failing to provide any significant biological or medical facts. Madsen said he did not even seem to understand that many of the researchers he was citing were themselves supporters of the disease concept. He concluded by considering Fingarette's impact on people working in the alcoholism field. "Fingarette has administered a totally undeserved and a very vicious slap in the face to these sacrificing people as well as to every sufferer of the disease of alcoholism," he wrote.[41]

Some of the depressing facts cited by Fingarette could not be denied even by people who were working hard to help alcoholics. Dr. George E. Vaillant was one of them. A graduate of Harvard Medical School, he became interested in alcoholism in the early 1970s when relatives of an alcoholic friend asked him for help. He was a psychiatrist who was considered knowledgeable about addiction generally, but he had to call some senior members of the Harvard faculty for advice. No one was able to help.

His curiosity piqued, Vaillant signed on as a consultant and ultimately codirector of an ambitious project to help alcoholics in the neighboring cities of Cambridge and Somerville, Massachusetts. "To me, alcoholism became a fascinating disease," Vaillant wrote.

> It seemed perfectly clear that by meeting the immediate individual needs of the alcoholic, by using multi modality therapy, by disregarding "motivation," by turning to recovering alcoholics rather than to Ph.D.'s for lessons in breaking self-detrimental and more or less involuntary habits, and by inexorably moving patients from dependence on the general hospital into the treatment system of A.A., I was working for the most exciting alcohol program in the world.

Anxious to prove the effectiveness of their program, Vaillant and the director checked on the progress of the first one hundred patients to undergo detoxification two years after their discharge. Only five of the patients had remained abstinent for the entire period, which was a success rate of just 20 percent. Since that was about the rate at which untreated alcoholics stopped on their own, it appeared they were not helping. "Not only had we failed to alter the natural history of alcoholism, but our death rate of three per cent a year was appalling," Vaillant recalled.[42]

Facing layoffs, closings, a loss of public confidence, and self-doubt, the people who were lucky enough to still have jobs in the addiction field in the 1990s were severely demoralized. William L. White spoke for them in 1997 as he wrote the final words of his comprehensive study, *Slaying the Dragon: The History of Addiction Treatment and Recovery*. He had worked as a counselor, clinic director, and researcher since the late 1960s and had experienced the great excitement surrounding the growth of treatment. Now he wondered if he was watching its collapse. "America is moving addiction once again from the arena of public health to the arena of public morality," he wrote. "If this trend continues, it is likely that addiction will be de-medicalized and increasingly criminalized for all but the most affluent of our citizens."[43]

White believed the threat came from within as well as without. As the treatment industry became increasingly professional, it had lost its passion for service. The sober alcoholics who had once played such a prominent role as counselors were disappearing from the field. The professionals who replaced them had been trained for the work, but they lacked the experience of personal recovery that gave sober drunks credibility with still bleary alcoholics. White, whose book documented the collapse of many previous recovery efforts, knew that it could happen again. "How much of the current system of addiction treatment will survive and be recognizable a decade from now is open to question," he wrote. But history also gave White hope:

> The movement to generate and sustain support systems for recovering alcoholics and addicts in this country has been, and will continue to be, unstoppable. Every time formal systems of treatment collapse, new grassroots movements rise up to rebuild or replace those systems.

White was counting on the passion of drunks and drug addicts who had survived their addiction.[44]

CHAPTER TEN

Waves of Sobriety

ON MARCH 25, 2000, an alcoholic in a blackout drove her pickup truck onto a freeway going the wrong direction in rural Washington State and collided with a car, killing thirty-eight-year-old Richard Davis and his twelve-year-old daughter, LaSchell. Such accidents rarely made national news. But the driver of the pickup was Audrey Kishline, the founder of Moderation Management, a mutual aid group that tries to help people with alcohol problems control their drinking.

Two months earlier, Kishline had admitted to members of the group that her drinking was out of control and that she was trying to stop with the help of several sobriety groups, including AA. She also reaffirmed her belief that Moderation Management worked for people who were not addicted to alcohol. In July, when she pleaded guilty to two counts of vehicular homicide, her view appeared to have changed. According to her lawyer, Kishline now believed that Moderation Management contained many people like her—"alcoholics covering up their problem."[1]

Kishline's accident reignited a bitter dispute that had begun almost forty years earlier between the alcoholism treatment community, which regarded abstinence as the goal of all alcoholics in recovery, and its critics, including many who rejected the idea that alcoholism was a disease. The controversy began in 1962 when a British psychiatrist, D. L. Davies, reported that alcoholism patients treated at a London hospital had been able to start drinking again without further problems; some had been drinking safely for as long as eleven years. Only ninety-three drunks were studied, and just seven were judged to have resumed "normal" drinking. Davies was quick to acknowledge that most alcoholics would never drink normally. But his study challenged the idea that alcoholism is inevitably progressive and that loss of control is irreversible.

Davies's findings were received with great skepticism by most alcoholism experts. Some questioned whether the men who had returned to drinking successfully were the alcoholics described by Jellinek. "One possible explanation of Doctor Davies' findings derive[s] from the fact that there are undoubtedly degrees of alcoholism," one commentator observed. "All patients are not equally ill."[2]

But many of those who criticized Davies did not want to debate the fine points of his research. They were alarmed by the danger that sober alcoholics would be encouraged to drink again. "For every alcohol addict who may succeed in reestablishing a pattern of controlled drinking, perhaps a dozen will kill themselves trying," a doctor commented in the *Quarterly Journal of Studies on Alcohol*.[3]

The Davies study probably didn't get anyone drunk. The debate over controlled drinking was confined to the pages of academic journals until 1976, when the RAND Corporation published a report that provided support for the idea. The National Institute on Alcohol Abuse and Alcoholism had commissioned RAND to evaluate the effectiveness of alcoholism treatment at forty-four federal treatment facilities. To the surprise of many, the authors of *Alcoholism and Treatment*, which became known as the RAND Report, concluded that the number of patients who had achieved abstinence was "relatively small."[4] Most of those who had improved were drinking again at "moderate" levels or were alternating periods of drinking and abstention. Overall, 22 percent of those receiving treatment had become "normal drinkers."

The national press expressed skepticism about the RAND Report, but the controversy grew more heated when two behavioral psychologists, Mark and Linda Sobell, published a book two years later in which they claimed they had succeeded in training alcoholics to drink safely.[5] They had studied seventy alcoholics at a state hospital in California, dividing them into a control group that was urged to pursue abstinence and a controlled drinking group that was trained to limit consumption and treated with aversive conditioning, including electric shocks.

Following up with their subjects two years later, the Sobells found that the controlled drinking group had significantly more "days functioning well" than those whose goal was abstinence.[6]

The National Council on Alcoholism (NCA) was horrified. At a news conference, NCA executives called the RAND Report "dangerous and misleading." "My concern is that a lot of people will try to drink again, and a lot of people will die as a result," said Dr. Nicholas A. Pace, the president of NCA's New York City affiliate. The Sobells were also harshly criticized. The prestigious *Science* magazine published an article that challenged their results, reporting that eight years after the Sobells claimed their patients were drinking normally, eight were drinking excessively, six were abstinent, and four were dead. The article claimed that most of the subjects had failed to drink safely from the very beginning, raising questions about the Sobells' honesty. One of the authors put his suspicions in so many words. "Beyond any reasonable doubt, it's fraud," he said. Several investigations cleared the Sobells of any wrongdoing.[7]

The Kishline accident in 2000 brought the bitter dispute over controlled drinking back to center stage. NCA, which had been renamed the National Council on Alcoholism and Drug Dependence (NCADD), issued a statement that blamed the accident on Kishline's failure to acknowledge her alcoholism. This was not her fault, it said. "Unfortunately, the disease of alcoholism, which is characterized by denial, prevented this from occurring." But there were people to blame, NCADD said. The accident "provides a harsh lesson for all of society, particularly those individuals who collude with the media to continually question abstinence-based treatment for problems related to alcohol and other drugs." The advocates of controlled drinking had done great harm:

> What makes Ms. Kishline's present situation even more distressing is the fact that her denial, amplified by the media, undoubtedly contributed to the progression of alcoholism and other alcohol-related problems for thousands more unidentified Americans and their families. . . . [W]e should all remember the names of Richard and LaSchell Davis the next time a problem drinker claims to be able to "drink a little" without harm.

Defenders of controlled drinking were stung by the charge that they were responsible for the accident. Stanton Peele, a leading critic of the disease concept of alcoholism who had endorsed Moderation Management, sought to distance himself from Kishline by saying he hadn't spoken to her in five years. He also claimed that her decision to join AA made her drinking worse.[8]

As the backlash over the Kishline accident grew, many prominent alcoholism experts began to worry that the reputation of alcoholism treatment was being badly damaged. Three weeks after the NCADD statement, Dr. Alexander DeLuca, the director of the Smithers Addiction Treatment and Research Center in New York, found himself caught in the controversy when *New York* magazine reported that Smithers was offering its patients treatment that included Moderation Management. This news was shocking because Smithers had been founded with a $10 million gift from the Christopher D. Smithers Foundation, which strongly supported abstinence for alcoholics. DeLuca insisted that the report had exaggerated the changes at Smithers. "Our treatment programs never changed," he said. But DeLuca had agreed to allow Moderation Management to begin holding meetings at Smithers in January. In the atmosphere created by the Kishline accident, the Smithers board of directors concluded that DeLuca had gone too far and forced him to resign.[9]

On the same day that DeLuca's firing was announced, thirty-four scholars and prominent treatment professionals issued a statement that attempted to bring the controlled drinking controversy to an end. Ernest Kurtz, a historian of the alcoholism movement, had drafted the statement and sent it to people on both sides of the debate. He was the perfect intermediary because he was both an AA member and someone who had endorsed Moderation Management, which he believed would make it easier for many people to recognize their alcoholism. Above all, he shared the fear of many that the alcoholism community was tearing itself apart and undermining its ability to help alcoholics get sober. The statement addressed this problem directly:

> That Ms. Kishline was intoxicated at the time of the crash has been claimed to indicate the failure of the approach of one or another of the mutual-help groups Ms. Kishline has attended. Such claims

are not in accord with everyday experience in the field, in which relapse is common, whichever approach the drinker adopts. Recovery
from serious alcohol problems is a difficult goal and there are many
paths to it.

The final paragraph proposed a compromise. "We believe that the approach represented by Alcoholics Anonymous and that represented by
Moderation Management are both needed," it said.[10]

Under different circumstances, Kishline would probably have endorsed the statement, but she was awaiting the final disposition of the
criminal charges against her. A month later, she was sentenced to four
and a half years in prison. She continued to struggle with sobriety after
her release and committed suicide in 2015.

The compromise over controlled drinking was the first sign of a moderating tone in the debate over alcoholism. There was still plenty of
disagreement over many issues, but much of the heated rhetoric disappeared. One factor contributing to this de-escalation was a growing knowledge about the physiology of alcohol and drug addiction. In
1988, Henry Fingarette claimed that his survey of experts in "biology,
medicine, psychology, and sociology" had found no evidence to support
Jellinek's concepts of tolerance, craving, withdrawal, and "loss of control." But back in the mid-1970s, biologists and pharmacologists had
conducted thousands of experiments on the effects of alcohol on ani-
mals, and many were convinced that addiction originated in the brain.

Over the next two decades, researchers identified the existence of
a brain reward system that begins in the brain stem, which controls
heartbeat, respiration, and other functions that ensure survival, and
connects through the limbic system, the center of emotion and motivation, with the cerebral cortex. The primary function of this circuit is to
reward eating, sex, and other behavior that is biologically beneficial by
releasing into the limbic system a pleasure-causing neurotransmitter
called dopamine.[11]

Scientists theorized that alcohol and other psychoactive drugs
hijack the brain reward system, flooding a section of the limbic system with dopamine and producing a rush of pleasure that is far more

powerful than natural neurotransmitters. But the power of alcohol and drugs wanes for regular users, creating a craving for more drugs. Alcoholics and addicts become victims of the very system that once ensured survival, seeking out drugs with the same desperation that they once sought food and water. The brain reward system becomes the instrument of their self-destruction.

In 1997, Allan I. Leshner, the director of the National Institute on Drug Abuse (NIDA), gave the government's seal of approval to this new theory of addiction. "Dramatic advances over the past two decades in both the neurosciences and behavioral sciences have revolutionized our understanding of drug abuse and addiction," he announced.[12]

As in all matters pertaining to science and public policy, however, this was not the final word in the debate. In 2014, ninety-four addiction researchers and clinicians sent a letter to the editors of *Nature* magazine disputing an article stating that the brain disease model of alcoholism represented a consensus among people who study addiction. One of the signers later joined two colleagues in publishing a more detailed critique of the neurobiology of addiction in the *Lancet*, a British medical journal. The authors raised questions about the results of the animal experiments that had played such an important role in verifying the brain disease theory, expressed doubt about the usefulness of research into the genetics of addiction, and rejected claims that the neuroimaging technologies that had made it possible to provide live pictures of brain activity during intoxication proved that drug taking is a compulsion. They concluded that NIDA's decision to spend 40 percent of its budget on neuroscience research was not justified in light of what it had accomplished for addicts.[13]

Nora D. Volkow, Leshner's successor, responded to the criticism in the *Lancet*. Volkow is a psychiatrist who played a pioneering role in the use of PET scans, a type of MRI imaging that was being used to study the brain of addicts. Her own research suggested modifications to the brain disease model, but she firmly defended the importance of neuroscience. "These findings, along with ongoing research, are helping us understand the neurobiological processes associated with loss of control, compulsive drug taking, inflexible behaviour, and negative emotional states associated with addiction," she and George Koob wrote. The research had made possible several medications, including naloxone and acamprosate that helped reduce craving in alcoholics, buprenorphine-naloxone for opioid addiction, and varenicline for tobacco addiction.[14]

It also provided a basis for experimenting with the use of deep brain stimulation, which involved the implanting of a stimulator to send electrical impulses to parts of the brain. The technique, which was developed to treat Parkinson's disease, chronic pain, and depression, was showing "promising results" in addiction treatment, Volkow and Koob wrote. She reproved the critics for believing "that science should immediately translate into transforming solutions." She also asked why some people were having trouble "accepting as a bona fide disease one that erodes the neuronal circuits that enable us to exert free will." No one questioned the importance of basic research in Alzheimer's disease or schizophrenia.[15]

But the disagreement over the brain disease theory was not as great as the battle over whether alcoholism was a disease. The authors of the *Lancet* article acknowledged that changes in physiology played an important role in addiction. "Addiction is a complex biological, psychological, and social disorder that needs to be addressed by various clinical and public health approaches," the authors of the *Lancet* article acknowledged. Volkow and Koob agreed on the importance of approaching alcoholism from multiple directions. "Understanding how genetic, developmental and environmental (including social) factors affect the susceptibility for substance abuse disorders helps develop better prevention strategies," she and Koob wrote.[16]

There was also rising confidence in recovery. Once twentieth-century doctors accepted the fact that alcoholism was an illness, they had to recognize that it was not something that they could cure. George Vaillant and his associates in the Cambridge-Somerville alcoholism program, who were doing everything possible to help their patients, were naturally disappointed when they discovered that 95 percent relapsed in the first year. They had to relearn the lesson that guided the work of Albert Day and the first generation of addiction specialists. "Some men . . . *must* fall, at least once," Day told his patients at the Washingtonian Home. Sometimes they relapsed repeatedly before they could accept the fact that they are addicted. AA acknowledged this in the advice it offered to alcoholics who were having doubts about quitting. "Step over to the nearest barroom and try some controlled drinking," the Big Book suggested. "Try to drink and stop abruptly. Try it more than once." Of course, there was a chance that you would start another binge. But "it may be worth a bad case of the jitters if you get a full knowledge of your condition." Relapses were part of the learning process for most alcoholics.[17]

Vaillant came to realize this as his study of drunks continued. In addition to managing the alcoholism program, he was conducting one of the first studies to follow several groups of alcoholics for forty years. Using data from the Harvard Medical School's Study of Adult Development that began in 1940, Vaillant and his fellow researchers were able to watch the development of alcoholism in 660 men from its first appearance. The results, which were published in 1983 as *The Natural History of Alcoholism,* convinced Vaillant that the goal of treatment should not be a cure. "[A]lcoholics recover not because we treat them but because they heal themselves," he wrote.[18]

The most powerful evidence for this in Vaillant's study was the dramatic increase in the number of men who became abstinent over time. While most of the men were drinking at the end of the first year, four times as many had quit eight years later. Vaillant had never stopped believing that treatment was important. "I have no doubt that by providing consultation, detoxification, welfare and shelter, we stop hemorrhage," he wrote. "At the same time, we may need to recognize that the recovery process in alcoholism is best catalyzed not by a single episode of treatment but by fostering natural healing processes over time." Vaillant believed that AA supported these healing processes. Two-thirds of the men who stopped drinking had eventually found their way into AA. "Joining any club takes time," he wrote. He also pointed to other programs that worked. "[T]here are many paths to recovery in alcoholism," he concluded.[19]

Then, in 1989, the National Institute on Alcohol Abuse and Alcoholism (NIAAA) funded Project MATCH, the largest clinical study of psychotherapies that had ever been undertaken. The goal of the study was not to determine whether treatment worked. The assumption was that some therapies were certainly effective. What the

NIAAA was trying to determine was whether drunks shared characteristics that made some treatments more effective than others. Researchers recruited 1,726 patients who had reported alcohol problems and divided them into groups that were given one of three treatments: twelve-step facilitation (TSF), cognitive behavior therapy (CBT), and motivational enhancement therapy (MET).

Members of the TSF group were encouraged to attend AA meetings, find a sponsor, and work through the first five steps. Patients in the CBT group were taught skills to avoid relapse, including drink-refusal techniques and ways to manage negative moods. MET therapists used motivational psychology to encourage individuals to consider the effect of alcohol on their lives and to develop and execute a plan to stop drinking. Individuals in the TSF and CBT groups met with their therapists once a week for twelve weeks. MET consisted of four sessions over twelve weeks.[20]

In 1996, the NIAAA announced a surprising result: matching did not work; the patients fared the same in all three groups. But Project MATCH also showed that all three treatments had been effective. One year after the study, half of the subjects reported they were no longer drinking heavily, and the number of days they were drinking each month had declined from twenty-five to six. These results provided important validation of the effectiveness of alcoholism treatment at a moment when it was under heavy attack from Herbert Fingarette and others. They had argued that in its heavy dependence on AA's twelve steps, the treatment industry was perpetrating a fraud. Project MATCH provided the first scientifically valid evidence of the effectiveness of the Minnesota model. In addition, it was certainly good news that the other approaches were effective since this strengthened the argument that alcoholism was a treatable illness. Even the critics of the Minnesota model could take some satisfaction in the results, since they had argued that other treatments were more cost effective than twenty-eight-day inpatient rehabilitation.

The argument for the effectiveness of treatment was strengthened by the development of a new paradigm for understanding addiction. The advocates of this view acknowledged that alcoholism and drug addiction were not like most diseases, because drinking and drug taking were voluntary in the beginning. Yet there were other diseases that closely resembled addiction, including type 2 diabetes, hypertension, and asthma.

In a 1996 article in the *Lancet*, Charles P. O'Brien and A. Thomas McLellan observed that these are "conditions that show a similar confluence of genetic, biological, behavioral and environmental factors." All three were regarded by the medical profession as "chronic" disorders because there was no expectation of a cure. They were also treated successfully as long as patients followed a strict diet and proper exercise regimen. But patients often failed to follow a doctor's orders and experienced a recurrence of their symptoms. O'Brien and McLellan argued that there were also effective treatments for alcoholism and drug addiction and that their rate of relapse was actually lower than some other chronic diseases. "Is it not time that we judged the 'worth' of treatments for chronic addiction with the same standards that we use for treatments of other chronic diseases?" they asked.[21]

Four years later, McLellan and O'Brien renewed their plea in an article in the *Journal of the American Medical Association*. Physicians continued to see addiction as a social problem instead of a health issue, they said. Few medical schools required their students to take an adequate course on the subject, and most doctors were not asking about alcohol or drug use during routine exams. A survey of general practitioners and nurses found that a majority were unaware of effective medical treatments for addiction.

McLellan and O'Brien acknowledged that the rate of relapse one year after alcohol or drug treatment was high—between 40 and 60 percent. But they reiterated the fact that the relapse rates for patients with diabetes, hypertension, and asthma were also high, and this did not mean that the treatments were ineffective. In this article, they also went into great detail on some of the proven methods of treating opioid and alcohol addiction. The relapse rate for addictions would decline when alcohol and drug dependence were treated properly. "It is essential that practitioners adapt the care and medical monitoring strategies currently used in the treatment of other chronic illnesses to the treatment of drug dependence," they concluded.[22]

There was already an outstanding example of a program that was executing the policies they were describing. In the 1970s, state medical boards began to respond to rising concern over addiction in the medical profession by creating physician health programs (PHP). The PHPs investigated reports of impaired doctors and then gave them a choice—accept treatment or lose your license to practice medicine. Unlike many employee assistance programs, however, the PHPs retained the commitment to rehabilitation that had inspired the sober drunks who started the first industrial alcoholism programs. Physicians who were in recovery played a key role in the program, counseling the newcomers during treatment and then helping them connect with other recovering doctors and twelve-step programs on their release. What made the PHP programs unique, however, was the fact that they played an active role in the lives of their patients for five years and sometimes more. They conducted periodic interviews and random drug tests. When doctors relapsed, they reevaluated them, deciding whether to require more treatment or to recommend disciplinary action. License revocation was relatively rare. While 25 percent suffered a relapse, many of them got sober again. PHPs reported success rates between 70 and 96 percent.

William L. White was enthusiastic about the success of the PHPs. In 2008, he sensed "an historical opportunity." He joined McLellan in publishing an article that urged "re-engineering addiction treatment into a system of sustained recovery support." White believed that the philosophy of addiction treatment was returning to its roots. While the members of the American Association for the Cure of Inebriety considered alcoholism a disease, they had also recognized that it was a complex disorder that resembled other chronic illnesses in its most extreme form. But this understanding disappeared with the AACI. "The emphasis on alcoholism as a *chronic* disease was lost in the larger battle to convey to the American public and policy makers that alcoholism was a disease," White and McLellan wrote. Although the idea of alcoholism as chronic illness had been reborn, it had yet to change much:

> While many in our field have come to consider some (not all) forms of addiction as chronic—this change in thinking has not been followed by changes in treatment strategy, monitoring methods, insurance coverage or outcome expectations.

The purpose of the article was to outline the wide-ranging changes that had to be made.[23]

White and McLellan began their task by attempting to clear away the wreckage of decades of debate over the nature of alcoholism. They wrote:

> Our focus in this article is not on what addiction is—a disease, illness, disorder, habit, problem, etc.—but on the temporal course of addiction and how the span of the disorder from onset through sustained recovery can be most effectively managed at personal and professional level.

The first step was to make clear that not all alcohol or drug (AOD) problems were chronic. "[M]ost do NOT have a prolonged and progressive course," they wrote. "All persons with AOD problems do NOT need specialized, professional, long-term monitoring and support— many recover on their own, with family or peer support." But the line between problem drinking and alcoholism was hard to decipher in the early years of a drinking career. White and McLellan called for research to identify early signs of progression.[24]

They also sought to reassure alcoholics, drug addicts, and their families. "Among those who do need treatment, relapse is NOT inevitable, and all persons suffering from substance dependence do NOT require multiple treatments before they achieve stable, long-lasting recoveries," they wrote. Even in the most difficult cases, partial recoveries were possible:

> Recovery management strategies for persons with the most severe and persistent disorders include multiple goals: reducing the number, intensity, and duration of relapse episodes; strengthening and extending the length of remission periods; reducing the personal and social costs associated with relapse; reducing the propensity for drug substitution and other excessive behaviors during early periods of recovery initiation; and enhancing the quality of personal/family life through both the remission and relapse phases of the disorder.

Abstinence remained the goal of treatment, but under the chronic care model, it was no longer the sole measure of success.[25]

White and McLellan pointed to a 2006 study that concluded that the recovery rate from alcoholism was almost 50 percent. Only 18 percent of those in recovery were abstinent. The rest were still drinking but had not reported symptoms of abuse or dependence during the previous twelve months. Many had no desire to quit drinking and might have succeeded in their goal of moderating their drinking. But others continued to try to achieve abstinence. The promise of the chronic disease model was that it would develop strategies to identify all these people and help them achieve their goals. "We invite those on the frontlines of addiction treatment to join us in writing this new future for addiction recovery in America," they wrote.[26]

As professionals reimagined addiction treatment, an advocacy movement was organizing to press for its realization. The spirit that had animated recovering alcoholics in the 1950s and 1960s to staff hospital wards, open chapters of the National Council on Alcoholism, and lobby for the Hughes bill faded after 1970. One exception was a sober drunk named Paul Molloy who joined with other occupants of a county-run halfway house in Silver Springs, Maryland, in taking over the lease in 1975. Molloy later launched Oxford House, which began renting homes for alcoholics and addicts who were trying to stay sober. But activism was declining. Harold Hughes attempted to reinvigorate it by organizing a Society for Americans in Recovery in 1991, but the organization closed several years later.

It was only in 1996 that veteran activists began to notice new local groups organizing around issues like the need for detox services for indigent patients or a decision to reduce the number of beds in a treatment facility. "We came from the grassroots," one activist said. In Santa Barbara, California, one group gathered a large number of supporters at a board of supervisors meeting. "They asked all those in recovery to stand, and the whole room stood up. . . . They invited us to the table in a strategic planning process," an organizer reported.[27]

The federal government attempted to encourage these new groups. In 1998, the Center for Substance Abuse Treatment, a division of the Substance Abuse and Mental Health Services Administration (SAMHSA), issued grants to nineteen community groups to assist them in organizing people in recovery to advocate for improved addiction treatment. At the same time, the Johnson Institute Foundation, which was formed to promote the early-intervention strategy of Vernon Johnson, was funding regular meetings of leaders in the addiction field.

Recognizing the potential of the community groups, organizers began to outline a plan for a public awareness campaign that would be launched at a summit meeting in St. Paul, Minnesota, in October 2001. The first step was to identify participants who represented every aspect of "the national recovery community."

Organizers sent a questionnaire to representatives of sixty-six groups actively promoting recovery at the local level and individuals who had recovered from alcohol or drug addiction. Whenever possible, a balance was sought based on geography and cultural diversity. There was also an attempt to ensure that different methods of recovery were represented by including people from secular, twelve-step, and religious groups. A special effort was made to include those who had recovered with the assistance of medicine like methadone.

Six hundred questionnaires were distributed, and two hundred people who responded were chosen to attend, including some family members of alcoholics and addicts and representatives of recovery organizations, many of whom were also in recovery.

The Faces & Voices of Recovery Summit had two major goals. The first was to get people in recovery to identify themselves publicly. The news media were full of stories about addicted people, but almost all were active alcoholics or addicts. The few who were sober or clean were generally early in their recoveries, including celebrities who were still cycling in and out of rehabs. The public needed to see that alcoholics and addicts were living full and satisfying lives; engaged in demanding, important careers; raising children; and contributing to their communities. There were millions of potential role models. But few people were speaking up, in part because there was a widespread belief that it violated AA and NA traditions of anonymity. One of the first speakers confronted this issue directly on the opening night of the St. Paul summit. "By our silence, we let others define who we are," she said.[28]

The other objective was to plan an advocacy campaign to seek changes in laws and government policies that would enhance the prospects for recovery. Summit participants were polled to identify the most important issues, and there was strong support for a campaign to end discrimination against people in recovery. At the time of the summit, one of the most pressing issues was the failure of insurance companies to provide adequate coverage for behavioral illnesses, including alcohol and drug addiction.

Legislation had been introduced in Congress and state legislatures to force the companies to provide equal treatment of mental and physical illness. But the insurance companies were lobbying hard against the parity bills. In California, they had succeeded in getting the legislature to drop addiction treatment, although recovery groups there were fighting hard to restore it. Other goals included ending job discrimination against people who had been in treatment and allowing people who had been convicted of drug offenses to gain access to government welfare and education programs that would help them make a new start.

While these were ambitious goals, a national poll conducted by the organizers showed that there was strong support for them among people in recovery. A random survey of drunks and addicts in recovery revealed that 87 percent agreed that it was important for the American people to understand the basic facts of addiction and recovery. More surprisingly, half said they were willing to talk about their experience publicly.

The 2001 summit put the recovery movement on a new footing. Faces & Voices of Recovery, which began as a publicity campaign, was incorporated in 2004, making it the national voice of the recovery community organizations (RCO). The summit also encouraged the creation of new groups, which proliferated rapidly. By 2016, there were one hundred local, regional, and state RCOs

Some of the RCOs operated community centers that helped people in recovery find services and advice. There were twenty-five recovery community centers in New England in 2012, including three centers operated by the Connecticut Community for Addiction Recovery (CCAR). In 2013, the CCAR centers recorded fifty-nine thousand visits and hosted eleven hundred events, including support meetings, GED classes, and computer classes. CCAR also sponsored a hot line that received more than fourteen hundred calls that year from people who were in danger of relapsing.

In addition, the RCOs were seeking to reverse the sharp decline in the number of people in recovery who were working in the addiction field. CCAR trained seventeen hundred "recovery coaches" in 2013 and established a Recovery Technical Assistance Group to help other RCOs establish coaching programs.

The birth of an organized movement of former drunks and addicts played an important role in expanding government support of recovery. When Senator Paul Wellstone addressed the Faces & Voices of Recovery Summit in 2001, he said there was no chance of passing his insurance parity bill if it contained addiction treatment. But, by 2008, people in recovery were making themselves heard. Wellstone had died in an airplane crash, but by the time his bill came up for a final vote in 2008, it included coverage for addiction treatment. When the Mental Health Parity and Addiction Equity Act was sitting in committee in the House of Representatives, recovery groups generated ten thousand calls to Speaker Nancy Pelosi to help move it to the floor, where it passed.

An even more important victory followed two years later with the enactment of the Patient Protection and Affordable Care Act. The centerpiece of President Barack Obama's legislative agenda, the Affordable Care Act (ACA), expanded health-insurance coverage for millions of Americans. It had great significance for alcoholics and addicts because it defined addiction treatment as an "essential" health service and required insurance companies to provide it to all their customers. The law prohibited insurance companies from denying coverage to people with preexisting conditions, making it possible for people in recovery to seek further medical help if they relapse. The ACA also encouraged the states to extend Medicaid to make it possible for poor people, who are disproportionately affected by addiction, to receive treatment for the first time.

The Obama administration went even further in its effort to help alcoholics and addicts. Although the Clinton and Bush administrations had launched several helpful programs, the Obama administration was the first to officially embrace recovery as a cornerstone of US drug policy. The first signal of a dramatic change in policy came soon after the new president took office in 2009. The White House Office of National Drug Control Policy (ONDCP) had been established by the Reagan administration to lead the war on drugs. The leader of the ONDCP was known to the nation as the "drug czar" and had usually been a man with military or law enforcement background. After Obama was elected, a new office was added to the ONDCP and charged with encouraging recovery. Leaders of the recovery movement were invited to consult with White House officials, and recovery was announced as one of the four principles of a new national drug control strategy.

The administration also began to add recovery leaders to the ONDCP. McLellan, whose articles comparing addiction to other chronic diseases had been highly influential in the recovery movement, was hired as deputy director in 2012. He was succeeded two years later by Michael Botticelli, who had directed the Massachusetts Bureau of Substance Abuse Services. Botticelli was also an alcoholic who had quit drinking in 1988 following his arrest for drunk driving. In 2015, he succeeded his boss, becoming the new drug czar.

What was happening around the United States, however, may have been even more important in encouraging new efforts to help the addicted. The problem of alcohol and drug addiction had certainly not improved in the opening decades of the twenty-first century. As this book goes to press, the United States is in the midst of an epidemic of opioid addiction that killed 29,467 people in 2014. The Substance Abuse and Mental Health Services Administration has said that twenty-two million Americans are addicted to alcohol or drugs. Fifteen million are alcoholics; another three million are addicted to both alcohol and drugs, and four million are drug addicts.

These numbers are daunting. But the number of people in recovery is also large and growing. In January 2016, there were more than 117,000 AA groups worldwide with over 2 million members, including 1.2 million in the United States. The Partnership for Drug-Free Kids and the New York State Office of Alcoholism and Substance Abuse Services commissioned a national poll in 2011 that asked 2,526 adults, "Did you once have a problem with alcohol and drugs, but no longer do?" Ten percent of the 2,526 adults who responded said yes. A survey of more than four hundred studies on remission rates put the number of alcoholics and addicts in recovery at between 25 million and 40 million. The ranks of the recovering are growing rapidly. There were 1.8 million in treatment in 2013.[29]

But before this army could begin to march, the recovery movement had to persuade the troops to begin identifying themselves publicly. This was the challenge of the St. Paul summit in 2001, but it was not easily accomplished. People had to be willing to face the consequences of challenging a stigma that was still strong. There was good reason to fear that their honesty would cost them.

It was also not immediately clear whether this strategy, which was largely driven by public relations, violated the traditions that guided millions of AA, NA, and Al-Anon members. AA's tradition six opposes endorsing, financing, or lending AA's name to any "outside enterprise." Tradition ten says that the organization has "no opinion on outside issues" and should not be drawn into "public controversy." Tradition eleven is potentially the most troublesome. "Our public relations policy is based on attraction rather than promotion; we need always maintain personal anonymity at the level of press, radio and films," it says. NA and Al-Anon adopted the same language. Many members of these anonymous fellowships were bound to have questions about the wisdom of "coming out."[30]

As a practical matter, this problem was easily solved. "You can speak about your own recovery and advocate for the rights of others, as long as you do not involve the twelve-step group by name," Faces & Voices of Recovery declared in a pamphlet, *Advocacy with Anonymity*. The pamphlet suggested language that made it clear that alcoholics and addicts were only speaking for themselves:

> I'm (your name) and I am in long-term recovery, which means that I have not used (insert alcohol of drugs or the name of the drugs you used) for more than (insert the number of years that you are in recovery) years. . . . I am now speaking out because long-term recovery has helped me change my life for the better, and I want to make it possible for others to do the same.

The pamphlet appeared to settle the matter for many. Alcoholics and addicts began identifying themselves as people "in long-term recovery" in a growing number of public places, including a 2013 documentary, *Anonymous People*, which tells the story of the emerging recovery movement. New groups were formed to encourage the trend. Two of them, Facing Addiction and I Am Not Anonymous (IANA), feature the names and pictures of their supporters on their websites. They sell T-shirts, buttons, and other promotional items that identify the wearer as "In Recovery" and urge people to "Unite to Fight Addiction." An IANA T-shirt reads, "IANA: If Not Us, Then Who?"[31]

People in recovery began showing up at public events. SAMHSA launched Recovery Month in 1989, but it was only after the St. Paul summit that large numbers began showing up at events sponsored by local groups around the country. In 2002, more than two hundred events were listed on the Recovery Month online calendar, including the Texas Soberfest in Austin, which drew five thousand people, and Hands Across the Bridge, which involved two hundred people holding hands across the Interstate 5 bridge connecting Portland, Oregon, and Vancouver, Washington. By 2008, the number of events had tripled. The highlight of that year's celebration was a march across the Brooklyn Bridge by ten thousand people. The federal government was represented by the national drug czar.

In 2013, it was estimated that more than 125,000 people participated in Recovery Month events, which included dances, workshops, conferences, parades, rallies, walks, and runs. Two years later, recovery advocates began organizing their biggest event yet, the Unite to Face Addiction rally and concert, which it was hoped would draw as many as a hundred thousand people to the National Mall in Washington, DC. A threatened hurricane led organizers to consider canceling the event, but the concert proceeded when the hurricane missed the city. Tens of thousands heard rock stars Steven Tyler, Joe Walsh, and Sheryl Crow perform.

Despite the reduced turnout, the Unite to Face Addiction event was a landmark in the growth of the recovery advocacy movement. On the National Mall, surrounded by the government institutions and national monuments, formerly anonymous people in recovery asserted their right to full citizenship. One of those who spoke to the crowd expressed the thoughts of many. William Cope Moyers, the son of journalist Bill Moyers, is vice president of public affairs and community relations at the Betty Ford Hazelden Foundation. He is also an addict and alcoholic who relapsed several times before he established long-term sobriety in 1994. Moyers was well qualified to speak for the crowd:

> For too long, addiction has been an illness of isolation. For too long, addiction has been cloaked in the stigma of private shame . . . the stigma of public intolerance . . . the stigma of discriminating public policy.
>
> But today . . . today TOO LONG . . . IS NO LONGER. Because today . . . HERE WE ARE!
>
> Today on this national mall we stand TOGETHER as the antidote to addiction. . . .
>
> WE unite to face addiction. WE unite to prove with our faces and our voices and our lives that addiction does not discriminate. . . . And to prove that recovery should not discriminate either. Because WE are the fortunate ones. The ones who got well. And it is our responsibility, our opportunity . . . to come together as one, for the sake of those who still suffer. . . . WE unite to let them know, that they are not alone. WE unite to reassure them—that it is okay to ask for help. WE unite to tell their families that there is hope. WE unite, to keep the doors of treatment open . . . and open wide, no matter how often those who suffer need to walk through them again.
>
> NO longer do we simply dream on about the promise and possibility of recovery. Today we live on, in our reality that recovery is real. Because it sounds and looks and lives like us. All of us. United.[32]

There is a long way to go before the recovery advocacy movement achieves all of its goals. The latest victory is the passage of the Comprehensive Addiction and Recovery Act (CARA) of 2016. It took several years of hard work by advocacy leaders and strong support from their clean and sober supporters to pass the bill, which creates new policies and additional funds to improve prevention, treatment, and recovery support. Even as they expressed satisfaction at the passage of the bill, however, recovery leaders acknowledged that it did not go as far as they hoped. CARA will authorize only a million dollars a year for the vital support services provided by RCOs. The fact that CARA passed by overwhelming majorities in both houses of a bitterly divided Congress is not evidence that our elected representatives have suddenly recognized the importance of recovery. It is a response to the crisis caused by opioid addiction. CARA is an important step forward, but the fight for recovery will go on.

Sobriety has always come in waves that carried us forward and then receded. At times, we seemed in danger of losing all of our gains. The Washingtonians faded quickly. Prohibition sent the country in the wrong direction in its search for a solution. When interest in alcoholism as a medical problem revived after the repeal of Prohibition, no one remembered the work of J. Edward Turner, Albert Day, and the American Association for the Cure of Inebriety. Even after the importance of treatment was widely recognized in the second half of the twentieth century, drug addicts were sent to prison instead of treatment.

But the search for sobriety never ended. Handsome Lake's Good Word was being read at Iroquois religious ceremonies more than 150 years after his death. Many Washingtonians joined the sober fraternities, which provided a home until the rise of the ribbon clubs. Leslie Keeley got rich claiming he had a gold cure for alcoholism, but he also helped tens of thousands get sober and provided the spark for a national league of sober men. Religion was a powerful force for recovery that worked through Jerry McAuley and the Salvation Army. The discoveries of science inspired Elwood Worcester and Courtenay Baylor.

In 1935, a new wave began to form. AA proved again that drunks could get sober, and as it prospered, it showed that they could stay sober for a lifetime. Sober alcoholics believed in the importance of treatment, and they convinced political leaders that it was important for the country. This argument lost ground during the 1980s and 1990s, but the treatment advocates won the war. Today, the US government recognizes that medical treatment for alcoholics and addicts is a basic human right.

There is always a possibility that this latest wave will recede. But it seems unlikely that people in recovery will allow it to happen. There are too many of them, and there has been a significant change in the way they think about themselves. For many years, AA members believed they were different from addicts. This attitude is waning as younger alcoholics join. Alcoholics and addicts in recovery are beginning to understand that what they are addicted to is less important than addiction itself and are working together to ensure that everyone has an opportunity to recover. Throughout American history, people who have survived addiction have carried the promise of recovery to fellow sufferers. Today, they are speaking directly to their fellow Americans.

MY FATHER TOLD ME the same story many times when I was growing up. My grandfather Mike sat him down at the kitchen table of their modest home in a hard-drinking steel town in western Pennsylvania. I don't know how old my dad was at the time—maybe a navy recruit on leave during the last days of World War II or a theater student attending college on the GI Bill. He may even have been a disk jockey by then. Mike was not much of a talker, but he was determined to make an impression on his son. His father was an alcoholic who died young, leaving Mike to raise two brothers and a sister. All three were heavy drinkers.

So was Mike. He put a bottle of Kessler's whiskey on the table and poured two large drinks. Raising his glass, he looked my dad in the eye.

"You drink too much," he said.

Mike was right about my dad, and if he had lived long enough, he would have seen right through me. When he died, my dad and I got drunk on shots and beers in a dark neighborhood bar around the corner from the funeral home.

So my grandfather never knew that he had started something. My father continued to drink, often having his first martini of the day at 10 a.m. following his radio show. But he was haunted by what alcoholism had done to his family, and the stories he told me were warnings. I wasn't completely surprised when he finally quit drinking.

That decision changed his life. He was not a bad man, but he was a selfish one. Then he joined Alcoholics Anonymous and started to repair the damage that he had done to his wife and children. He tried to help others. He was like Scrooge on Christmas morning. In his own words, he took his head out of his ass.

I watched his progress without understanding it because I was struggling with my own alcoholism. Then I quit drinking, too.

And it all began with a story. Mike introduced my father to the family ghosts, and he passed them along to me. Later I told our story so often that my sons begged for mercy.

But stories can inspire as well as warn.

From the time of Handsome Lake and the Washingtonians, sober drunks have shared their stories with people like my dad and me. They have shown us that we are not alone and introduced us to a worldwide community of people who are living happily without drugs or alcohol. They have told us how their lives were saved.

Today, we number in the millions, and our story grows louder with every retelling.

ACKNOWLEDGMENTS

MORE THAN TWENTY YEARS AGO, my adviser in graduate school, Walter P. Metzger, suggested that I write this book. I had just told him that I was a recovering alcoholic. He replied with his customary enthusiasm that the history of recovery would make a great subject for someone who had actually experienced it. Professor Metzger died earlier this year. I remain very grateful for his encouragement.

Every writer on the history of addiction and recovery stands on the shoulders of William L. White, author of *Slaying the Dragon: The History of Addiction Treatment and Recovery in America*. Published in 1998 and revised in 2014, *Slaying the Dragon* is a comprehensive history of the subject told by someone who has been personally involved in the recovery movement since the 1960s. Bill has worn many hats during his career: counselor, clinical director, researcher, trainer, and consultant. He has authored or coauthored eighteen books and more than four hundred articles, monographs, research reports, and book chapters. I am grateful to Bill for offering advice at key points in my research and for introducing me to Patty McCarthy Metcalf at Faces & Voices of Recovery and Greg Williams at Facing Addiction, who provided information about recent developments in the recovery movement.

Early in my research, I was fortunate to participate in the Addiction Studies Program for Journalists that was sponsored by the Wake Forest University School of Medicine and National Families in Action. The program brought together science reporters and other people writing about addiction and recovery for a two-day program in Washington, DC, which included presentations by experts on the physiology of alcoholism, drug prevention, and treatment for alcohol, and drug addiction. I want to thank the program director, Professor David Friedman of Wake Forest, and codirector Sue Rusche, the president and chief executive officer of National Families in Action.

Several libraries provided invaluable assistance. The Center for Alcohol Studies Library at Rutgers University is a gold mine for researchers. The Rutgers School of Alcohol Studies is the successor of the pioneering alcohol studies program established at Yale University in the 1940s, and its library inherited and expanded the collection of books, magazines, and other material started at Yale. The Rutgers library is headed by the expert and accommodating Judit H. Ward. Like so many other researchers, I have benefited from a temporary home in the Wertheim Room of the New York Public Library, which has been ably administered by Jay Barksdale and Melanie Locay. I also want to thank the librarians at the Syracuse University Library and the Illinois State Library as well as the General Service Office of Alcoholics Anonymous.

One of the pleasures of writing this book is that it has given me another opportunity to work with Beacon Press. Helene Atwan, the director, showed enthusiasm for the subject even before there was a formal proposal, and the manuscript has benefited enormously from her rigorous editing. I am delighted to be working again with my friends Tom Hallock and Pam MacColl, and with the rest of the wonderful staff at Beacon.

I am also grateful to Jill Marr at the Sandra Dijkstra Literary Agency for championing the book and for her expert shepherding.

Finally, I want to express my love and appreciation to Dan Cullen and Mary Chris Welch, who listened to years of talking and complaining about the book. Of course, the top prize in this category goes to my wife, Pat Willard, who told me to shut up and keep writing.

INTRODUCTION

1. David McCullough, *John Adams* (New York: Simon & Schuster, 2001), 529.

2. Paul C. Nagel, *Descent from Glory: Four Generations of the John Adams Family* (New York, Oxford: Oxford University Press, 1983), 79; McCullough, *John Adams*, 548.

3. Nagel, *Descent from Glory*, 80; McCullough, *John Adams*, 555.

4. Increase Mather, *Wo to Drunkards: Two Sermons Testifying Against the Sin of Drunkenness* (Boston: Printed and Sold by Timothy Green, 1712), 7.

5. Seneca, quoted in ibid, 18, 23, 24; Nathan Crosby, *Inebriate Asylums: Remarks in Opposition to Them Before the Committee on Charitable Institutions* (Boston: Nation Press, 1871), 3, 4, 5, 10.

CHAPTER ONE: MOUNTAIN OF BONES

1. Arthur C. Parker, *The Code of Handsome Lake, the Seneca Prophet* (Albany: State University of New York, 1913), 20, 22. Handsome Lake's descriptions of himself, his journey home, and its consequences are contained in the *Gaiwiio*, a record of his teachings that became the foundation of a new religion. The *Gaiwiio* (Good Word) was translated and published by Parker, an archeologist.

2. Ibid., 20–21. The language used to refer to indigenous people is often contested. I have used tribal names when possible. I use "Indian" to refer to indigenous people as a whole or to describe multiple tribes collectively.

3. Ibid., 21–22.

4. Anthony F. C. Wallace, *The Death and Rebirth of the Seneca* (New York: Alfred A. Knopf, 1970), 240–41; Parker, *The Code of Handsome Lake*, 24.

5. Parker, *The Code of Handsome Lake*, 24, 27.

6. Wallace, *The Death and Rebirth of the Seneca*, 242.

7. Ibid., 260, 307.

8. Kenneth T. Jackson, ed., *The Encyclopedia of New York City*, 2nd ed. (New Haven, CT: Yale University Press, 2010), 786.

9. Peter C. Mancall, *Deadly Medicine: Indians and Alcohol in Early America* (Ithaca, NY: Cornell University Press, 1995), 43–44.

10. Ibid., 69, 75.

11. Ibid., 12.

12. Ibid., 68–69, 70, 75; Alden T. Vaughan, *New England Frontier: Puritans and Indians, 1620–1675* (Boston: Little, Brown, 1965), 46.

13. Vaughan, *New England Frontier*, 43; Bartlett B. James and J. Franklin Jameson, *Journal of Jasper Danckaerts, 1679–1680* (New York: Charles Scribner's Sons, 1913), 179–80.

14. Mancall, *Deadly Medicine*, 46.

15. Ibid., 52.

16. James and Jameson, *Journal of Jasper Danckaerts*, 180; William E. Johnson, *The Federal Government and the Liquor Traffic* (Westerville, OH: American Issue Publishing, 1911), 176–77; Mancall, *Deadly Medicine*, 99.

17. Mancall, *Deadly Medicine*, 91, 96, 97.

18. Ibid., 107, 123.

19. Don L. Coyhis and William L. White, *Alcohol Problems in Native America: The Untold Story of Resistance and Recovery—"The Truth About the Lie"* (Colorado Springs, CO: White Bison, 2006), 69; Mancall, *Deadly Medicine*, 120.

20. Mancall, *Deadly Medicine*, 52, 91, 120.

21. Ibid., 93.

22. Anthony F. C. Wallace, *Jefferson and the Indians: The Tragic Fate of the First Americans* (Cambridge, MA: Harvard University Press, 1999), 296.

23. Wallace, *Death and Rebirth of the Seneca*, 120.

24. Gregory E. Dowd, *A Spirited Resistance: The North American Indian Struggle for Unity, 1745–1815* (Baltimore: Johns Hopkins University Press, 1992), 126.

25. Ibid., 142.

26. Ibid., 138.

27. Wallace, *Death and Rebirth of the Seneca*, 244. Subsequent quotes in this chapter are from pp. 284, 278, 301, 304, 305, 306, 307, 309, 310, 318, and 319–20.

CHAPTER TWO: OUT OF THE GUTTER

1. William George Hawkins, *The Life of John H. W. Hawkins* (Boston: John P. Jewett, 1859), 71.

2. Rev. O. W. Morris to Rev. William G. Hawkins, October 25, 1858, quoted in ibid., 72.

3. Hawkins, *The Life of John H. W. Hawkins*, 73.

4. David Rothman, *The Discovery of the Asylum: Social Order and Disorder in the New Republic* (Boston: Little, Brown, 1971), 76.

5. Edwards quoted in Jed Dannenbaum, *Drink and Disorder: Temperance Reform in Cincinnati from the Washingtonian Revival to the WCTU* (Urbana: University of Illinois Press, 1984), 38.

6. Hawkins, *The Life of John H. W. Hawkins*, 4, 5–6.

7. Ibid., 26, 40.

8. Ibid., 40.

9. Ibid., 59.

10. Ibid., 92.

11. Ibid., 71, 92.

12. Ibid., 92–93.

13. David Harrisson Jr., *A Voice from the Washingtonian Home* (Boston: Redding & Co., 1860), 47.

14. John Zug to Editor, *Journal of the American Temperance Union* (December 12, 1840), quoted in Hawkins, *The Life of John H. W. Hawkins*, footnote, 67–68.

15. Hawkins, *The Life of John H. W. Hawkins*, 86.

16. Ibid., 84–85.

17. Ibid., 85, 87.

18. Ibid., 86; *Mercantile Journal* quoted in ibid., 89.

19. Ibid., 95–96.

20. Leonard U. Blumberg and William L. Pittman, *Beware the First Drink! The Washington Temperance Movement and Alcoholics Anonymous* (Seattle: Glen Abby Books, 1991), 76; Sean Wilentz, *Chants Democratic: New York City and the Rise of the American Working Class* (New York: Oxford University Press, 1984), 307.

21. Ruth M. Alexander, "'We Are Engaged as a Band of Sisters': Class and Domesticity in the Washingtonian Temperance Movement, 1840–1850," *Journal of American History* 75, no. 3 (December 1988), 771.

22. Blumberg and Pittman, *Beware the First Drink!*, 145.

23. Hawkins, *The Life of John H. W. Hawkins*, 301.

24. Ibid., 197.

25. Ibid., 189.

26. Abraham Lincoln, "An Address Delivered before the Springfield Washington Temperance Society, on the 22nd of February, 1842," *The Collected Works of Abraham Lincoln*, vol. 1, ed. Roy P. Basler (New Brunswick, NJ: Rutgers University Press, 1953), 275, 276–77.

27. Ibid., 273–74, 277, 278.

28. Ibid., 273, 276.

29. Abraham Lincoln, *Great Speeches* (New York: Dover Publications, 1991), 8; Lincoln, "An Address Delivered Before the Springfield Washington Temperance Society," 279.

30. John B. Gough, *Autobiography and Personal Recollections of John B. Gough, with 26 Years' Experience as a Public Speaker* (Springfield, MA: Bill, Nichols & Co., 1870), 175, 179.

31. *Journal of the American Temperance Union*, 6 (October 1842), 154; John Marsh, *Temperance Recollections: Labors, Defeats, Triumphs; an Autobiography* (New York: Charles Scribner, 1866), 128.

32. *The Crystal Fount and Rechabite Recorder*, 2, no. 2 (September 23, 1843), 26–27.

33. "Temperance Changes," *Journal of the American Temperance Union*, 8 (October 1844), 154.

34. John Marsh quoted in Milton A. Maxwell, "The Washingtonian Movement," *Quarterly Journal of Studies on Alcohol* 11 (1950): 12.

35. Mark Edward Lender and James Kirby Martin, *Drinking in America: A History*, rev. and enl. ed. (New York: Free Press, 1987), 55.

36. Almost Over, *Crystal Fount and Rechabite Recorder* 3 (November 2, 1844), 120.

37. Alexander, "'We Are Engaged as a Band of Sisters,'" 780.

38. David M. Fahey, *Temperance and Racism: John Bull, Johnny Reb, and the Good Templars* (Lexington: University Press of Kentucky, 1996), 20.

39. Hawkins, *The Life of John H. W. Hawkins*, 272.

40. Ibid., 284, 293.

41. Ibid., 349.

42. Ibid., 350–51.

43. Ibid., 400.

CHAPTER THREE: DISCOVERY OF THE DISEASE

1. J. Edward Turner, *The History of the First Inebriate Asylum in the World* (New York: n.p., 1888), 16.

2. John W. Crowley and William L. White, *Drunkard's Refuge: The Lessons of the New York State Inebriate Asylum* (Amherst: University of Massachusetts Press, 2004), 29–31.

3. "Significant Scots: George Cheyne," http://www.electricscotland.com /history/other/cheyne_george.htm.

4. George Cheyne, *An Essay on Health and Long Life* (London: George Strahan, 1724), 43–44, 51–53.

5. David Freeman Hawke, *Benjamin Rush: Revolutionary Gadfly* (Indianapolis: Bobbs-Merrill Co., 1971), 86.

6. Ibid., 101.

7. Ibid., 177.

8. Ibid., 303.

9. Benjamin Rush, *An Inquiry into the Effects of Spirituous Liquors on the Human Body, and Their Influence upon the Happiness of Society* (Philadelphia: Thomas Bradford, 1784), 4.

10. Ibid., 6, 7.

11. Ibid., 10, 11.

12. Benjamin Rush, *An Inquiry into the Effects of Ardent Spirits upon the Human Mind and Body with an Account of the Means of Preventing and of the Remedies for Curing Them*, 6th ed. (New York: Cornelius Davis, 1811), 2–3, 7.

13. Benjamin Rush, *Medical Inquiries and Observations upon the Diseases of the Mind*, 5th ed. (Philadelphia: Grigg & Elliot, 1835), 264; ibid., 4, 9.

14. Rush, *Inquiry into the Effects of Ardent Spirits*, 4, 21.

15. Ibid., 28, 32.

16. Benjamin Rush, *Autobiography of Benjamin Rush; His "Travels Through Life," Together with His* Commonplace Book *for 1789–1813* (Westport, CT: Greenwood Press, 1970), 354.

17. Rush, *Medical Inquiries and Observations upon the Diseases of the Mind*, 265–66.

18. Rush to John Adams, June 28, 1811, *Letters of Benjmin Rush*, vol. 2 (Princeton NJ: Princeton University Press, 1951), 1086–87; Rush, *Inquiry into the Effects of Ardent Spirits*, 25–26.

19. Samuel Bayard Woodward, *Essays on Asylums for Inebriates* (Worcester, MA: n.p., 1838), 1.

20. James Parton, *Smoking and Drinking* (Boston: Ticknor and Fields, 1868), 119.

21. Harrisson, *A Voice from the Washingtonian Home*, 114.

22. Albert Day, *Methomania: A Treatise on Alcoholic Poisoning* (Boston: James Campbell, 1867), 32–33.

23. Ibid., 35, 39.

24. Parton, *Smoking and Drinking*, 138–39.

25. Harrisson, *A Voice from the Washingtonian Home*, 122.

26. Day, *Methomania*, 51; Parton, *Smoking and Drinking*, 145.

27. Harrisson, *A Voice from the Washingtonian Home*, 124.

28. Ibid., 204.

29. Ibid., 204, 212, 223.

30. Ibid., 204, 231, 232.

31. [John W. Palmer], "Our Inebriates, Harbored and Helped," *Atlantic Monthly* 24 (July 1869): 109.

32. T. D. Crothers, "Sketch of the Late Dr. J. Edward Turner, the Founder of Inebriate Asylums," *Quarterly Journal of Inebriety* 9, no. 4 (October 1889): 311–12.

33. Crowley and White, *Drunkard's Refuge*, 36–37, 43.

34. J. Edward Turner, *The History of the First Inebriate Asylum in the World* (New York: privately published, 1888), 234–35.

35. Ibid.

36. Palmer, "Our Inebriates, Harbored and Helped," 109, 110.

37. Parton, *Smoking and Drinking*, 135; Palmer, "Our Inebriates, Harbored and Helped," 112, 114.

38. Parton, *Smoking and Drinking*, 127; Palmer, "Our Inebriates, Harbored and Helped," 112.

39. Palmer, "Our Inebriates, Harbored and Helped," 113.

40. Ibid., 114–15.

41. Ibid., 115, 116.

42. Joseph Parrish, "Historical Sketch of the American Association for the Cure of Inebriety," *Quarterly Journal of Inebriety* 10 (1888): 189.

43. Joseph Parrish, "The Philosophy of Intemperance," American Association for the Cure of Inebriety, *Proceedings of the First Meeting Held in New York, Nov. 29 and 30, 1870* (Philadelphia: Henry B. Ashmead, 1871), 26, 27, 28, 29.

44. Ibid., 29–30, 30–31, 32.

45. Ibid., 33, 40.

46. Parrish, "Historical Sketch," 190; "Disabilities of Inebriates; a Communication from the Inmates of the Pennsylvania Sanitarium," *Proceedings*, 41, 42.

47. "Disabilities of Inebriates," 43, 44.

48. Parrish, "Historical Sketch," 190.

49. Parrish, "Philosophy of Intemperance," 33; Nathan Crosby, *Inebriate Asylums: Remarks in Opposition to Them Before the Committee on Charitable Institutions* (Boston: Nation Press, 1871), 3, 4.

50. Crosby, *Inebriate Asylums*, 5, 10.

51. Parrish, "Historical Sketch," 189; Joseph Parrish, "Opening Address," American Association for the Cure of Inebriety, *Proceedings of the Second Meeting Held in New York, Nov. 14 and 15, 1871* (Philadelphia: Henry B. Ashmead, 1872), 4, 5, 6, 7.

52. Parrish, "Opening Address," 7.

53. Parrish, "Historical Sketch," 189.

CHAPTER FOUR: SEARCH FOR HIGHER POWER

1. Robert M. Offord, *Jerry McAuley: An Apostle to the Lost*, 2nd ed. (New York: George H. Dorran Co., 1907), 64.

2. Arthur Bonner, *Jerry McAuley and His Mission*, rev. ed. (Neptune, NJ: Loizeaux Brothers, 1990), 15.

3. Offord, *Jerry McAuley*, 13.

4. Bonner, *Jerry McAuley and His Mission*, 19.

5. Offord, *Jerry McAuley*, 14, 16, 17, 18, 19.

6. Ibid., 22.

7. Ibid., 23.

8. Ibid., 28, 29.

9. Bonner, *Jerry McAuley and His Mission*, 38.

10. Ibid., 46.

11. Ibid., 60.

12. Ibid., 54, 60, 63.

13. Carroll Smith Rosenberg, *Religion and the Rise of the American City: The New York City Mission Movement, 1812–1870* (Ithaca, NY: Cornell University Press, 1971), 182; Bonner, *Jerry McAuley and His Mission*, 66.

14. Bonner, *Jerry McAuley and His Mission*, 64.

15. Ibid., 10.

16. Annie Wittenmyer, *History of the Woman's Temperance Crusade* (Philadelphia: Office of the Christian Woman, 1878), 724, 725.

17. Ibid., 728–29.

18. Ibid., 729.

19. W. H. Daniels, *The Temperance Reform and Its Great Reformers* (New York: Nelson & Phillips, 1878), 378–79.

20. Ibid., 377–78, 392.

21. Ibid., 389.

22. Ibid., 382, 384, 402.

23. Ibid., 378, 387.

24. Ibid., 402–3.

25. Ibid., 467.

26. Ibid., 468.

27. Ibid., 470–71.

28. Frederick B. Hargreaves, *Gold as a Cure for Drunkenness, Being an Account of the Double Chloride of Gold Discovery Recently Made by L. E. Keeley of Dwight, Illinois*, 3d ed., rev. and enl. (Dwight, IL: n.p., July 1880), 2.

29. "Inside History of the Keeley Cure," *Journal of the American Medical Association* 49 (1907): 1862. Seventy years after Keeley and Hargreaves began their experiments, two Danish researchers discovered a chemical, disulfiram, that could produce the same effect as nauseants without being added to alcohol. Marketed as Antabuse, it is still used in the treatment of some alcoholics.

30. Ibid.

31. Ibid., 1863.

32. Ibid.

33. Ibid.

34. R. H. Harris, "Hope for Drunkards," *Chicago Daily Tribune*, March 18, 1891, 7; John Hudspeth, "A Disease and Not a Crime," *Chicago Daily Tribune*, March 20, 1891, 9.

35. F. M. Havens to Henry Coleman, March 12, 1891, quoted in Alfred R. Calhoun, *Is It "A Modern Miracle?": A Careful Investigation of "The Keeley Gold Cure" for Drunkenness and the Opium Habit* (New York: People's Publishing, 1892), 130, 131.

36. Hudspeth, "A Disease and Not a Crime."

37. "Editor Medill Honored," *Banner of Gold* 23, no. 26 (December 29, 1894): 823.

38. "Many Cures Effected," *Chicago Daily Tribune*, February 10, 1891, 1; "He Has Cured 5,000 Drunkards," *Chicago Daily Tribune*, February 14, 1891, 1; "Dr. Keeley's Dipsomania Cure," *Chicago Daily Tribune*, February 18, 1891, 4.

39. C. S. Clark, *The Perfect Keeley Cure: Incidents at Dwight, and "Through the Valley of the Shadow" into Perfect Light* (Milwaukee: Armitage & Allen, 1892), 48, 54. Drug addiction was a growing problem at the time. Keeley advertised the double chloride of gold as a cure for opium and other addictive drugs, including tobacco, "cocaine, chloral, hasheesh, atropia, strychnia, and such others as are formed by humanity." William L. White, *Slaying the Dragon: The History of Addiction Treatment and Recovery in America*, 2nd ed. (Bloomington, IL: Chestnut Health Systems, 2014), 74.

40. Ibid., 53.

41. Ibid., 42.

42. Ibid., 102.

43. John Flavel Mines, "Drunkenness Is Curable," *North American Review* 153, no. 419 (October 1891): 447.

44. H. Wayne Morgan, *Drugs in America: A Social History, 1800–1980* (Syracuse, NY: Syracuse University Press, 1981), 80.

45. Ibid.; Ben Scott, "Keeleyism: A History of Dr. Keeley's Gold Cure for Alcoholism," master's thesis, Illinois State University, 1974, 80.

46. George A. Barclay, "The Keeley League," *Journal of the Illinois State Historical Society* 57 (Winter 1964): 349–50, 352.

47. Ibid., 354.

48. Ibid., 356.

49. "Dr. Leslie Keeley Dead," *Chicago Daily Tribune*, February 22, 1900.

50. "Doings at Dwight," *Banner of Gold* 15, no. 9 (September 1900): 141.

51. "Reunion and Celebration of the Anniversary of Mr. Hegner's Graduation," *Banner of Gold* 15, no. 5 (May 1900): 71; *Banner of Gold* 15, no. 6 (June 1900): 93; "Doings at Dwight," *Banner of Gold* 15, no. 7 (July 1900): 107.

CHAPTER FIVE: FALSE DAWN

1. *Kansas City Star*, January 31, 1901, quoted in Kansas Museum of History, "Carry A. Nation," online exhibit, http://kshs.org/p/carry-a-nation-1901-story/10601.

2. Dorothy Caldwell, "Carry Nation, a Missouri Woman, Won Fame in Kansas," *Missouri Historical Review* LXIII, no. 4 (1969): 474.

3. "Hurrah for Carrie," *Emporia Gazette*, February 11, 1901.

4. Mark Lender and James Martin, *Drinking in America: A History*, ed., rev. and enl. (New York and London: Free Press, 1987), 69.

5. Leonard U. Blumberg and William L. Pittman, *Beware the First Drink! The Washington Temperance Movement and Alcoholics Anonymous* (Seattle: Glen Abby Books, 1991), 62.

6. Lender and Martin, *Drinking in America*, 73; Charles T. Woodman, *Narrative of the Life of Charles T. Woodman: A Reformed Inebriate, Written by Himself* (Boston: Theodore Abbot, 1843), 12.

7. John Allen Kraut, *The Origins of Prohibition* (New York: Alfred A. Knopf, 1925), 205.

8. Hawkins, *The Life of John H. W. Hawkins*, 348.

9. Ibid., 375.

10. Caldwell, "Carry Nation, a Missouri Woman," 464.

11. Jack London, *John Barleycorn*, introduction by Pete Hamill (New York: Modern Library, 2001), xv, 4.

12. John Gardner Greene, "The Emmanuel Movement, 1906–1929," *New England Quarterly* 7, no. 3 (September 1934): 502.

13. Elwood Worcester, Samuel McComb, and Isador H. Coriat, *Religion and Medicine: The Moral Control of Nervous Disorders* (New York: Moffat, Yard & Co., 1908), 134.

14. Horatio W. Dresser, ed., *The Quimby Manuscripts*, 2nd ed. (New York: Thomas Y. Crowell Co., 1921), 194.

15. Eric Caplan, *Mind Games: American Culture and the Birth of Psychotherapy* (Berkeley: University of California Press, 1998), 68.

16. Henry Wood, "Does Bi-Chloride of Gold Cure Inebriety?," *Arena* 7 (January 1893): 147.

17. Ibid., 148, 149, 150.

18. Ibid., 151.

19. Caplan, *Mind Games*, 123; Elwood Worcester, "The Results of the Emmanuel Movement," *Ladies' Home Journal* 25 (February 1909): 16.

20. Elwood Worcester and Samuel McComb, *Body, Mind and Spirit* (Boston: Marshall Jones, 1931), 235.

21. Worcester quoted in Richard M. Dubiel, *The Road to Fellowship: The Role of the Emmanuel Movement and the Jacoby Club in the Development of Alcoholics Anonymous* (Lincoln, NE: iUniverse, 2004), 82; "Men Help Themselves by Helping Others," *Boston Daily Globe*, July 27, 1913.

22. Worcester, "The Results of the Emmanuel Movement," 16; Dubiel, *The Road to Fellowship*, 87.

23. Dubiel, *The Road to Fellowship*, 88.

24. Dwight Anderson and Page Cooper, *The Other Side of the Bottle* (New York: A. A. Wyn, 1950), 152, 154.

25. Courtenay Baylor, *Remaking a Man: One Successful Method of Mental Refitting* (New York: Moffat, Yard & Co., 1919), 2.

26. Ibid., 8, 10, 11, 12.

27. Ibid., 7, 21, 51.

28. Ibid., 22, 61.

29. Ibid., 85.

30. Nathan G. Hale Jr., *Freud and the Americans: The Beginning of Psychoanalysis in the United States, 1876–1917* (New York: Oxford University Press, 1971), 227.

31. "Is This Why You Drink?," *McClure's Magazine* 49, no. 5 (September 1917): 16.

32. Ibid.

33. Ibid., 16, 17.

34. Sarah W. Tracy, *Alcoholism in America: From Reconstruction to Prohibition* (Baltimore: Johns Hopkins University Press, 2005), 136.

35. Ibid., 134.

36. Ibid., 128.

37. Ibid., 201, 214.

38. Ibid., 207.

39. Ibid., 217.

40. Ibid., 171.

41. Ibid., 185.

42. Ibid., 250, 262.

43. Ibid., 261, 262.

44. Thomas C. Maroukis, *The Peyote Road: Religious Freedom and the Native American Church* (Norman: Oklahoma University Press, 2010), 33; J. S. Slotkin, *The Peyote Religion: A Study in Indian-White Relations* (Glencoe, IL: Free Press, 1956), 140.

45. Robert H. Ruby and John A. Brown, *John Slocum and the Indian Shaker Church* (Norman: Oklahoma University Press, 1996), 6, 26.

46. S. C. Gwynne, *Empire of the Summer Moon: Quanah Parker and the Rise and Fall of the Comanches, the Most Powerful Indian Tribe in American History* (New York: Scribner, 2010), 314.

47. Hazel W. Hertzberg, *The Search for an American Indian Identity: Modern Pan-Indian Movements* (Syracuse, NY: Syracuse University Press, 1971), 266–67.

48. Ibid., 266, 267, 268.

49. Clarence W. Hall, *Out of the Depths: The Life Story of Henry F. Milans* (New York: Fleming H. Revell, 1930), 134.

50. Ibid., 124.

51. Ibid., 140.

52. Ibid., 153.

53. "The Salvation Army's 'Lost Drunks,'" *Literary Digest* 66, no. 12 (September 18, 1920): 38.

54. "A Salvation Army Report on Prohibition," *Literary Digest* 71, no. 2 (October 8, 1921): 32.

55. Alcoholics Anonymous, *Dr. Bob and the Good Oldtimers: A Biography, with Recollections of Early A.A. in the Midwest* (New York: Alcoholics Anonymous World Services, 1980), 30.

56. John C. Burnham, "New Perspectives on the Prohibition 'Experiment' of the 1920s," *Journal of Social History* 2, no. 1 (Autumn 1968): 60.

57. "A Salvation Army Report on Prohibition."

58. Deborah Blum, "The Chemist's War: The Little-Told Story of How the US Government Poisoned Alcohol During Prohibition with Deadly Consequences," *Slate*, February 19, 2010, http://www.slate.com/articles/health _and_science/medical_examiner/2010/02/the_chemists_war.html; "Government to Double Alcohol Poison Content," *New York Times*, December 30, 1926, 2.

59. Alcoholics Anonymous, *Dr. Bob and the Good Oldtimers*, 32.

CHAPTER SIX: TWO DRUNKS

1. Lois Wilson, *Lois Remembers: Memoirs of the Co-Founder of Al-Anon and Wife of the Co-Founder of Alcoholics Anonymous* (New York: Al-Anon Family Group Headquarters, 1987), 39, 72.

2. Ibid., 37, 72.

3. Alcoholics Anonymous, *"Pass It On": The Story of Bill Wilson and How the A.A. Message Reached the World* (New York: Alcoholics Anonymous World Services, 1984), 24.

4. Ibid., 30.

5. Wilson, *Lois Remembers*, 13–14, 98.

6. Ibid., 72.

7. Ibid., 69.

8. Ibid., 72, 81.

9. Alcoholics Anonymous, *"Pass It On,"* 101, 104–5.

10. Wilson, *Lois Remembers*, 86; Alcoholics Anonymous, *"Pass It On,"* 98, 108.

11. Alcoholics Anonymous, *"Pass It On,"* 111.

12. Alcoholics Anonymous, *Alcoholics Anonymous: The Story of How Many Thousands of Men and Women Have Recovered from Alcoholism*, 3rd ed. (New York: Alcoholics Anonymous World Services, 1976), 10.

13. Alcoholics Anonymous, *"Pass It On,"* 115; Alcoholics Anonymous, *Alcoholics Anonymous: The Story of How Many Thousands of Men and Women Have Recovered from Alcoholism*, 11–12.

14. William G. Borchert, *The Lois Wilson Story: When Love Is Not Enough* (Center City, MN: Hazelden, 2005), 164.

15. Alcoholics Anonymous, *"Pass It On,"* 120.

16. Ibid., 120, 121.

17. Alcoholics Anonymous, *Alcoholics Anonymous: The Story of How Many Thousands of Men and Women Have Recovered from Alcoholism*, 14; Wilson, *Lois Remembers*, 89.

18. Alcoholics Anonymous, *Alcoholics Anonymous Comes of Age: A Brief History of A.A.* (New York: Alcoholics Anonymous World Services, 1957), 64.

19. Ibid.
20. Alcoholics Anonymous, *"Pass It On,"* 131.
21. Borchert, *Lois Wilson Story*, 170.
22. Alcoholics Anonymous, *Alcoholics Anonymous Comes of Age*, 68.
23. Wilson, *Lois Remembers*, 82.
24. Borchert, *Lois Wilson Story*, 172.
25. Alcoholics Anonymous, *Alcoholics Anonymous Comes of Age*, 65.
26. Alcoholics Anonymous, *"Pass It On,"* 136.
27. Ibid., 137.
28. Alcoholics Anonymous, *Dr. Bob and the Good Oldtimers*, 66.
29. Ibid., 12; Alcoholics Anonymous, *Alcoholics Anonymous: The Story of How Many Thousands of Men and Women Have Recovered from Alcoholism*, 172.
30. Alcoholics Anonymous, *Dr. Bob and the Good Oldtimers*, 18.
31. Ibid., 19.
32. Ibid., 32, 34.
33. Ibid., 50–51.
34. Alcoholics Anonymous, *Alcoholics Anonymous Comes of Age*, 69–70.
35. Alcoholics Anonymous, *Alcoholics Anonymous: The Story of How Many Thousands of Men and Women Have Recovered from Alcoholism*, 180.
36. Alcoholics Anonymous, *Dr. Bob and the Good Oldtimers*, 71.
37. Ibid., 72.
38. Alcoholics Anonymous, *"Pass It On,"* 148–149.
39. Alcoholics Anonymous, *Dr. Bob and the Good Oldtimers*, 83, 84; Alcoholics Anonymous, *Alcoholics Anonymous, The Story of How Many Thousands of Men and Women Have Recovered from Alcoholism*, 185.
40. Alcoholics Anonymous, *Alcoholics Anonymous, The Story of How Many Thousands of Men and Women Have Recovered from Alcoholism*, 185.
41. Ibid., 185, 186, 188.
42. Ibid., 186.
43. Ibid., 186–87.
44. Ibid., 187, 188.
45. Ibid., 189.
46. Alcoholics Anonymous, *Dr. Bob and the Good Oldtimers*, 90.
47. Ibid., 91.
48. Ibid., 105–6, 107.
49. Ibid., 117.
50. Ibid., 101.
51. Ibid., 87, 118, 147.
52. Ibid., 98.
53. Ibid., 113.
54. Ibid., 147.
55. Alcoholics Anonymous, *Alcoholics Anonymous Comes of Age*, 76.

CHAPTER SEVEN: THE BIRTH OF ALCOHOLICS ANONYMOUS

1. Alcoholics Anonymous, *Alcoholics Anonymous Comes of Age: A Brief History of A.A.* (New York: Alcoholics Anonymous World Services, 1957), 144.
2. Ibid., 144–45.
3. Ibid., 145.
4. Ibid.
5. Frank Buchman, *Remaking the World: The Speeches of Frank N. D. Buchman*, new and rev. ed. (London: Blandford Press, 1961), 29.
6. "Oxford Group," *Wikipedia*, https://en.wikipedia.org/wiki/Oxford_Group.
7. Garth Lean, *Frank Buchman: A Life* (London: Constable, 1985), 46, posted on http://www.frankbuchman.info, accessed December 19, 2016.
8. Ibid., 31.
9. Buchman, *Remaking the World*, 46.
10. The Layman With a Notebook, *What Is the Oxford Group?* (New York: Oxford University Press, 1933), 9.
11. Susan Cheever, *My Name Is Bill; Bill Wilson: His Life and the Creation of Alcoholics Anonymous* (New York: Simon & Schuster, 2004), 134.
12. Alcoholics Anonymous, *Dr. Bob and the Good Oldtimers*, 55–56.
13. Ibid., 58.
14. Mitchell K., *The Story of Clarence H. Snyder and the Early Days of Alcoholics Anonymous in Cleveland, Ohio* (Washingtonville, NY: A.A. Big Book Study Group, 1999), 25.
15. Alcoholics Anonymous, *Dr. Bob and the Good Oldtimers*, 101; Ernest Kurtz, *Not-God: A History of Alcoholics Anonymous* (Center City, MN: Hazelden Educational Services, 1979), 54.
16. Alcoholics Anonymous, *"Pass It On,"* 130–31; Alcoholics Anonymous, *Dr. Bob and the Good Oldtimers*, 100–101.
17. Kurtz, *Not-God*, 45.
18. Mitchell K., *The Story of Clarence H. Snyder*, 34.
19. Alcoholics Anonymous, *Alcoholics Anonymous Comes of Age*, 159.
20. Ibid.
21. Ibid., 160, 161.
22. Alcoholics Anonymous, *"Pass It On,"* 198–99. A disclaimer from AA: "The Twelve Steps and the Twelve Traditions are reprinted with permission of Alcoholics Anonymous World Services, Inc. ('A.A.W.S.') Permission to reprint the Twelve Steps and the Twelve Traditions does not mean that A.A.W.S. has reviewed or approved the contents of this publication, or that A.A. necessarily agrees with the views expressed herein. A.A. is a program of recovery from alcoholism *only*—use of the Twelve Steps and Twelve Traditions in connection with programs and activities which are patterned after A.A., but which address other problems, or in any other non-A.A., does not imply otherwise."
23. Ibid., 161, 162; Alcoholics Anonymous, *"Pass It On,"* 198.
24. Alcoholics Anonymous, *Alcoholics Anonymous Comes of Age*, 162.

25. Ibid.

26. Mitchell K., *The Story of Clarence H. Snyder*, 39; Alcoholics Anonymous, *Alcoholics Anonymous Comes of Age*, 163.

27. Alcoholics Anonymous, *Alcoholics Anonymous Comes of Age*, 167.

28. Ibid.

29. Alcoholics Anonymous, *Dr. Bob and the Good Oldtimers*, 163, 167.

30. Ibid., 164.

31. Ibid., 218.

32. Ibid., 200; *Salvation Nell* was a 1931 film in which a young woman joins the Salvation Army and tries to convert her father on his release from prison.

33. Elrick B. Davis, "Alcoholics Anonymous Makes Its Stand Here, Part 1," *Cleveland Plain Dealer*, October 21, 1939, http://www.silkworth.net/ebd/plndlr1.html.

34. Elrick B. Davis, "Alcoholics Anonymous Makes Its Stand Here, Part 2," *Cleveland Plain Dealer*, October 23, 1939, http://www.silkworth.net/ebd/plndlr12.html; "Alcoholics Anonymous Makes Its Stand Here, Part 4," October 25, 1939, http://www.silkworth.net/ebd/plndlr4.html.

35. Alcoholics Anonymous, *Dr. Bob and the Good Oldtimers*, 206, 207.

36. Alcoholics Anonymous, *Alcoholics Anonymous Comes of Age*, 21.

37. Ibid., 25.

38. Ibid., 183.

39. Ibid., 186.

40. Alcoholics Anonymous, *"Pass It On,"* 245, 246.

41. Alcoholics Anonymous, *Alcoholics Anonymous Comes of Age*, 190, 191.

42. Alcoholics Anonymous, *Alcoholics Anonymous: The Story of How Many Thousands of Men and Women Have Recovered from Alcoholism*, 3rd ed. (New York: Alcoholics Anonymous World Services, 1976), xiii–xiv.

43. Alcoholics Anonymous, *Twelve Steps and Twelve Traditions* (New York: Alcoholics Anonymous World Services, 1953), 173–74.

44. Alcoholics Anonymous, *Alcoholics Anonymous*, 62.

45. Mitchell K., *The Story of Clarence H. Snyder*, 54, 63.

46. Alcoholics Anonymous, *Alcoholics Anonymous: The Story of How Many Thousands of Men and Women Have Recovered from Alcoholism*, xiv; Alcoholics Anonymous, *Twelve Steps and Twelve Traditions*, 139–40.

47. Alcoholics Anonymous, *Twelve Steps and Twelve Traditions*, 147, 149, 156.

48. Ibid., 129, 130.

49. Alcoholics Anonymous, *Twelve Steps and Twelve Traditions*, 160.

50. William Wilson, "Our A.A. Experience Has Taught Us That," *AA Grapevine* 2, no. 11 (April 1946): 2–3.

51. "The Twelve Traditions of Alcoholics Anonymous" (short form), Alcoholics Anonymous, rev. October 2014, http://www.aa.org/assets/en_US/smf-122_en.pdf. See reference in note 22.

52. Alcoholics Anonymous, *"Pass It On,"* 339, 342.

53. Alcoholics Anonymous, *Alcoholics Anonymous Comes of Age*, 214.

54. Ibid., 218.

55. Ibid., 214.

CHAPTER EIGHT: RISE OF THE SOBER DRUNK

1. Blake Bailey, *Farther and Wilder: The Lost Weekends and Literary Dreams of Charles Jackson* (New York: Alfred A. Knopf, 2013), 4.

2. Ibid., 202.

3. Jeffrey Meyers, ed., *The Lost Weekend: Screenplay by Charles Brackett and Billy Wilder* (Berkeley: University of California Press, 2000), 15; Bailey, *Farther and Wilder*, 202.

4. Bailey, *Farther and Wilder*, 202, 204.

5. Charles Jackson, *The Lost Weekend*, Time Reading Program Edition (New York: Farrar & Rinehart, 1963), xv.

6. National Committee for Education on Alcoholism (NCEA), "New Public Health Movement Started to Educate Public on Alcoholism," October 3, 1944, Papers of Marty Mann, Syracuse University Libraries, Syracuse, NY, 1, 2.

7. Ibid.

8. NCEA, "New Public Health Movement Started to Educate Public on Alcoholism," 1.

9. Sally Brown and David R. Brown, *A Biography of Mrs. Marty Mann: The First Lady of Alcoholics Anonymous* (Center City, MN: Hazelden Information and Educational Services, 2001), 3–4.

10. Ibid., 26.

11. Anderson and Cooper, *The Other Side of the Bottle*, 214.

12. Ibid., 214–15.

13. Harold H. Moore, "Activities of the Research Council on Problems of Alcohol," *Quarterly Journal of Studies on Alcohol* 1, no. 1 (June 1940): 105–6.

14. Anderson and Cooper, *The Other Side of the Bottle*, 12, 20.

15. Dwight Anderson, "Alcohol and Public Opinion," *Quarterly Journal of Studies on Alcohol* 3, no. 3 (December 1942): 388.

16. Ibid., 377, 378, 390.

17. Brown and Brown, *A Biography of Mrs. Marty Mann*, 162.

18. NCEA, "New Public Health Movement Started to Educate Public on Alcoholism," 1.

19. Marty Mann, undated memo, Papers of Marty Mann.

20. Marty Mann, "The National Committee for Education on Alcoholism, Inc., a Division of the Yale Plan on Alcoholism," September 1949, Papers of Marty Mann, 5–6.

21. "Marty Interviewed on Committee," *AA Grapevine* 1, no. 5 (October 1944).

22. Ralph M. Henderson to John C. Myers, October 31, 1947, Papers of Marty Mann, 2.

23. Quoted in Anderson, "Alcohol and Public Opinion," 385–86.

24. Marty Mann, "Alcoholism, America's Fourth Greatest Public Health Problem: An Address Given Before the Joint Session of the Legislature of the State of South Carolina," March 6, 1946, Papers of Marty Mann, 6; Anderson, "Alcohol and Public Opinion," 387.

25. Marty Mann, "The Alcoholic in the General Hospital," manuscript of article for *Southern Hospitals*, October 1948, Papers of Marty Mann, 2.

26. Ibid.; Marty Mann, "What Shall We Do About Alcoholism," *Vital Speeches of the Day* 13 (1947): 254.

27. Mitchell K., *The Story of Clarence H. Snyder*, 55.

28. Mary C. Darrah, *Sister Ignatia: Angel of Alcoholics Anonymous*, 2nd ed. (Center City, MN: Hazelden Pittman Archives Press, 2001), 11.

29. Ibid., 303.

30. Mann, "The Alcoholic in the General Hospital," 6.

31. NCEA, "How to Set Up a Clinic or Information Center in Your Community," Papers of Marty Mann, n.d.

32. Alcoholics Anonymous, *Alcoholics Anonymous: The Story of How Many Thousands of Men and Women Have Recovered from Alcoholism*, 141, 146.

33. Harrison M. Trice and Mona Schonbrunn, "A History of Job-Based Alcoholism Programs, 1900–1955," in *Employee Assistance Programs: Wellness/ Enhancement Programming*, 4th ed., ed. Michael A. Richard, William G. Emener, and William S. Hutchison Jr. (Springfield, IL: Charles C. Thomas, 2009), 13.

34. Ibid., 15.

35. Ibid., 16.

36. Ibid., 14.

37. Sgt. Bill S. with Glenn F. Chestnut, *On the Military Firing Line in the Alcoholism Treatment Program: The Air Force Sergeant Who Beat Alcoholism and Taught Others to Do the Same* (Lincoln, NE: iUniverse, 2003), 85, 214.

38. Ibid., 214.

39. Marty Mann, "Memo to the Executive Committee," November 10, 1954, Papers of Marty Mann, 1.

40. Ibid.

41. Quoted in White, *Slaying the Dragon*, 260.

42. "A.A.s to Be Asked for Information," *AA Grapevine* 3, no. 3 (August 1946).

43. E. M. Jellinek, "Phases of Alcohol Addiction," *Quarterly Journal of Studies on Alcohol* 13 (1952): 674.

44. Ibid.; E. M. Jellinek, *The Disease Concept of Alcoholism* (New Haven, CT: College and University Press, 1960), 12.

45. Harold E. Hughes and Dick Schneider, *The Man from Ida Grove: A Senator's Personal Story* (Lincoln, VA: Chosen Books, 1979), 103.

46. Quoted in "Harold Hughes, Iowa Trucker Turned Politician, Dies at 74," *New York Times*, October 15, 1996.

47. Hughes and Schneider, *The Man from Ida Grove*, 277.

48. Lyndon B. Johnson, *Public Papers of the Presidents of the United States: Lyndon B. Johnson, Containing the Public Messages, Speeches, and Statements of the President, 1966* (Washington, DC: Government Printing Office, 1967), 1: 243; Nancy Olson, *With a Lot of Help from Our Friends: The Politics of Alcoholism* (New York: Writers Club Press, 2003), 72.

49. Olson, *With a Lot of Help from Our Friends*, 40.

50. Ibid., 53, 54.

51. Ibid., 79.

52. Ibid., 83.

53. Ibid., 103.

CHAPTER NINE: BOOM AND BUST

1. Betty Ford and Chris Chase, *Betty: A Glad Awakening* (New York: Doubleday, 1987), 18, 22, 41.

2. Ibid., 20.

3. Ibid., 9, 11.

4. Ibid., 60.

5. Ibid., 53–54, 55.

6. Ibid., 54, 55, 58.

7. Ibid., 60, 61.

8. Damian McElrath, *Hazelden: A Spiritual Odyssey* (Center City, MN: Hazelden, 1987), 30–31.

9. Ibid., 31.

10. Ibid., 71.

11. Ibid., 75–76.

12. Ibid., 76

13. Ibid., 69, 77.

14. Ibid., 77.

15. Ibid., 102.

16. Ibid., 108.

17. Alcoholics Anonymous, *Twelve Steps and Twelve Traditions*, 23.

18. Jerry Spicer, *The Minnesota Model: The Evolution of the Multidisciplinary Approach to Addiction Recovery* (Center City, MN: Hazelden Educational Materials, 1993), 39; Daniel J. Anderson, "The Psychopathology of Denial," paper presented at Alcoholism: A Major Challenge for the '80s seminar, Eisenhower Medical Center, Rancho Mirage, CA, February 16, 1981; reprinted in Damian McElrath, *Dan Anderson: A Biography* (Center City, MN: Hazelden, 1999), 116.

19. McElrath, *Hazelden*, 128.

20. Anderson, "The Psychopathology of Denial," 120–21.

21. Vernon E. Johnson, *I'll Quit Tomorrow* (New York: Harper & Row, 1973), 3.

22. Ibid., 4.

23. Ibid., 3–4, 59.

24. White, *Slaying the Dragon*, 381.

25. Ibid., 382.

26. Kurtz, *Not-God*, 271.

27. Ibid., 266.

28. Roger C., "A History of Secularism in A.A.," address delivered at Widening the Gateway, a conference for secularists in AA, Olympia, WA, January 16, 2016, William L. White Papers, http://www.williamwhitepapers.com/pr /A%20History%20of%20Secularism%20in%20A.A.pdf.

29. White, *Slaying the Dragon*, 479.

30. Ibid., 480.

31. Thomas F. McGovern and William L. White, eds., *Alcohol Problems in the United States: Twenty Years of Treatment Perspective* (New York: Haworth Press, 2002), 92; White, *Slaying the Dragon*, 461.

32. Milan Korcok, *Addiction Treatment in Crisis* (Providence, RI: Manisses Communications Group, 1999), 17.

33. White, *Slaying the Dragon*, 396.

34. Ibid., 397.

35. Ibid.

36. Korcok, *Addiction Treatment in Crisis*, 4, 9.

37. Wendy Kaminer, *I'm Dysfunctional, You're Dysfunctional: The Recovery Movement and Other Self-Help Fashions* (New York: Vintage Books, 1993), 10, 21–22, 28.

38. Herbert Fingarette, "Alcoholism: The Mythical Disease," *Public Interest* 81 (Spring 1988): 4, 11; Herbert Fingarette, *Heavy Drinking: The Myth of Alcoholism as a Disease* (Berkeley: University of California Press, 1988), 1, 38.

39. Fingarette, *Heavy Drinking*, 70.

40. Ibid., 73.

41. William Madsen, *Defending the Disease: From Facts to Fingarette* (Akron, OH: Wilson, Brown & Co., October 1988), 1, 2, 33.

42. George E. Vaillant, *The Natural History of Alcoholism* (Cambridge, MA: Harvard University Press, 1983), 283–84, 284–85.

43. White, *Slaying the Dragon*, 341.

44. Ibid.

CHAPTER TEN: WAVES OF SOBRIETY

1. Audrey Kishline to members of Moderation Management, January 20, 2000, http://www.doctordeluca.com/documents/kishlinetoldMM.htm; Sam Howe Verhovek, "Advocate of Moderation for Heavy Drinkers Learns Sobering Lesson," *New York Times*, July 9, 2000.

2. Brook Hersey, "The Controlled Drinking Debates: A Review of Four Decades of Acrimony," 2001, http://www.drbrookhersey.com/uploads/3/1/9 /2/31926129/controlled_drinking.pdf, 7.

3. R. G. Bell, "Comment on the Article by D. L. Davies," *Quarterly Journal of Studies on Alcohol* 24 (1963): 322.

4. David J. Armor, J. Michael Polich, and Harriet B. Braiker, *Alcoholism and Treatment* (Santa Monica, CA: RAND Corporation, 1976), v; http://www.rand.org/pubs/reports/R1739.html.

5. Mark B. Sobell and Linda C. Sobell, *Behavioral Treatment of Alcohol Problems: Individualized Therapy and Controlled Drinking* (New York: Plenum Press, 1978).

6. Hersey, "The Controlled Drinking Debates," 11.

7. Jane Brody, "Alcohol Council Rejects Rand Report on Drinking," New York Times Syndicate, published in *Wilmington Morning Star*, June 11, 1976; Hersey, "The Controlled Drinking Debates," 12.

8. National Council on Alcoholism and Drug Dependence, "Statement Re: Vehicular Manslaughter Charges Against Author of Moderation Management," June 20, 2000, http://www.charitywire.com/charity109/02018.html.

9. Jennifer Steinhauer, "Addiction Center's Director Quits in Treatment Debate," *New York Times*, July 11, 2000.

10. "Statement Re: Audrey Kishline's Fatal MVA from Addiction Clinicians, Researchers, and Scholars—Circa 8/2000," copy in possession of author.

11. Fingarette, *Heavy Drinking*, 1–2.

12. Alan I. Leshner, "Addiction Is a Brain Disease, and It Matters," *Science* 278 (October 3, 1997): 45.

13. Wayne Hall, Adrian Carter, and Cynthia Forlini, "The Brain Disease Model of Addiction: Is It Supported by the Evidence and Has It Delivered on Its Promises?," *Lancet* 2 (January 2015): 105–10.

14. Nora D. Volkow and George Koob, "Brain Disease Model of Addiction: Why Is It So Controversial?," *Lancet* 2 (August 2015): 677.

15. Ibid., 678.

16. Hall et al., "The Brain Disease Model of Addiction," 109; Volkow and Koob, "Brain Disease Model of Addiction," 678.

17. Parton, *Smoking and Drinking*, 138–39; Alcoholics Anonymous, *Alcoholics Anonymous: The Story of How Many Thousands of Men and Women Have Recovered from Alcoholism*, 31–32.

18. Vaillant, *The Natural History of Alcoholism*, 314.

19. Ibid., 293, 294, 315.

20. National Institute on Alcohol Abuse and Alcoholism, *Alcohol Alert* 36 (April 1997), http://pubs.niaaa.nih.gov/publications/aa36.htm.

21. Charles P. O'Brien and A. Thomas McLellan, "Myths About the Treatment of Addiction," *Lancet* 347 (January 27, 1996): 240.

22. A. Thomas McLellan et al., "Drug Dependence, a Chronic Medical Illness: Implications for Treatment, Insurance, and Outcomes Evaluation," *JAMA: Journal of the American Medical Association* 284, no. 13 (October 4, 2000): 1694.

23. William L. White and A. Thomas McLellan, "Addiction as a Chronic Disorder: Key Messages for Clients, Families and Referral Sources," *Counselor* 9, no. 3 (2008): 2, 4, 14.

24. Ibid., 10.

25. Ibid., 10, 12, 14.

26. D. A. Dawson et al., "Recovery from DSM-IV Alcohol Dependence: United States, 2001–2002," *Addiction* 1 (2005): 281–92.

27. Alliance Project, *Proceedings*, Faces & Voices of Recovery Summit, October 5–7, 2001, St. Paul, MN, 14, http://www.facesandvoicesofrecovery.org /sites/default/files/2001_summit_report.pdf.

28. Ibid., 13.

29. Josie Feliz, "Survey: Ten Percent of American Adults Report Being in Recovery from Substance Abuse or Addiction," news release, Partnership for Drug-Free Kids, March 6, 2012, http://www.drugfree.org/newsroom/survey -ten-percent-of-american-adults-report-being-in-recovery-from-substance -abuse-or-addiction/; William L. White, *Recovery/Remission from Substance Use Disorders: An Analysis of Reported Outcomes in 415 Scientific Reports, 1868–2011* (Philadelphia: Great Lakes Addiction Technology Transfer Center, Philadelphia Department of Behavioral Health and Intellectual Disability Services, March 2012), http://www.naadac.org/assets/1959 /whitewl2012_recoveryremission_from_substance_abuse_disorders.pdf.

30. Alcoholics Anonymous, *Twelve Steps and Twelve Traditions*, 11, 12.

31. Faces & Voices of Recovery, *Advocacy with Anonymity*, brochure, http:// www.facesandvoicesofrecovery.org/sites/default/files/resources/Advocacy _with_Anonymity_brochure.pdf, 1, 2.

32. William Cope Moyers, speech, Unite to Face Addiction Rally, October 4, 2015, Washington, DC, http://www.hazeldenbettyford.org/articles/gardner /unite-to-face-addiction.

ELKHART PUBLIC LIBRARY

3 3080 01652 8468

WITHDRAWN

Educate • Enlighten • Entertain

ELKHART PUBLIC
LIBRARY
myEPL.org   Elkhart, Indiana